Alex Aniel originally hails from Sa[...] Tokyo since 2007. He began play[...] aged thirteen, which led him to vis[...], study the language and eventually move there permanently. He has over a decade of experience in the video game industry, and currently works for game music label Brave Wave Productions and physical game publisher Limited Run Games, specializing in the production of game music albums and business development for both companies.

ITCHY, TASTY

An Unofficial History of Resident Evil

Alex Aniel

unbound

First published in 2021
This paperback edition first published in 2022

Unbound
Level 1, Devonshire House, One Mayfair Place, London W1J 8AJ
www.unbound.com

Unbound does not have any control over, or responsibility for, any third-party
websites referred to in this book. All internet addresses given in this book
were correct at the time of going to press. The author and publisher regret any
inconvenience caused if addresses have changed or sites have ceased to exist, but can
accept no responsibility for any such changes.

Text design by PDQ Digital Media Solutions Ltd

A CIP record for this book is available from the British Library

ISBN 978-1-80018-212-7 (paperback)
ISBN 978-1-78352-948-3 (hardback)
ISBN 978-1-78352-949-0 (ebook)

Printed in Great Britain by Clays Ltd, Elcograf S.p.A

1 3 5 7 9 8 6 4 2

PATRONS

Daniel Acedo Calderón
Albert Alonso
Dimitri Awesometh
Philipp Bader
Christine Bagarino
Peter Baines
Jake Baldino
Bradley Biglin Sr
Michael Billing
Jontahn Brantner
Rocco Buffalino
Adam Cherneski
Joey Chiu
Jonathan Clark
Michael Anthony Clemmer
EteRnal PAL - Phong T. Le
Diamond Feit
Michael Ferguson
José Pedro Gonçalves Fernandes
Florian Fischer
Jeff Foertsch
Connor Foss
fred_derf
William Golden
Jairo Gonzalez Cardenas
Alexander Hartley
James Hollifield - Steinmann
    (BBMACK)
Gregory Kinstetter
Tyler Kozimor
Thomas Kozlowski III
Fionna Kuhn
Zig Kusnierz
Blackarachnia Lavigne
Alexandria Lee
Chris Liabotis
Leon Luo

Lynsey M
Mark Major
Robbie "Rombie" McGregor
George Melita
Stephen Meyerink
Jacob Montalvo
Joerg Mueller-Kindt
mzx666
Andy Nichol
Honza Olejník
Jonathan Ondriezek
Harley Osborne
Austin Parish
Luke Parry
Luca Pelliciari
Christopher "Distant Memories 1996"
    Prettyman
Jeremy Pryer
Nadeem Rasool
Sidney Richardson
Michael Ripka
William Stuart Robertson
Marten Schenk
Chris Schulte
Steve Sitjar
Joshua J. Slone
Jakob Soto
Mathew Stickles
Jim Stirrup
Mohammed Taher
Claire Turner
Anthony Velez
Ashley Washington
Steve Wright
xZombieAlix
Al Yang

CONTENTS

FOREWORD

A predominantly black screen that plays host to a door-opening sequence. Have you ever thought about just how many times you've seen the mysterious door enveloped in the shadows? A door of uncertainty, suspense and oftentimes horror. Will you survive?

I remember the first time I experienced the *Resident Evil* style of survival horror. I was in high school at the time, and I went to the local game store to pick up a copy of the game along with the strategy guide. I was a spoiled youth and my parents supported my gaming hobby as long as I was a good kid. I didn't know much about this game other than what I'd seen in magazines at the time, so it was a leap of faith with Capcom. I loved fighting games so I knew the company mainly for games like *Street Fighter* and awesome arcade experiences such as *Final Fight*... but a scary 3D game on the new PlayStation console? This was even before the genre was defined as survival horror. This was an age of discovery.

I can see it clear as day. Everything about the game is ingrained in my mind. Alongside it, the memories of my youth are embedded in these experiences like it was just yesterday. That's how much of an impact Chris, Jill and the incident in the Arklay Mountains had on me. I remember discussing the upcoming Capcom horror game with my gaming friends during art class and the skepticism from everyone because they'd never played anything like it.

All that changed after a few weeks, once we got to play the game. There was genuine horror and fear embedded in our gaming DNA. We hadn't felt this way before. One morning, before heading out to school, I remember showing my older sister the opening scene, where you encounter the first zombie. She screamed and cowered in fear, and had nightmares for quite some time after that. Everything in this era of gaming was new. It paved the way for an interesting future and taught me skill sets that would benefit me in my gaming life – which had parallels with real life, oddly enough. I mean, I was just a young kid. How was I supposed to know I needed a memory card for this game? I hadn't needed it for fighting games or for *Ridge Racer*... but I sure needed it after playing six hours straight and losing my progress while getting skewered in the underground laboratory. Lesson learned? Plan ahead.

Impressions and experiences are everything. It was during this mighty age of gaming that I decided I wanted to work within the video game industry and be part of something that I enjoyed. I never looked back. Over the years I was lucky enough to get to know Alex Aniel, or "cvxfreak" as he was known on internet message boards, and eventually met him at one of the many gaming events around the world. My fondest memory, however, is of us exchanging ideas and discussing the industry in the most unlikely of places. At the Capcom booth during E3 2017, we bonded over games new and old as we sat in their VIP area. I always knew he was a big-time *Resident Evil* fan and collector. I guess you can say his influence sort of rubbed off on me. Almost like a virus.

I don't get scared of video games anymore. I'm more afraid that I won't have time to enjoy them. I'm writing this a mere few weeks before Capcom releases the reimagined adventure of *Resident Evil 2* for a new generation of gamers.

Once you get past the loading screen that is the door in the darkness, you'll see that the doors lead to infinite opportunities and possibilities for the future. Long live *Resident Evil*.

Mark Julio

January 2019

INTRODUCTION

I can still remember the excitement I felt one late winter afternoon in 2015. I was visiting the San Francisco Bay Area for the annual Game Developers Conference (GDC), where members of the game industry gather in one place in their pursuit of newfound knowledge, ranging from insider information on new technologies and products to potential new business partnerships. I work in the video game industry, and 2015 was my fifth year of making the pilgrimage. Though I now live in Tokyo, the Bay Area is where I was born and raised, and where my family lives. GDC is something I've always viewed as a homecoming paired with the joys and stresses of networking.

On this particular day in early March, before heading over to GDC in downtown San Francisco, I had a special assignment: to visit the US office of Capcom, the Osaka-based developer and publisher of video games and other amusement products – including *Resident Evil*, known in Japan as *Biohazard*. Technically, most of the magic happened over in Osaka, not at the US branch, but still, it was a moment of personal excitement to finally visit the company that made this iconic series.

Like many of my contemporaries (I was born in 1987), I have loved video games for as long as I can remember. As a teenager, I discovered that many of my favorite games were made in Japan, which eventually led to my decision to study Japanese upon entering university in the US in 2005 and move to Tokyo two years later. Even earlier in the 2000s, I wrote free online walkthroughs for various *Resident Evil* games, which represented my first work in the industry. Then, in late 2010, right before graduating from my master's program in Tokyo, I interned at localization company 8-4, where I observed how various companies in the industry collaborate to bring games to audiences globally. The following April, I joined a game developer, where I worked on localization and production for two years. In January 2014, I went on to establish Brave Wave Productions with my best friend, Mohammed Taher, to help him achieve his goal of connecting Japanese retro game music composers with fans all around the world.

The whole time, I remained a *Resident Evil* fan. Over those years, I played all the versions and frequently engaged with the game's large community through social media. So, perhaps the reader can imagine just how utterly thrilled I was when I stepped through the entrance of the offices of Capcom USA in San Mateo. This was the home of *Resident Evil* and, for the first time ever, I was welcomed inside. If I could have told my thirteen-year-old self that this day would eventually come, I am sure he would have completely lost it.

Two years on from that momentous day in 2015, I was once again in San Francisco for GDC. It was barely a month since the release of *Resident Evil 7: Biohazard* – a game I consider as one of my favorites and one that was a critical success for Capcom

– and Capcom Japan had sent several members of the *Resident Evil 7* team to deliver talks on the game's development history. Director Koshi Nakanishi discussed the difficulties in deciding on a new direction for *Resident Evil* following the critical struggle of its predecessor, *Resident Evil 6*, and I wondered, did every *Resident Evil* game have such a fascinating story behind its development?

After the talks, I conversed in Japanese with Nakanishi and the rest of the team, complimenting them on their success. As a fan, I felt a connection with them, and I genuinely believe Nakanishi and the others felt that same connection with me. The vast majority of GDC attendees speak no Japanese and only one of the Capcom staff spoke English, so our conversation was their only opportunity to directly engage with a non-Japanese *Resident Evil* fan without the aid of an interpreter. We were speaking amongst the large crowds typical of GDC, yet no one else nearby could understand what we were saying. At that precise moment, I felt very proud of myself for being able to talk to them – this was something few, if any, *Resident Evil* fans in the West could do.

Japanese game companies have not always been so forthcoming with their history. In the 1980s, Capcom and some of its competitors had been so secretive that pseudonyms had been used in game credits to prevent the aggressive headhunting of talent in what was then an immature industry. Three decades later, Capcom, by now a larger and more globalized operation, was opening up and acknowledging its past while looking toward the future. But aside from rare moments like the one at GDC, such developer anecdotes like those about *Resident Evil 7: Biohazard* either remain stuck in Japan, intended for Japanese audiences, or presented in isolation with little context as to what had occurred beforehand.

Those conversations at GDC are why I decided to write this book. My passion for *Resident Evil*, combined with my bilingual abilities, industry connections, research background, sheer luck, hard work and unwavering love for gaming, motivated me to assemble nearly a decade of insider information that I hereby present to you. The *Resident Evil* series has developed an infamously intricate lore and universe, full of characters and plot lines that have captivated fans from game to game, but from my perspective, what are infinitely more intriguing are the stories of the people behind it all. These untold tales are finally coming to light, in many cases for the first time, thanks to exclusive interviews with key *Resident Evil* staff, including its original creator, Shinji Mikami. Through long and detailed conversations, I asked each creator to tell their own story, allowing me to assemble all of their accounts into one overarching narrative. It has been an honor and a privilege to speak with these talented creators and, from here, I present to you their stories.

"You are about to enter the world of survival horror. Good luck!"

CHAPTER 1: THE ORIGINS OF SURVIVAL HORROR

TOKURO FUJIWARA AND CAPCOM ACTION GAMES

By early 1996, Capcom had an enviable thirteen-year history of releasing high-quality action games. In an industry with relatively few big-name players, Capcom saw itself as *the* action game company, with its own unique approach to game production. Within gaming and broader pop culture, Capcom was a widely recognized brand. The company had released a number of popular arcade and console games, from *Bionic Commando* and *UN Squadron* to *Ghosts 'n Goblins*, *Mega Man* and *Street Fighter II*. The company even dabbled in collaborations with Disney for video game adaptations of *DuckTales* on the NES (Nintendo Entertainment System) and *Aladdin* on Super NES. All these titles heavily emphasize action and combat. I use the term "action" as

Japanese game developers tend to: referring to the heavy focus on fighting and a lighter focus on exploration. In terms of genre, *Street Fighter II* is a fighting game, while *Mega Man* and *Ghosts 'n Goblins* are side-scrolling platformers, but what the three have in common is their focus on attacking and defeating opponents.

There are design intricacies in Capcom games that make them unique – they're usually very difficult to beat, and even though the action is at the center of the gameplay experience, the protagonists often have limitations that contribute to said difficulty. This contrasts with Nintendo, for example, whose games usually focus more on a deeper exploration experience with fairly well-equipped characters.

So how did Capcom become the action game company, anyway? Several individuals have been integral to the shaping of Capcom's identity since its establishment as a video game company in 1983, but one person is particularly noteworthy: Tokuro Fujiwara. Hailing from the Kansai region of Japan, Fujiwara graduated from Osaka Designers' College in 1982 and initially joined Konami, then located near Osaka, working there for a year as a game planner for an arcade title called *Pooyan*. His stint at Konami would prove short, however, because in 1983 he was invited by an acquaintance to join Capcom, another Osaka-based game company. Fujiwara accepted. He joined at the same time as Yoshiki Okamoto, Capcom's other notable creator from this era, and along with three others the group ended up forming Capcom's first official game development team, sowing the seeds for the brand it was to eventually become.

Fujiwara directed a number of Capcom titles in the mid-1980s, but the most notable from this era is the aforementioned

1985 arcade platformer *Ghosts 'n Goblins* (known as *Makaimura* in Japan). Taking place in a medieval fantasy world populated with an amalgamation of monsters from different mythoi such as demons, zombies, ghosts, magicians and bats, players must guide a knight named Arthur (not related to King Arthur) and venture into the Demon Realm to rescue Princess Prin Prin. The premise sounds similar to the *Super Mario* series, but *Ghosts 'n Goblins* is notoriously difficult thanks to aggressive enemy AI, Arthur's low character health and the difficult obstacles in all the stages. "We focused on our own specific style of action game because our priority was for Capcom to offer something different from other companies," Fujiwara explains. Indeed, while most stages in *Super Mario Bros.* can be completed without killing a single enemy by cleverly timing Mario's jumps, in *Ghosts 'n Goblins* the action itself is the gameplay experience – players must kill or be killed. Arthur, despite being a knight, is highly vulnerable to damage and will die after only two hits, like Mario. He can also jump, but he cannot change direction midair like Mario can. According to Fujiwara, this design was completely intentional. "Back in the eighties, we made games difficult because we wanted players to spend a lot of time playing and make the experience very rewarding at the end. We needed the arcade version to be difficult so recurring players could make the game profitable for arcade operators." *Ghosts 'n Goblins* is infamous for making players beat the game *twice* before seeing the ending, prompting Jeremy Parish of the Retronauts podcast to once say, jokingly, that "[Fujiwara] is the most hateful man alive."

HOME *SWEET HOME*: THE FIRST CAPCOM HORROR GAME

By the late 1980s, Capcom had built a solid reputation as an action game publisher, but the company wanted to diversify its game catalog and to create games that were more likely to succeed commercially. So, the company collaborated with other entertainment entities, allowing Capcom to combine its development prowess with a partner's intellectual property and marketing muscle. The most prominent collaboration of this time was Disney's *DuckTales* on the NES, a 1989 platforming title based on the popular American cartoon TV series. Produced by Fujiwara, *DuckTales* sold well and is often regarded as one of the best games on that system. However, it wasn't the only licensed Capcom title of the era; the same year, Capcom also released a game called *Sweet Home* for the Famicom (the Japanese version of the NES), which was based on a Japanese horror film of the same name by famed filmmaker Kiyoshi Kurosawa.

Directed by Fujiwara himself, *Sweet Home* uses the story, characters and setting of Kurosawa's film. The game takes place in Japan, where a small film crew explores a large mansion once owned by artist Ichiro Mamiya in order to procure valuable antique frescos he left behind. However, the crew soon discovers that the manor is haunted by the ghost of Lady Mamiya, Ichiro's wife, and they must escape without getting killed by her or other demons. The mansion is filled with monsters, locked rooms, hidden passageways and death traps. Players control one of five characters and pair up with a partner character to explore the building. The mystery surrounding the Mamiya family can be uncovered by reading detailed files scattered throughout the game. Careful and meticulous item management is another key gameplay element. In a departure from prior Capcom games, *Sweet Home* is a role-playing game (RPG) with random encounters and first-person battles against ghosts and other monsters, similar to Enix's *Dragon Quest*. *Sweet Home* also contains what *Shenmue* creator Yu Suzuki would eventually call "quick time events" (QTE), a gameplay mechanic that requires players to press a button within a very short time interval to avoid being killed by a trap.

Even before the idea of a *Sweet Home* video game came up, Fujiwara believed that horror could become a genre of its own; Capcom obtaining the license gave him the opportunity to try to make it happen. Despite its RPG elements, he emphasizes that *Sweet Home* is a horror title first and foremost, and that he considers Capcom's later *Breath of Fire* series to be the company's first genuine RPG. "I made the *Breath of Fire* series because I wanted Capcom to branch out from action games to other genres, including RPGs. I made *Sweet Home* earlier, but I consider it a horror game rather than an RPG," Fujiwara clarifies.

Because the Famicom/NES was an 8-bit 2D console incapable of generating realistic graphics, there were limits to what Fujiwara's team could achieve in terms of creating a horror title with credible audio and visual expression. Even so, Capcom gave *Sweet Home* a considerable production budget: development took about two years, which was longer than for other games of its time, especially within Capcom, whose games could usually be finished in as little as three months. While the visuals are great for an 8-bit title, the dot-pixel graphics don't instill the levels of fear befitting a horror game. And while composer Junko Tamiya's chiptune soundtrack is moody, compositionally interesting and matches the pacing of the game quite well, it doesn't exactly frighten viewers like a true horror film can.

The *Sweet Home* brand never gained much commercial traction, either as a movie or as a video game. The film wasn't a blockbuster in Japanese theaters, and Capcom's game failed to sell as well as its more popular hits such as *Ghosts 'n Goblins*, *Mega Man 2* or *Bionic Commando*. The game was never released outside of Japan due to regional licensing restrictions, denying Capcom the ability to increase sales through overseas markets. The film itself was eventually released on VHS, but as of 2019 has been long out of print, with no disc or digital release planned. Due to licensing, the game edition has met a similar fate to the film, having never been rereleased on any platform, physically or digitally. However, regardless of the game's relative obscurity, Fujiwara considers *Sweet Home* to be a personal success story and a product he's particularly proud of. "I think it turned out quite well, all things considered," he concludes.

Due to its interesting production history, unique traits and lack of release outside Japan, retro enthusiasts often give *Sweet Home* a shot, considering it a piece of gaming history. I asked Fujiwara if he'd like to see *Sweet Home* come back in some form. "That would be great, wouldn't it?" he says, with a nostalgic smile on his face.

However, in some respects, *Sweet Home* has actually been back for a very long time – since March 22, 1996, in fact, when Capcom released another attempt at a horror title: *Resident Evil*.

ENTER SHINJI MIKAMI: *RESIDENT EVIL* BEGINS DEVELOPMENT

After the release of *Sweet Home*, Capcom eventually moved on from the 8-bit video game era. The company's arcade business, while already flourishing in the 1980s, experienced a boom in 1991 with the massive, unprecedented success of Yoshiki Okamoto's *Street Fighter II*, which dramatically transformed Capcom's image, reflecting the game's tremendous cultural influence. For many young gamers in the early 1990s, Capcom might as well have been "the *Street Fighter* brand."

Meanwhile, Capcom continued to develop its console game business as well. NES remained a popular system through the early 1990s, but the game industry continued to evolve technologically and demographically as audiences grew older and gaming became more popular beyond Japan and the US. In October 1988, Sega released the 16-bit Genesis (known as the Mega Drive in most territories outside North America), eventually making the firm a viable competitor to Nintendo. Nintendo responded with its own 16-bit console, the Super NES. For Fujiwara, as general manager of Capcom's console games division, the 16-bit era provided the opportunity to create games with better graphics, sound and gameplay. After *Sweet Home*, he went on to produce several NES and Super NES games, such as *Mega Man 3* through *Mega Man 7*, the *Breath of Fire* series, *Demon's Crest* and *Super Ghouls 'n Ghosts*. He also oversaw the production of collaborative products with Disney, such as *Disney's Aladdin*.

Even as the 16-bit era kept him busy, Fujiwara never lost sight of his lofty goal to make his original vision for *Sweet Home* a reality and invent the horror game genre. While Capcom couldn't revisit the *Sweet Home* property itself due to its being owned by a different company, Fujiwara constantly sought out an opportunity to develop another horror game. But despite their audio-visual advancements over the NES, the predominantly 2D, 16-bit consoles still weren't advanced enough to express a credible vision of horror. "The NES limited what we could achieve in terms of horror," Fujiwara admits. "The next set of consoles, like the Super Famicom, were better but still not enough." But in 1993, Fujiwara finally got his chance. In that year, 3D graphics began to gain traction in Japan thanks to games such as Nintendo's *Star Fox,* a Super NES rail-shooter title whose cartridge was equipped with a special chip enabling the system to display polygons, which are relatively more advanced visual shapes used to comprise video game graphics than the pixels commonly used in 2D titles. Another notable title was Sega's *Virtua Fighter*, a polygonal competitive fighting game made possible through advancements in arcade hardware.

Even more significant was the entry of Japanese electronics manufacturing giant Sony into the video game hardware market. Following a failed collaboration with Nintendo to develop a CD-ROM drive add-on for the Super NES, Sony decided to go head-to-head with Nintendo and Sega through a 32-bit disc-based game console, PlayStation. Sony's system was capable of 3D graphics and it supported CD-ROMs, which gave developers opportunities to offer more content in their games, thanks to the discs' higher storage capacities and lower manufacturing costs; Nintendo's and Sega's 16-bit consoles used low-capacity, high-cost cartridges to store game data, which was prohibitive to creating a lengthy cinematic experience. Thanks to its more advanced capabilities and use of CD-ROMs, Fujiwara felt that PlayStation could finally bring the horror games genre to life. This was Fujiwara's long-awaited chance to strike while the iron was hot.

As the game industry continued to evolve, Capcom itself continued to grow and change. A few of the employees who had joined Capcom in the 1980s, such as *Mega Man* creator Akira Kitamura and the company's chiptune composers Manami Matsumae and Takashi Tateishi, had left the company by 1990. However, Capcom was far from experiencing a brain drain. In 1990, a twenty-four-year-old man from Yamaguchi, south-west Japan, named Shinji Mikami joined the company as a designer. Fujiwara, whose duties included managing the development of new personnel, placed Mikami on a number of projects early in his career, including the licensed titles *Disney's Goof Troop* and *Disney's Aladdin*. Both Disney collaborations were critically and commercially successful, particularly the latter.

By 1993, Fujiwara was no longer directing games himself, instead handing such duties to younger creators to give them opportunities for professional growth. He was particularly impressed with Mikami's work ethic and strong sense of game

Shinji Mikami

design on the Disney titles, so he reached out to him about the creation of a *Sweet Home*-inspired horror game with Mikami as director. In a 2016 interview with video game news website GameSpot, Mikami recalled his meeting with Fujiwara: "We were in Capcom's Osaka development studio and my [boss at the time], Tokuro Fujiwara, called me in to talk to him. He said that he wanted us to make a horror game using systems from *Sweet Home*... I was actually a big fan of *Sweet Home*, and [Fujiwara] was someone that I really respected, so I was excited about the project from the beginning."[1] Fujiwara explains his own perspective, stating that "Mikami proved himself as a capable individual immediately after he joined Capcom. I learned of his talents while observing his work on the Super NES games. That's why I chose him to work on *Resident Evil*." An enthusiastic Mikami accepted the offer, and, under Fujiwara's guidance, got to work on a new horror game.

BRINGING THE SURVIVAL AND THE HORROR: THE WORLD OF *RESIDENT EVIL*

Video game fans will remember the original 1996 *Resident Evil* as being a unique game for its time. As part of the product's branding, Capcom crafted the term "survival horror" for the game's genre to emphasize the fact that the game was every bit as much about fighting for one's life as it was about experiencing fear, uncertainty and tension. *Resident Evil* is renowned for delivering both the survival and the horror with equal success, therefore allowing the "survival horror" name to become part of the gaming mainstream.

The basic premise of *Resident Evil* sees members of a police unit known as the STARS (Special Tactics and Rescue Service) Alpha Team heading towards the last known coordinates of their counterparts, Bravo Team, who have gone missing during an investigation of several grisly murders that took place in Raccoon Forest. Soon enough, Alpha Team discovers the source of these violent killings: they are the work of zombies created by an evil pharmaceutical corporation operating out of a laboratory buried deep beneath the Spencer Estate, a large and mysterious mansion. The Estate is nestled away in the aforementioned forest, which lies on the outskirts of a fictional Midwestern US town known as Raccoon City.

Resident Evil contains what could be considered a rudimentary version of what gamers now call "open world" because – door-opening loading sequences notwithstanding – the game comprises an expansive, interconnected arrangement of rooms and corridors with access consistent with the real world. Here, you will not find any magic green pipes that teleport your character to the other side of the world in two seconds. The lone exception to this rule is the "Item Box." Due to the characters being able to hold only six or eight items at a time, items not currently required need to be deposited into Item Boxes, which are scattered throughout the game. The Item Boxes are all magically connected to each other for later item retrieval – the only element of the game that breaks the universe's space–time continuum.

The world of *Resident Evil* is a drastic departure from earlier Capcom 2D games, such as *Mega Man*, which features distinct stages completely disconnected from one another, or *Street Fighter II*, whose country-themed stages are connected via a world map that players don't interact with directly. In *Resident Evil*, players must unlock doors to progress through the environment, which often involves solving puzzles or locating unusual objects, such as crests engraved with emblems like animals or weather elements. Opening these doors yields new items and weapons, which bring players one step closer to the end.

The gameworld map of *Resident Evil* is made possible thanks to its 3D gameplay and graphics engine. Initially, the development team had conceptualized a game with a first-person viewpoint, but this required more polygons and processing power than the team was capable of extracting out of PlayStation this early in the system's lifecycle. Instead, the team achieved a realistic look by employing a clever mix of polygonal character models and pre-rendered photo-like backgrounds. The characters are ordinary human beings who wander through rooms containing mundane objects such as typewriters, kitchen tables, bookshelves, keys, bathtubs, diaries that players can read to uncover clues, and so forth. These objects are no longer stylized pixel renders, as commonly seen in previous console generations. Many at the time of release considered *Resident Evil* a graphical masterpiece for PlayStation. While not exactly *Toy Story* quality, the game looked considerably more advanced than anything that had come before it. The benefits of the pre-rendered backgrounds are the increased detail of the visuals, the smoother frame rate and the claustrophobic, yet atmospheric angles from which players can view the action. What prevents *Resident Evil* from being a true open-world game is the fact that the rooms are separated by non-skippable door-opening loading animations that are at least five seconds long, a conscious design decision by the development team to account for the limited system memory of

PlayStation, which could only render one room at a time while maintaining the game's visual fidelity.

The game's enemy characters also lend much credence to the survival horror genre name. Easily the series' signature enemies, the existence of zombies is justified by the mysterious "T-virus" created by the enigmatic Umbrella Corporation. Of course, the use of zombies wasn't itself an original idea; by 1996 the creatures had already been popularized in films such as George Romero's *Night of the Living Dead*, but the zombie concept evolved through *Resident Evil* because, by being in a video game, zombies were no longer relegated to movies, whose endings viewers had no control over, or to cheesy costumes seen at Halloween parties. The game offered players their first credible opportunity to interact with zombies directly. Players could fight them with firearms or combat knives, while the zombies could, in turn, bite the character back and eventually kill them if enough damage was sustained. The audience no longer had to just sit back and watch the action unfold in a predetermined manner; they now had direct control over their experience and the fate of their characters.

The game features more enemies than just zombies. The scene early on in the game in which two Cerberus (the game's name for zombified dogs, named after the "Hound of Hades" in Greek mythology) jump through a window unannounced has become one of the most memorable and iconic set pieces in gaming history. It's probably the scene that defines most players' first recollection of the game because it happens so unexpectedly. As soon as the Cerberus appear, the music changes to a frantic percussion track that ratchets up the tension to almost unbearable levels. That said, the Cerberus aren't overly dangerous; they don't deal a ton of damage. They may be more difficult to shoot than zombies, but they require fewer bullets to kill, making them more of a nuisance than a real threat, assuming the player can regain his or her composure following their surprise appearance.

But then there are the Hunters, which appear halfway through the game to up the challenge. These green-skinned, hunchbacked reptilian creatures are outfitted with sharp claws on their hands and feet, making them faster and more dangerous than zombies as they can decapitate players with a devastating leap-slash attack in unguarded moments. The initial appearance of a Hunter is another iconic scene, as the creature is introduced entirely through a computer-generated (CG) movie. As the player enters a previously visited room during the game's second act, a cut-scene depicts a more agile yet clearly very deadly creature running towards the player – all from the point of view of the actual creature. Players have no idea what they are up against until the scene ends, when the Hunter comes into view and gameplay resumes. Players have mere seconds to deal with this new threat and must choose a powerful weapon like the Shotgun to survive.

Each of the game's enemies contributes to the challenge of surviving a horrific nightmare no matter how overwhelming the odds. The player is in complete control of the character's destiny, and it's up to them to exercise the right combination of calculation, judgment and skill to get through the game. For Mikami, it was this key difference between video game and cinema that motivated him to choose zombies as the game's primary antagonists. In a NowGamer interview, Mikami declared how unfortunate it was that the cast of *Dawn of the Dead* could never survive their ordeal no matter what the audience wanted, something he wanted to change with *Resident Evil*.[2]

That said, it's somewhat ironic to describe *Resident Evil* as a game that lets players take "complete control" of the experience, considering the awkwardness of the game's so-called "tank controls," as they are referred to in English. These controls have been criticized throughout the years for their complexity and low level of intuitiveness; indeed, maneuvering the characters is akin to driving a military tank, which can be a clumsy endeavor. In Japanese, the tank controls are referred to as *rajikon-sousa*, with *rajikon* being a portmanteau of the English words "radio" and "controls." In turn, *rajikon-sousa* refers to a toy race car operated with a twin-stick remote control – one stick for pushing the wheels forward or backward, and the other for moving them sideways. The controls enable the in-game character to move forward when the player presses Up on the gamepad and to step back when they press Down, regardless of the actual direction the character faces relative to the television screen. A contrasting approach is found in the real-time controls featured in *Super Mario 64*, to cite another 1996 game, where Up always moves Mario forward and Down always turns him around and sends him in the opposite direction.

The issues with *Resident Evil*'s controls are exacerbated by the pre-rendered backgrounds, which sometimes leaves enemies hidden in plain sight. Players are aware that enemies are in the room because they can hear them, but they can't actually see the enemies because they aren't within view of the camera. But being attacked by unseen enemies is part of the fabric of classic *Resident Evil*, even if it can be frustrating. The Japanese version mitigated this problem with auto-aiming weapons; pressing R1 on the PlayStation controller makes the character aim directly at the enemy so players can shoot with confidence. However, auto-aim functionality was removed from the North American version to increase the difficulty level, therefore encouraging North Americans to buy the game rather than rent it (games are not available for rental in Capcom's native Japan in any case).

The development team wasn't unaware of the potential pitfalls the controls presented. When Yoshiki Okamoto joined the team in late 1995 to replace outgoing executive producer Tokuro Fujiwara, one of the first requests he made to Shinji Mikami was to determine which controls were more suitable for the game – tank or real-time. The development team tried both schemes in pre-release builds and concluded that the game was scarier with the tank controls. "We implemented *Devil May Cry*-style real-time controls into a pre-release build, but the game lost its sense of fear and challenge because the zombies were far too easy to avoid. So, we ended up dropping them from the game and keeping the tank controls," Okamoto recalled.* He also asked Mikami to look into implementing other adjustments, such as increasing the number of Ink Ribbons, which are used on typewriters found throughout the gameworld to save the player's progress onto a PlayStation memory card, from one to three per set. In a May 1998 interview with Japanese print publisher Micro Design Publishing, Okamoto joked that without this change "the game would become one where players spend the entire time looking for Ink Ribbons." When he joined the team, Okamoto believed that *Resident Evil* was shaping up to be a "shitty game," but that it could become good if a few adjustments were made.[3][†] His advice proved to be pivotal.

---

* *Devil May Cry*, released by Capcom in 2001, features *Super Mario 64*-style movement.
† In this interview, Okamoto used the term *kusoge*, which translates as "shit game."

For all its touted innovations in game design, *Resident Evil* isn't actually the first horror game ever made. Looking beyond the Capcom catalog, some argue that the honor belongs to *Mystery House* on the Atari 2600 or perhaps *Alone in the Dark* on PC. However, I can say with confidence that *Resident Evil* was the first survival horror game ever released, thanks to its combination of realistic 3D gameworld, a line-up of genuinely terrifying enemies, and controls that let players confront zombies without making them too easy to defeat. It's thanks to the game's genre-defining elements that the survival horror name has resonated with the entire gaming community and become the standard moniker for just about any kind of video game that contains horror and fear elements, even if its use for non-Capcom games is technically unofficial. Konami refers to its *Silent Hill* series as "Horror Adventure," while Koei Tecmo calls *Fatal Frame* (*Project Zero* in

Yoshiki Okamoto

Europe) "Horror Action Adventure." But in the eyes of the average gamer, they're all still survival horror. And despite all its technical limitations, the realistically crafted world of *Resident Evil* allows for the survival and the horror to successfully come together in a way that *Alone in the Dark*, *Clock Tower* and *Sweet Home* could only have dreamed of. In a 2010 retrospective with NowGamer, Shinji Mikami admitted that you "couldn't really call [*Resident Evil*] 'beautiful' now." But he also reminded the audience that it was "incredibly difficult to produce the game for the PlayStation hardware back then." *Resident Evil* may be a relic by today's standards, but at the time creating such a game was a gargantuan task, and the impact it had on the medium was immeasurable.

THE MASTER OF UNLOCKING: LOCALIZATION AND VOICE ACTING IN *RESIDENT EVIL*

The original *Resident Evil* would have become iconic solely on the basis of its survival and horror elements. Yet, the game boasts an iconic cast of characters that have contributed to its strong presence in video game pop culture. The characters consist of Chris Redfield, Jill Valentine, Albert Wesker, Barry Burton and Rebecca Chambers, all of whom belong to STARS. Chris, Jill, Wesker and Barry belong to Alpha Team, while Rebecca belongs to Bravo Team. Created by scenario writer Kenichi Iwao and named by game planner Hideki Kamiya, the characters are caricatures of American superheroes and villains, each crafted by Japanese people who in the 1990s relied on mass media to help shape their image of Americans.

Even if they are unrealistic exaggerations of American people, each of the STARS members has become a video game icon with their own sizeable fanbase. Chris, twenty-five, an ex-Air Force pilot, is a flawed tough guy who means well and carries a keen sense of justice. Jill, twenty-three, is a strong, fierce and independent ex-Delta Force heroine who is also an expert pianist and lock picker. Wesker, thirty-eight, sports slicked-back hair, sunglasses and a black police uniform, and is the cool-headed yet enigmatic villain. In contrast, Rebecca, who wears an olive-green medical uniform, is a highly intelligent, resourceful and clairvoyant young woman who has already graduated college by the age of eighteen. Chris's, Jill's and Rebecca's résumés may be unrealistically impressive (and in Jill's case completely impossible, as the Delta Force only enlists male participants) but the characters nonetheless succeed in capturing the imaginations of people looking for an escape from reality when playing video games. Many *Resident Evil* fans find the characters attractive and appealing, and even fans not yet born in 1996 can be seen cosplaying the original characters.

Barry also has a following, and is a favorite of many *Resident Evil* fans. Both he and Albert are thirty-eight, making them the oldest of the main characters, while Barry is the only one who is a parent during the events of *Resident Evil*. He has a distinctive beard that adds to his sense of authority and to his quasi-parental role to the younger Chris and Jill. However, what makes Barry so memorable is not so much his appearance, but what he says. Barry has become particularly infamous for the rather unfortunate dialogue he delivers early in the game: not everyone who plays *Resident Evil* will make it to the end, but most players will get to witness at least two of Barry's classic lines. The game has been universally panned for its poorly delivered, stilted voice-overs, resulting in lines that have unrealistic intonation and emphasis. Thanks to Barry, gaming pop culture contains references to quotes such as "It might be better if you, the master of unlocking, take it with you," and "You were almost a Jill sandwich!" Although unintentionally funny, there's no denying these words are badly written. The awkward dialogue results from a combination of low production budget, cultural differences and differing priorities between the development team, the voice cast and those tasked with managing their relationships.

Shinji Mikami offers one take on how the voice-acting ended up the way it did. I joined him for dinner in Osaka in January 2007, back when I did not yet speak conversational Japanese. Mikami himself did not speak conversational English, so the two of us communicated through a mutual friend and interpreter. With the two of us unable to really say anything to each other directly, Mikami attempted to make conversation by humorously holding out his right hand and pointing out his index finger so his hand resembled a gun. He then looked at me and said, in accented English, "I have THIS!" He was referring to a line spoken by Barry early on in *Resident Evil*. Mikami explained that the dialogue had been kept intentionally simplistic so that even ordinary Japanese people could understand it (*Resident Evil* does not have a Japanese dub, even for the Japanese version). Many Japanese people are not fully conversant in English, but because it is a compulsory subject in Japan's educational curriculum, the average person is likely to understand at least some English if it is spoken in simple sentences, slowly and clearly.

More than a decade has passed since my dinner with Mikami. I moved to Tokyo eight months later, in September 2007, and still live there today. I am now fluent in Japanese and, armed with a dictionary for the occasional new word, I can comfortably play through any *Resident Evil* in the language, whether it's Japanese text and English voices, or entirely Japanese (*Resident Evil* games began offering Japanese dubs in 2012). After a decade spent in the country and all the grammatical and spelling errors in English one will inevitably encounter during that time, I can see where Mikami was coming from. In my experience, most Japanese people in large cities, like Tokyo and Osaka, understand simple English phrases from *Resident Evil*, such as "Stop it! Don't open that door!" and "Oh no! It's a monster!" The game's lines do not get any more complex than that. In 2016, the average Japanese person's knowledge of English was parodied in the hit music video "PPAP" by Japanese comedian Pikotaro. His yellow leopard-print outfit, simplistic yet mesmerizing choreography and bizarre facial expressions make for a hilarious video on their own, but the main lyrics – "I have a pen, I have a apple" [sic] – also poke fun at Japanese people's English. Of course, there are many Japanese people who are fluent in English (certainly a great many more than the number of Westerners fluent in Japanese), but the reality is that the dialogue in *Resident Evil* is not that much more difficult than the lyrics of "PPAP." The game's oversimplistic dialogue was a deliberate choice by Mikami to accommodate Capcom's domestic audience at the expense of a more realistic portrayal for the West.

Even when considering the intentional simplification of the game's dialogue, there are still some deficiencies in the game's overall English localization, a video game term that refers to a product whose content is intentionally modified to suit a different linguistic audience, not just translated directly from the original.

In 1996, the concept of a high-quality game localization, and even the term "localization" itself, was still unusual. Shinsaku Ohara, a bilingual designer who entered Capcom in 1999, recalls that the company did not have a localization team when he joined. "If you compare *Resident Evil* with previous Capcom games, you'll see that there wasn't much to translate before it. Therefore, it was enough for the game to just be in English without regard to quality," Ohara explains.

The voice recordings themselves took place during August and September 1995, in Tokyo. At this point in time, the use of full-fledged professional recording studios for video games was still years away from being commonplace. With a very limited budget and no precedent for carrying out complex voice recordings, Capcom (and other publishers) could only afford to look for people close to home. There was, and still is, a relatively small pool of native English speakers in Japan, so the people who were recruited for recording gigs were not necessarily trained professionals. They may have been English teachers, DJs, religious missionaries, or relatives of Japanese nationals. In most cases, their actual talent did not matter, if it was even perceptible to begin with; they just needed to be native English speakers.

Two voice actors and actresses who worked on *Resident Evil* offer their own perspectives on why the dialogue turned out the way it did. Lynn Harris was the voice actress of Rebecca, and also oversaw the casting of the other characters. Harris ascribes the camp, over-the-top feel of her performance to the fact that she didn't have sufficient background knowledge of the game during the recording. She also notes how disconnected every segment of the production was. "I was not provided with enough information to know exactly what was going on in each scene," Harris says. "That's the way it was. Thus, decisions on how and where to use the voices, and in which context, were made by game editors who I assume had little or no English language skills." Harris defends her work on the game, explaining, "People keep saying the acting was bad, but that's not so. It's just that the lines weren't used in the way we thought they'd be."

Barry's voice actor, Barry Gjerde, concurs with Harris about their having been in the dark regarding the game's content, presuming that the secrecy was intentional for competitive reasons. Gjerde says, "I also noticed that there seemed to be a reluctance on the part of clients or agents to tell the name of the game, as if it were a secret so the competition wouldn't know." The Japanese game industry was infamous for its wide-ranging protection of trade secrets in the 1980s and 1990s, so Gjerde's assumption certainly has merit.

Gjerde also explains that his most memorable lines were part of the script written by Capcom. "For those people who are dying of curiosity, no, I did not improvise or make up those corny lines – 'Jill sandwich,' etc. They were in the script, and, as a voice actor, it was my job to read them. Recording sessions are not a democracy, and if you want to work, you don't complain much." It didn't help matters that the recording set-up, also, had its limitations. Gjerde recalls his experience in the cramped studio: "Sometimes as many as four of us had to squeeze into a totally inadequate narration booth, holding our scripts, deftly moving out the way when it was someone else's turn at the one microphone, and getting to the mic when it was our turn." Many would agree with Gjerde that a job is a job, and that regardless of the voice cast's actual talent, the combination of low-budget production values, different cultural backgrounds, everyone's lack of experience and the only recent incipience of fully voiced video games made high-quality voice-acting in *Resident Evil* unfeasible in 1995.

Seeing how things turned out, perhaps Capcom would not have wanted it any other way. The voice-acting of *Resident Evil* is every bit as vital to the game's identity as the "survival horror" slogan, the gameplay, the pre-rendered graphics, tank controls and sci-fi story. There are several fan-made parody videos on the internet that manipulate the voice-overs to make them sound more comedic or sexual. Lines from the original game's dialogue would go on to be referenced several times over in future *Resident Evil* editions, with comedic effect. In 2002, a remake of *Resident Evil* was released with a tremendous visual makeover. The dialogue, too, was revamped with better voice-acting (though it was still imperfect). Yet while the remake is considered one of the best entries in the series, the improved voice-acting means that it is seen very differently from the original, which holds a unique place in the canon thanks to Barry's classic lines. The remake is lauded for being a great game, but is not necessarily a beloved object of pop culture. More recently, 2015's *Resident Evil: Revelations 2*, the first game in the canon since the original to feature Barry as protagonist, apes a number of his original lines, to the amusement of long-time fans.

RESIDENT EVIL SAVES CAPCOM

Many, if not most, will agree that game development is universally difficult. The production of *Resident Evil,* in particular, was far from smooth sailing, from start to finish, with several hurdles specific to the project: it was a 3D game being developed for new hardware; it was on a larger scale than anything Capcom had produced before; and the majority of the team members, Shinji Mikami included, were new to their jobs, so there was very little experience to go around. The only true veteran on the team was executive producer Tokuro Fujiwara, but despite his long-running desire to create the Horror video game genre, he had very little active involvement in the game's specific direction, leaving those responsibilities to Mikami. Thus, Mikami found himself leading a team of green but talented people that included planners Koji Oda, Hideki Kamiya, Kazuhiro Aoyama, and Hiroki Kato, character animator Jun Takeuchi, programmers Yasuhiro Anpo and Hiroyuki Kobayashi, gameplay designer Katsutoshi Karatsuma, scenario writer Kenichi Iwao, and sound designer Ippo Yamada.

The team initially experimented with utilizing ghosts for enemies, but this didn't stray far enough from *Sweet Home*, nor did it seem interesting to Mikami. They also tried to run a fully 3D engine with the game, offering a first-person perspective of the on-screen action, but technical limits forced them to adopt pre-rendered backgrounds instead. "We had originally attempted to have everything appear in full polygons. However, it became very clear early on that this wouldn't be possible given the limitation of the hardware at the time. [Mikami's] priority was making sure the zombies' visuals conveyed a sense of fear, so the decision was made to use polygons for them. The backgrounds were then swapped out to pre-rendered visuals, and this was when we decided to use the static camera as well," programmer Yasuhiro Anpo told GameSpot in a 2016 interview.[4] The tone of the game was meant to be more humorous (this is unrelated to the wonderful accident that is the game's voice-acting), but time constraints forced that approach to be dropped as well. Beyond such directional changes, the development was riddled with trial-and-error experimentation within every aspect of the game as the team explored what worked and what didn't.

Game development is seldom an easy affair, but for *Resident Evil* further difficulties arose due to the unfavorable financial situation Capcom found itself in by the mid-1990s. The company saw initial success with series like *Mega Man*, the collaborations with Disney and, especially, *Street Fighter II*, which nearly single-handedly carried Capcom through the first half of the 1990s. However, the so-called "*SFII* wave" came to an end and later *Street Fighter* sequels failed to perform as well as their predecessor. Meanwhile, game development costs were rising due to the advent of 3D games, which required longer development times and more personnel. Many Capcom employees assumed the company would eventually go bankrupt. Luckily for Capcom, in 1990 its then CEO, Kenzo Tsujimoto, purchased an area of land in California's Napa Valley that was famous for its red wine vineyards, both to pursue his interest in wine and as a personal investment. The income from this investment apparently helped Capcom stay in business through the mid-1990s.

Aside from Capcom's financial troubles, development of the original *Resident Evil* was facing its own external pressures. In late 1995, despite the game's development being nearly complete, Capcom considered cancelling *Resident Evil* altogether due to a recommendation from an American consulting firm, whose advisory services Capcom had sought in order to assess its struggling business. Capcom would have capitulated had it not been for Fujiwara's insistence that the game see its way to release. Fujiwara, whose dream to make survival horror a reality was nearly a decade old at this point, was a fervent believer in the game's potential to succeed. "No one, not even the development team, had high expectations for the game. Certain managers at Capcom wanted to cancel the game, and that's what nearly happened. However, I really pushed them to see production through to the end. I myself personally had a lot of faith in the game," Fujiwara explains. Shinji Mikami, despite being the game's director, did not himself learn of the near cancellation until nearly a decade later. In the *Resident Evil* series, injured characters can completely recover their health with an item called the First Aid Spray. Figuratively speaking, Fujiwara was the First Aid Spray that saved *Resident Evil*, bringing it back from red "Danger" status to green "Fine".

It turns out that *Resident Evil* couldn't have come at a better time for Capcom. After three years of production and development, the game was finally launched on March 22, 1996, in Japan, and on March 30 in North America. The game shattered Capcom's modest expectations both commercially and critically, receiving positive reviews from players and the game media alike. People lauded the game for its scare factor, detailed graphics and groundbreaking 3D gameplay. It earned the accolade of Game of the Year 1996 in the magazine *GamePro* and was voted Best PlayStation Game Overall in a North American PlayStation.com poll the same year. Reflecting on the game's success, Yoshiki Okamoto explains that "*Resident Evil* was the first PlayStation game that sold 1 million shortly after its release. Other titles gradually hit that mark as well, but *Resident Evil* got there the quickest." The original 1996 version sold 2.75 million by the end of its run, which would seem little compared to the likes of *Street Fighter II* if it weren't for the fact that *Resident Evil* would go on to be re-released multiple times, first in 1997. Sales of those versions are counted separately, but when combined the total sales of *Resident Evil* across its three releases on the original PlayStation stand at 5.08 million units, according to Capcom's own data.* Mikami told NowGamer, "To be honest, I was surprised by how successful it was. It was just a happy accident that the PlayStation market and the [salability] of *Biohazard* matched so perfectly. I think we were very lucky."[5]

In 2017, I met an individual who by sheer coincidence happened to be a relative of a former member of Capcom's board of directors. That board member resigned from Capcom in the mid-nineties, believing the company wouldn't survive into the second half of the decade. "Capcom managed to stay afloat thanks to Tsujimoto's investment in Napa Valley," the relative explained. "But afterwards, *Resident Evil* was released and became a huge hit, and the rest is history." Mikami concurs, having also believed that Capcom was going to go under. But company financial matters aside, as far as Mikami himself was concerned, it was mission accomplished. "I felt very strongly that I'd fulfilled my responsibility," he said, referring back to that which his boss, Fujiwara, had entrusted upon him when greenlighting the project years earlier.

It is ironic that a game featuring so much untimely death would help save its creator from the brink of bankruptcy. Or perhaps not; after all, scenario writer Kenichi Iwao, who meticulously created

* This figure combines *Resident Evil* (1996), *Resident Evil: Director's Cut* (1997) and *Resident Evil: Director's Cut Dual Shock Ver.* (1998).

the *Resident Evil* universe and all its characters, subplots, locations and thematic motifs, originally envisioned the T-virus as a means of bringing the dead back to life, a theme that would permeate throughout the series, from the first game onward. Now, having been resuscitated by to the unforeseen success of *Resident Evil*, Capcom's immediate priority was to maintain its momentum and make the new brand even bigger and better.

CHAPTER 2: FROM GAME TO FRANCHISE: *RESIDENT EVIL 2*

RESIDENT RESHUFFLE: THE HUMBLE BEGINNINGS OF HIDEKI KAMIYA

In the late eighties and early nineties, Capcom released games that achieved respectable, if not record-breaking sales. *Mega Man* and *Street Fighter* did not set sales charts alight when they were released in 1987, particularly compared to the success stories from other companies like Nintendo, but both performed well enough for Capcom to release sequels in the following years that put the two franchises firmly on the map. *Mega Man 2*, believed by many to be the best in the series, outsold the original and became a global million-seller. The success of *Street Fighter II* was even more remarkable: it blew the first game so far away that the original is barely a footnote in Capcom history.

Compared to *Mega Man* and *Street Fighter*, the first *Resident Evil* was a more immediate success, putting it ahead of Capcom's historical curve. *Resident Evil 2* was thus born. For Capcom to maintain its momentum in the newly christened survival horror genre, though, *Resident Evil 2* had to be better than its predecessor, much like *Mega Man 2* and *Street Fighter II* had been. The team wanted the sequel to be what James Cameron's *Aliens* was to *Alien*: even more groundbreaking and even more ambitious.

Ideally, any video game sequel is propped up by the experience gained by its creators during the production of the original. Creators aim to improve the quality for the sequel, usually adding new elements that were not previously possible due to constraints in time, technology or budget, all the while expanding the scale to offer customers better value for money. However, even before *Resident Evil 2* officially got off the ground, personnel shake-ups at Capcom ensured that it would be created in a different environment from its predecessor.

The first change was the Tokuro Fujiwara's departure from Capcom in late 1995, before the original game was even released. Having been the grand master of Capcom's console games since 1983 and a mentor to younger creators at the company, his departure marked the end of one era and the beginning of another. Fujiwara's decision to leave came down to his desire to make new and original games, something he says he would have been unable to do within Capcom. "Outside of *Resident Evil*, Capcom wanted to continue making franchise titles like *Street Fighter*. Meanwhile, I wanted to develop original games, but it didn't look like there'd be any opportunity to do so in the foreseeable future," Fujiwara says. Officially, he resigned from Capcom immediately after the release of *Resident Evil*, although in practice he stopped going into the office from December 1995 in order to use up his accumulated vacation days, of which there were plenty, given his thirteen-year tenure, during which he had amassed thousands of hours of overtime and unused days off, a pattern that was prevalent at Capcom during those years.

Fujiwara went on to establish his own independent development studio, Whoopee Camp. There, he assembled a team to develop a 2D platformer for PlayStation called *Tomba!* (known as *Tombi!* in Europe), which was released in December 1997. While not a tremendous commercial success, it performed well enough to receive a sequel two years later called *Tomba! 2: The Evil Swine Return* (*Tombi! 2* in Europe). Unfortunately, Fujiwara did not enjoy the same level of success at Whoopee Camp as he had at Capcom. Neither *Tomba!* title sold well enough to sustain the costs of operating the company, and as a result, Fujiwara placed Whoopee Camp into dormancy. The company continued to exist, but was effectively inactive.

Fujiwara went on to work on a number of games as a freelance consultant, such as the 2001 survival horror game *Extermination* for PlayStation 2. In 2006, he would reunite with Capcom for the first time in a decade for the PlayStation Portable (PSP) platformer *Ultimate Ghosts 'n Goblins*, a sequel to the game he had created two decades earlier. In 2009 he would work as a designer on PlatinumGames beat-'em-up title *MadWorld*. Afterwards, Fujiwara took a break from working on games for several years, due to health reasons. After his recovery, he quietly returned to the games industry in 2015 as a consultant. To perform his consulting services, Fujiwara brought Whoopee Camp out of dormancy, and as of 2020 he is operating under the banner once again, as its sole employee. His involvement in the *Resident Evil* series may have been brief, but had it not been for his seven-year-long desire to bring a legitimate horror experience to video games and his ability to recognize the talent of Shinji Mikami, *Resident Evil* as we know it today might never have existed. If Mikami is often credited as the father of *Resident Evil*, Fujiwara should certainly be considered its grandfather. But for *Resident Evil 2*, grandfather was no longer around.

The other notable departure was that of Kenichi Iwao, the scenario writer for *Resident Evil*. Iwao joined Capcom in the early 1990s, after the release of *Street Fighter II*, and initially worked on games such as the Super NES platformer *Demon's Crest*. Whereas Fujiwara, as executive producer, was more influential behind the scenes of *Resident Evil*, Iwao's contributions to the series are more direct and tangible. Iwao created the core elements of the *Resident Evil* game universe, like the T-virus, Umbrella Corporation, the STARS members, the zombies, the Tyrant, and all the other enemies. He also wrote the game's files, including the iconic line "Itchy. Tasty." from the Keeper's Diary. In Japanese, the line is *kayui uma*, which is more or less a direct translation, and the phrase has become a pop culture reference in Japan as the word *kayu* is a homonym that means either "itchy" or "rice porridge," while the word *uma* is a homonym meaning either "delicious" or "horse." Thanks to Iwao, Japanese *Resident Evil* fans can occasionally make jokes about the game featuring some combination of delicious porridge, itchy porridge, delicious horse, or itchy horse.

Upon departing Capcom, Iwao returned to his hometown of Tokyo and joined Square, where he went on to direct *Parasite*

Eve II, the sequel to a *Resident Evil*-inspired survival horror game whose plot is based on a 1995 Japanese science fiction novel of the same name. He also worked on the scenarios for the massively multiplayer online (MMO) RPGs *Final Fantasy XI* and *Final Fantasy XIV*. It is difficult to imagine the *Resident Evil* universe without the framework Iwao created for it early on. His departure meant the *Resident Evil* 2 team would have to find a new scenario writer, which would have profound consequences on the game's development.

Meanwhile, Shinji Mikami, whose success as the director of *Resident Evil* had made him an established figure within Capcom, decided for the sequel to take on the role of producer, a task more involved with budgeting and project management than with working one's creative juices. This meant having to choose someone else to direct *Resident Evil 2*. Mikami wanted to pass the

Hideki Kamiya

baton over to a younger colleague in order to foster his or her professional and creative development. Among the many talented people on Mikami's team was a twenty-five-year-old man who had recently joined the company, named Hideki Kamiya.

Hailing from Matsumoto in central Japan, Kamiya, like most game creators, had humble beginnings. He became an avid gamer during his childhood, when he owned a NES and played arcade games. He also enjoyed drawing. After graduating from university, Kamiya wanted to work in the games industry, leading him to apply to several companies. He received job offers from two major publishers: Capcom, for a game designer position, and Namco, who wanted him as an artist. Ultimately, Kamiya chose the former, joining the company in April 1994. He was soon put through his paces, as most new hires in Japanese companies are during their first year. Following his job training, Kamiya performed entry-level tasks such as quality assurance and basic planning before joining the *Resident Evil* team. Kamiya was a designer for certain environments in the Spencer Estate, though his most significant contribution to the series' lore was the naming of some of the characters, including Jill, Chris and Wesker. "I got the inspiration for their names from various media sources, including pornographic magazines," Kamiya recalls.

Of course, Kamiya's creative talents went beyond just naming characters, and Mikami soon took notice of his potential. Over drinks one night in mid-1994, Mikami told Kamiya, "You're the dark horse of the new recruits. You're either going to fail spectacularly, or you're going to be a huge success."[1] While Kamiya admits he was fairly boisterous in his twenties, his colleagues universally describe him as diligent, thoughtful, and hardworking, traits that Mikami saw as vital to successfully leading a project. In spring 1996, when the time came to choose a director for *Resident Evil 2*, Mikami called Kamiya into a meeting to formalize the decision, much like Fujiwara had done with Mikami nearly three years earlier. Kamiya, for reasons even he himself claims not to understand to this day, was now the director of *Resident Evil 2*.

RESIDENT EVIL 1.5 AND THE ARRIVAL OF NOBORU SUGIMURA

Survival horror games are not for everyone. Aside from being intended for mature audiences, their spookiness and haunting imagery require a certain level of mental preparedness, lest there be excessive screaming and panicking. It was ironic, then, that Hideki Kamiya was now in the director's seat for *Resident Evil 2*. Despite his newfound responsibility for overseeing the creative direction of the much-hyped sequel to the most successful horror game at the time, Kamiya was actually not, nor has he ever been, a fan of horror movies or games. He admits to being easily startled and having a soft stomach when it comes to violent and grotesque imagery, elaborating that even the gruesome death scenes in *Resident Evil* – from scenes of people being chewed by zombies to being decapitated by Hunters – can be far too much for him. However, Mikami chose him to direct *Resident Evil 2*, which meant that Kamiya needed to get over his distaste for horror or else hand off the responsibility to someone else. For the next two years, Kamiya would do his best to put on a brave face.

Unable to completely set aside his fear, Kamiya decided that

Resident Evil 2, while adhering to much of the core gameplay framework of its predecessor, would be more action-oriented, a reflection of his own preference for Hollywood action films. Being an early PlayStation title, the original *Resident Evil* neutered the combat abilities of its protagonists, resulting in a slow-paced action experience. *Resident Evil 2* would offer minor additions to the original's core formula, such as automatic weapons and faster and more numerous enemies, enhancements that were largely evolutionary rather than revolutionary. And instead of being located in an isolated mansion in the woods, the sequel would take place on the streets of Raccoon City. This meant more zombies on-screen at any one time – as many as seven, in fact, which is more than double the maximum of three seen in the original. The sequel would also star a new cast of characters across two scenarios, including officers Leon S. Kennedy and Marvin Branagh, civilians Ada Wong and Robert Kendo, young motorcyclist Elza Walker, and a teenage Sherry Birkin (most of their names were different earlier in production). Kamiya came up with unique and expansive scenarios for both Leon and Elza, much like the ones that set Jill and Chris apart in the original. And wanting *Resident Evil 2* to stand on its own, Kamiya decided that the game would have few direct connections to the story of the original game, although they take place in the same universe.

With *Resident Evil* having captured gamers' imaginations since 1996, the sequel garnered considerable media and consumer attention in both North America and Japan. *Resident Evil 2* was shown publicly for the first time at the spring 1996 Tokyo Game Show. While it was still early in production, players could already see improvements in the graphics and gameplay. Hype began to build among fans and expectations grew high, which in turn added to much of the pressure felt by Kamiya and his team. There was also considerable pressure internally from Capcom management. Having averted the threat of bankruptcy with the success of the original game, Capcom was now in better shape, but it was still far from being in the clear. A mishap or two could send the company back into difficult times. Thus, Capcom could not afford to squander the property's momentum. *Resident Evil 2* needed to be as successful as *Street Fighter II* had been earlier in the decade.

Throughout the summer and autumn of 1996, Kamiya's team continued to develop the environments, scenario, and gameplay system, managing to complete about 70 per cent of development by the end of that year. Now *Resident Evil 2* had to pass inspection by Yoshiki Okamoto, just like the original in late 1995. *Resident Evil* had been in rough shape when he took over from Tokuro Fujiwara as its executive producer, but Okamoto turned out to be even more dissatisfied with the status of *Resident Evil 2*. He felt that the visual premise, with its overly bright neon-lit environments and emphasis on Hollywood action elements, ran contrary to an authentic horror experience. Put simply, the game was not very scary. There was also a plethora of personnel issues impeding the project, which Mikami attributed to the high number of young, relatively inexperienced developers on the team.[2]

The story also proved to be a far bigger hurdle than anyone could have expected. Okamoto felt the plot and writing were subpar and uninteresting, with the game lacking originality. The *Resident Evil* series was Capcom's first game in which the plot was an important part of the overall connected universe – the *Mega Man, Street Fighter*, and *Ghosts 'n Goblins* series all had simple stories with little dialogue; for those games, the stories might as well not be there. The team's goals for *Resident Evil 2* were thus unprecedented in Capcom history as Capcom was attempting to offer a game with stronger gameplay and a more significant narrative than the original. Kamiya had taken charge of the story after Iwao left, carefully trying to work within Iwao's framework while injecting his own style. However, Kamiya's lack of hands-on experience in scenario-writing was evident. In its present state, *Resident Evil 2* was nowhere close to becoming the *Aliens* that Capcom originally set out to create.

The team needed to modify the scenario, but no one else at the company would make a credible replacement. Capcom therefore decided to look outside of the company for help. Okamoto got in touch with Noboru Sugimura, a well-known writer in Japan who by 1996 held an impressive two-decade pedigree for his work on Japanese television shows such as *Kyoryu Sentai Zyuranger* (adapted for the West as Saban Entertainment's *Mighty Morphin Power Rangers*) and *Kamen Rider* (adapted as *Masked Rider*, also through Saban). Sugimura happened to be a fan of the first game, so he accepted Okamoto's invitation and in late 1996 visited Capcom's Tokyo office to meet with Mikami and Kamiya, who were commuting from Capcom's headquarters in Osaka.

During his visit, Sugimura played Capcom's latest build of *Resident Evil 2*. Upon finishing, he immediately offered Mikami and Kamiya his feedback. As a writer, Sugimura felt that the story lacked both depth and thematic coherence, which he emphasized were key elements to creating a universe that would be engaging for gamers while surpassing what Capcom had already achieved with the first game. The idea of "thematic coherence" was particularly vital to Sugimura, who lambasted Kamiya for creating a story without any ties to the original. "That's terrible! You need to create a proper link between the two games!" he exclaimed. Sugimura believed that if *Resident Evil* was to evolve into a full-fledged game brand, then the games needed to be tied together in a way that went deeper than what Capcom was used to doing with the *Mega Man* and *Street Fighter* series, which did not depend on their minimalist plots to define their identities as game franchises. Sugimura proposed the provocative idea of having the team cease development of the current build and begin anew. Mikami and Kamiya could not make a decision like this during the meeting, so they told Sugimura they would discuss it with their team and get back to him.

After the meeting, Mikami and Kamiya rode the bullet train for the three-hour journey back to Osaka. During the ride, the two discussed Sugimura's feedback. While he was quite negative about the game, they agreed that he had raised many valid points that were difficult to ignore. This was the moment when Mikami and Kamiya realized what they needed to do: the existing build of *Resident Evil 2* would need to be completely overhauled, and they would need to bring Sugimura aboard to steer the ship in the right direction. Such a drastic move would result in a year-long delay, which was a long period of time in the PlayStation era. While a game created on schedule might take anywhere from three to five years to complete today, in the 1990s such long development periods were less common and often a sign of troubled production. Regardless of the lost productivity and financial impact on Capcom, Mikami and Kamiya had made up their minds. Okamoto analyzed Sugimura's feedback, much of which mirrored his own initial concerns, and backed Mikami and Kamiya, making the decision official: *Resident Evil 2* was to be scrapped, delayed, and re-created. "We decided to cancel it because we knew it wouldn't meet the expectations of players," Okamoto says.

When asked about his feelings the moment *Resident Evil 2* was officially canceled and whether he had any particular regrets about the experience, Kamiya unambiguously states that starting over was the correct decision. "It truly was a piece of shit. It was boring, devoid of vision, and a poor excuse for a horror game," he says colorfully. Armed with a strong choice of words, Kamiya appears steadfast and confident in a way that only someone with his experience could be. "To be honest, I was actually relieved when we canceled the game," he recalls. "It was my first time sitting in the director's seat, so I was quite inexperienced. I like to experiment with different ideas to see what works and what does not. Another thing that contributed to the failure of the game was my lack of vision. I do not usually have a specific vision going into a project. I like to experiment and see what sticks." When asked if he ever considered resigning – an act not unheard of in Japan, where a single failure can prematurely end one's career – Kamiya stoically says, "No, not at all."

When news of the cancellation made rounds within Capcom, a number of team members were dismayed. An entire year of development time had gone down the drain, and team morale had sunk. Certain team members even went as far as to arrange private meetings with Mikami to request that Kamiya be replaced as director. Mikami was not remotely impressed with such requests. He would flip the tables on the members and challenge them by rhetorically asking, "Why don't *you* direct the game, then?" No one offered to step forward to take over as director. Kamiya's position was safe – for the moment. But it was back to the drawing board for everyone. Kamiya certainly could not blow this second chance: another failed attempt would not be tolerated, even by Mikami, who was Kamiya's cheerleader at Capcom and the sole figure who stood between Kamiya and the more discontented members of the team.

The initial version of *Resident Evil 2* was gone, but not forgotten: the developers assigned it the codename *Resident Evil 1.5* in order to differentiate it from the release version of *Resident Evil 2* that they were now working on. Most games change between their initial conception and final release, and such transformations are usually kept out of the public eye until a game is close to its release date. But because *Resident Evil 1.5* was prominently covered by the game media prior to its reboot, Capcom has recognized and openly acknowledged its existence as a canceled *Resident Evil 2* prototype. To Capcom, it served as an object lesson in starting over from zero when the situation truly calls for it, and proved that the video game industry had now evolved to the point where seeking outside assistance could help improve a project's fortunes and set it on a path not previously available. Its cancellation was also pivotal in *Resident Evil* history because it was the first step in creating a sustained and interconnected narrative that endures to this day. Capcom also learned that some of its games could further the *Mega Man* or *Street Fighter* approach, where stories of subsequent versions need only be loosely connected. Meanwhile, some of the prototype's development engine found new life later on, in another action game, *Onimusha: Warlords*, which was released in 2001 for PlayStation 2.

A curated trailer of *Resident Evil 1.5* was included as a bonus with Japanese editions of *Resident Evil: Director's Cut Dual Shock Ver.*, which was released in August 1998 (after the final release of *Resident Evil 2*), giving fans a glimpse of what could have been. Fifteen years later, in 2013, an incomplete but playable prototype demo managed to leak onto the internet. The game-modding community has attempted to transform the demo into a playable product that adheres to the development team's original vision, with varying degrees of success. Although gamers might find the prototype an interesting relic of gaming history, Kamiya is unenthused by such efforts to bring back *Resident Evil 1.5*: "Honestly, no one needs to play through such a bad game."

KAMIYA STRIKES BACK: *RESIDENT EVIL 2* REBOOTED

Having been recruited onto the *Resident Evil 2* team to steer the ship in the right direction, writer Noboru Sugimura wasted no time getting his feet wet. Recognizing the value that well-written stories bring to games, in April 1997 Okamoto established an independent company called Flagship Co., Ltd. 1997 for the express purpose of developing game scenarios. With Okamoto in charge of the new company, Sugimura was designated head of scenario development. While technically working for a separate company outside of Capcom proper, Flagship and Sugimura were very much integrated into the *Resident Evil 2* team and would have hands-on involvement with the project's new direction.

First, Sugimura examined what could be salvaged from *Resident Evil 1.5* and repurposed for the new game. Although *Resident*

Evil 2 was being redesigned from the ground up, not everything from the previous version was getting thrown by the wayside. Sugimura decided to reuse some of the character designs to suit the new direction. He also decided that someone from the cast of *Resident Evil 2* should have direct ties to someone from the first game. As a result, he chose to replace Elza Walker with a similar but new character: nineteen-year-old Claire Redfield, who would be the younger sister of Chris Redfield. The game now contained that direct connection to the first game that *Resident Evil 1.5* was lacking. The designs for Leon S. Kennedy, Ada Wong, Sherry Birkin, Marvin Branagh, and Robert Kendo were largely carried over from the *1.5* version, and given expanded or modified roles.

Sugimura also decided to keep the Raccoon City backdrop, given that it was one of the few elements directly tied to the 1996 original. But, as with Hideki Kamiya's original concept *for Resident Evil 2*, the settings would be dramatically larger than those of the first game, with Raccoon City having been overrun with zombies, in contrast to the quieter, more isolated and claustrophobic corridors of the Spencer Mansion. The story is set three months after the original game, and Leon and Claire have arrived in Raccoon City, where they are unwittingly thrust into the zombie outbreak. They seek refuge in the Raccoon Police Department (RPD), perhaps the series' most iconic setting after the Spencer Mansion, and where the real fun begins. Sugimura suggested that the RPD be given a specific backstory to allow it to function as a puzzle-ridden maze. "During *Resident Evil 1.5*, the setup of the RPD made no sense at all," Kamiya explains. "Sugimura suggested making it so that the police building was formerly an art museum, explaining why there are bizarre puzzles throughout the building."

As in the original *Resident Evil* and *1.5*, the final version of *Resident Evil 2* would feature two protagonists. However, rather than have their stories occur in complete isolation, as had been planned, Kamiya and Sugimura worked together to come up with a new mechanic for *Resident Evil 2* called the "Zapping System." Leon and Claire explore the same locations and solve many of the same or similar puzzles, but because their stories occur simultaneously, players must finish both scenarios to witness the entire story and earn the true ending. Leon and Claire cross paths from time to time, so there are instances when the actions in one scenario directly affect what happens in the other. The most notable is when having to decide whether it should be Leon or Claire who acquires a specific weapon; players must weigh the pros and cons of the decision, as it could make things easier in the first scenario but more difficult in the second, and vice versa.

The Zapping System contained an additional layer of depth: the presence of multiple scenarios for each character. Leon's and Claire's scenarios serve as two sides of one story – an A side and a B side. The first character the player chooses takes on the A scenario, while the second character, who becomes playable following completion of the first scenario, is used for B. The two pairings are thus either Leon A–Claire B or Claire A–Leon B. The stories and gameplay elements, such as enemies and items encountered, change depending on which pairing is selected. Although largely identical to the A scenarios in terms of gameplay and basic story, the B scenarios offer a few extra challenges for players, such as the trenchcoat-sporting T-103 Tyrant, commonly referred to by Western fans as "Mr X," who would go on to become one of the more iconic monsters in the series.

While the Zapping System has come to define the identity of *Resident Evil 2*, neatly setting it apart from other entries, the developers only implemented the feature closer to the end of the project. Kamiya decided to incorporate the concept of two overlapping story arcs, an idea he originally came up with during the end of the first game's development, when it was too late to implement it. He admits that there are repetitive elements shared across all scenarios, such as both characters having to open the same doors with the same key, but also notes that making the game too realistic would have made it less entertaining.

On the technical side, the team managed to make tangible upgrades to the game's engine, and particularly to its graphics and animation. Whereas *Resident Evil* was an experiment in getting a 3D video game up and running on PlayStation, the team was now more skilled and experienced, and the technical improvements clearly showed in *Resident Evil 2*. The character models and backgrounds are more detailed, and characters slow down and clutch their sides as they sustain injuries. The enemies are faster and more aggressive, thanks to improvements made to the game's AI. This is most obvious with boss animations, which are speedier and more threatening than anything in the first game.

An accident during development led to *Resident Evil 2* becoming a game shipped across two CDs: in the final game, Disc 1 contains Leon's scenario, while Disc 2 features Claire's. It was technologically possible to have all of the final data for *Resident Evil 2* fit on a single, 700MB CD, just like the original, which is what Capcom had initially planned to do. However, the team ultimately miscalculated the size of the game's final audio data algorithm, which no one noticed until it was too late. Mikami recalls learning of the issue from programmer Yasuhiro Anpo. Anpo called Mikami, who was working on a different floor from the rest of the team. "Anpo told me there was a problem, but before he could explain, I actually hung up on him!" Mikami laughs. "Anpo eventually came over to my desk, where he told me that *Resident Evil 2* would require two discs instead of just one." Mikami remembers gasping in surprise. As producer, he was responsible for keeping the game within budget; this would surely force a recalculation. Capcom management was not at all pleased with the development. It would result in higher manufacturing and shipping costs due to the thicker, double-disc jewel case required. However, given that *Resident Evil 2* was already behind schedule at this point, rather than give the team time to reprogram the audio algorithms, Capcom conceded and allowed the game to ship on two discs. In a January 2018 tweet commenting on the game's 20th anniversary, Kamiya attributed the move to his youth and recklessness, but it certainly left its mark. Even though the team never conceptualized *Resident Evil 2* as a two-disc game, it had the positive net effect of making the game seem even longer, and therefore better, in the eyes of the average consumer, who knew nothing of the game's technical composition.

Meanwhile, Sugimura rewrote the sequel's plot to be more expansive and engaging than those of both the original and *Resident Evil 1.5*. He improved the story by affording more involved roles to the supporting cast, which consisted of Ada, an enigmatic spy operating for an unknown organization, and Sherry, the twelve-year-old daughter of the researchers at Umbrella Corporation responsible for developing the G-virus, which was capable of creating a more powerful BOW (bio-organic weapon) than the T-virus zombies from the first game. In contrast to the one-dimensional character interactions of the original that were stymied by budget limitations and poor voice-acting, the interactions between the characters in *Resident Evil 2* are much more varied, displaying qualities such as fear, tension, trauma, naivety and romance, as well as friendship and family.

Also, the story is presented more effectively in *Resident Evil 2* than in the original, thanks to the sequel's improved audio experience. This was the first time Capcom outsourced voice-acting to a professional recording studio outside of Japan. Whereas the original game had Mikami and other core staff members working with amateur or non-professional English voice actors who happened to be local, the talent pool improved greatly for the sequel. Notably, voice actress Alyson Court joined the series as Claire, a role she would reprise multiple times over the next fourteen years. Meanwhile, the soundtrack, composed by Masami Ueda, Shusaku Uchiyama, and Syun Nishigaki, featured moody and melodic tunes that managed to squeeze an orchestral sound out of PlayStation's sound chip. The music was so well received that in 1999 *Resident Evil 2*'s soundtrack, along with tracks from other *Resident Evil* games, was orchestrated for performance by the prestigious New Japan Philharmonic. Many fans still remember iconic themes such as the B-ending rock 'n' roll credits theme or the boss themes associated with the Birkin G-Type and T-103 Tyrant bosses.

Resident Evil 2 also has a greater number of extra gameplay modes than its predecessor. The most notable is "The Fourth Survivor," which stars the enigmatic Umbrella agent codenamed "HUNK." The mode was directed by system planner Kazuhiro

Aoyama as a bonus scenario that unlocks after you've met a specific set of conditions in the main game, and was the first time players could become one of the bad guys. The idea for the mini-game came late in production, when the development team had just enough time before the game was mastered for release to include an extra mode. "The Fourth Survivor" was crafted together from existing assets from the main scenarios, with Aoyama admitting that all of HUNK's animations were identical to Leon's. From a design perspective, giving HUNK a gas mask avoided having to create an entirely new character. The other mini-game, "The To-fu Survivor," features, as the name implies, a character resembling a giant block of bean curd with floating hands, holding nothing but a combat knife. This bonus is a remnant of the game's bug-testing phase, which used the tofu block to test the characters' ability to detect collision with enemies.

Due to its use of full capitals, fans over the years have speculated whether the name HUNK is an abbreviation for something, but Aoyama says that HUNK is just his name. An American on the *Resident Evil* team who wants to remain anonymous claims, "HUNK's name was actually supposed to be 'Hank,' but the developers misspelled it as 'hunk,' which they also wrote in all caps. That's why his name is stylized that way, even though it makes no sense." Indeed, in Japanese *katakana* (one of the language's three writing systems), "Hank" and "Hunk" are spelled the same way due to the lack of differentiation in Japanese between the U (/æ/) and U (/ʌ/) sounds. Kamiya, however, disagrees with the HUNK/Hank assertion.

Also, in Japan, nouns, proper or otherwise, are often written out in full caps. Most Japanese game developers are not fluent in English, and thus are less discerning about grammar and punctuation; many have told me that spelling everything in capitals makes it easier for developers to spot key terms in verbose conceptual documents. The same can be applied to "To-fu," which was the result of someone on the development team not realizing that in English "tofu" is spelled without a hyphen.

RESIDENT EVIL 2 BREAKS SALES RECORDS

At last, after an expensive and protracted production cycle that saw one prototype scrapped and development restarted from zero, *Resident Evil 2* was finally completed in December 1997. The game was scheduled to be released in North America on January 21, 1998, and in Japan on January 29. Capcom hoped to sell 2 million copies of the game in a short span of time, a very tall order for any video game in the 1990s, when the industry was far smaller than it is today. *Resident Evil 2* launched under the watchful eye of both Capcom and worldwide *Resident Evil* fans.

The response was far better than Capcom could ever have hoped. Straight out of the gate, *Resident Evil 2* sold a very large volume of copies and received a vast amount of critical acclaim. In Japan, the game sold nearly 1.4 million copies in just four days, making it an instant platinum-seller with sales figures it took the original game a year to achieve. In 1998, only Square's *Final Fantasy* and Enix's *Dragon Quest* series also sold more than a million copies at launch, indicating how popular the *Resident Evil* brand had become since 1996. *Resident Evil 2* was also very successful in the United States, where over 380,000 copies had been preordered, constituting 60 per cent of the initial manufacturing run of 633,000 units. The game grossed $19 million, earning it an accolade in the 1999 edition of the *Guinness Book of Records*. It outpaced even *Final Fantasy VII* and *Super Mario 64*. Despite Capcom USA still being a relatively small operation with limited marketing resources at the time, *Resident Evil 2* cemented the series as one of Capcom's most lucrative franchises, ultimately replicating what *Street Fighter II* and *Mega Man 2* had done for their respective series: taking something great and making it even greater. Capcom had succeeded in making the *Aliens* to its *Alien*.

The game's success brought Capcom financial gain that allowed it to pay dividends to its employees. By the time *Resident Evil 2* was released, Capcom had introduced an incentive-based bonus system in which a team's salaries would be commensurate with the sales of the games they developed. Having sold 4.96 million copies globally, *Resident Evil 2* was very lucrative for those who had worked on it. Mikami and Kamiya, in particular, had complained of low salaries during the time of *Resident Evil*, with Mikami admitting, "My salary on *Resident Evil* was probably less than a first-year employee would get today. I was actually unable to get married because of my financial situation."[3] *Resident Evil 2* allowed each member of the team to achieve greater financial stability in an industry infamous in Japan for its low salaries and long working hours.

Resident Evil 2 was critically successful as well. It was reviewed positively in all of the mainstream US game media at the time, including IGN, *Electronic Gaming Monthly*, GameSpot, and the *Official US PlayStation Magazine*. On Metacritic it enjoys a rating of 89 out of 100 and an average user rating of 9.2. out of 10.[4]

It cannot be overstated just how much of an improvement the sequel was over the original: it was larger and enhanced in nearly every respect. The only exception to this may be the actual horror elements, which some consider to be stronger in the original. But *Resident Evil 2* is no slouch, offering up its own fair share of frightening and disturbing moments, all while taking a more action-oriented approach that successors would also adopt in the years ahead. Combined with a more dramatic and elaborate storyline, thanks to Noboru Sugimura, one can certainly say that while *Resident Evil* certainly gave birth to this survival horror series, it was *Resident Evil 2* that ultimately transformed it into a full-blown game franchise.

ASK YOUR MOM: REFLECTIONS FROM HIDEKI KAMIYA

The tremendous success of *Resident Evil 2* was just what Hideki Kamiya needed after the arduous experience involved in bringing the game to fruition. The cancellation of *Resident Evil 1.5* had set the project back a year, cast doubt among some of his colleagues about his leadership skills, and nearly sent Capcom's franchise careening off a cliff to an untimely demise. But Kamiya never gave up on his goal of delivering a *Resident Evil 2* that would be groundbreaking and of high quality. He never fails to remind everyone that he would never have been able to make it without Mikami's support. "Without Mikami-san, I wouldn't be the person I am today," he proclaims.

But perhaps the most important relationship within the *Resident Evil 2* team was the one Kamiya had with Noboru Sugimura.

During our interview, Kamiya mentions Sugimura's name far more than anyone else's, even Mikami's. It is also significant that Kamiya always refers to Sugimura with the Japanese honorific title "sensei," which is commonly used to address teachers or people who are masters at their craft; for Kamiya, Sugimura was a master at creating stories whose guidance helped get *Resident Evil 2* back on track. "Sugimura-sensei was old enough to be my father," Kamiya muses, indicating the deference the Japanese give to their elders, who are often seen as sources of wisdom and guidance, with age and seniority forming the social fabric that profoundly shape how any two people interact with each other.

It was Sugimura who carefully constructed and contextualized nearly every story element of *Resident Evil 2*, wrapping it all up within a coherent and interesting universe. That said, few people would give the *Resident Evil* series credit for having a story befitting the great literary masterpieces of our time, but that is not what Sugimura ever set out to achieve. He gave *Resident Evil 2* the sort of characters and narrative that its fans would grow to care about, just like fans of Sugimura's other work, such as *Kamen Rider* and *Super Sentai*. More importantly, Sugimura was the leader that Kamiya needed. "He really loved *Resident Evil*," Kamiya explains. "I learned so much from him." In the years ahead, their relationship continued to grow, becoming more than just professional. Kamiya tells an anecdote about a motorcycle accident that left him hospitalized. He was lying on a hospital gurney recovering from surgery when his mother arrived with a get-well "gift" from Sugimura. Kamiya, believing it to be work material, opened the package up in front of his mother and found five pornographic books inside, much to his embarrassment.

Today, Kamiya is one of the game industry's most recognized creators and, as of 2020, is the senior vice president for the Osaka-based PlatinumGames. On social media he has earned a reputation for his colorful vocabulary and choice of words when interacting with followers. Tweeting in Japanese and English, Kamiya often mocks those who send him messages that he perceives to be inane, incomprehensible, redundant, false, or irrelevant. He particularly dislikes questions about games he didn't work on and subjects he has discussed previously. If one wants to communicate with Kamiya on Twitter, one would best first check his posting history for fear of getting publicly told to ask one's mother for the answer, or asked in turn, like one Kotaku writer, "Do you eat shit?", or perhaps worst of all getting blocked from viewing or responding to his tweets altogether.

From a distance, Kamiya looks rather like a grumpy, unapproachable celebrity. Even I was slightly nervous before meeting him for an interview in October 2017, apprehensive at the thought of asking him about something he may have answered countless times before. However, in real life, Kamiya is the complete opposite of his Twitter personality. He is very friendly, open, and hospitable. The Kamiya that most people witness on Twitter is, by his own admission, a character for show. His Twitter persona is an alter ego befitting a WWE actor. "When I post on Twitter, I talk as if I'm having drinks with someone at a bar. I'm not interested in maintaining a veil of formality like I do at work," Kamiya explains.

While Westerners may be accustomed to freedom of expression on social media, in Japan fewer people feel the same liberty. Often, famous people are expected to show restraint in how they express their opinions to avoid drawing undue attention to themselves. In the game industry, overt criticism on Twitter of fans, customers, competitors, or other companies is discouraged, which makes Kamiya a notable exception. Others in the game industry who tweet anything half as provocative as Kamiya have been reprimanded, but not Kamiya. In an April 2013 interview with Polygon, Tatsuya Minami, Kamiya's former boss, said of Kamiya's tweets: "Up until this point, everything he's said on Twitter has been on the very close side of the safe line. I've never asked him to delete anything. But he pushes that safe line when he decides to use some of the fouler language that he knows in English."[5] Perhaps Kamiya's online persona works well due to his status as an accomplished, charismatic creator in an industry where people are unfairly stereotyped as being socially awkward or lacking in communication skills. Whatever the reason, his colorful commentary dazzles observers time and time again.

Regardless of whether one agrees with his style of interacting with people on Twitter, Kamiya has certainly earned his privilege of being vocal and opinionated. Within the two-year development cycle of *Resident Evil 2* alone, he leaped from being a rookie director who depended on Mikami and Sugimura for guidance to the charismatic creative who helped Capcom reach new heights in the PlayStation era. He had tasted the bitterness of failure with *Resident Evil 1.5* and the sweet sensation of success following *Resident Evil 2*. Kamiya continued to be involved in the *Resident Evil* series in the years ahead, but it is *Resident Evil 2* that, for various reasons, remains his most notable and impactful contribution to the franchise.

CHAPTER 3: NEMESIS

NUMBERS AREN'T EVERYTHING

With video games, films and books, the line between the main
entry and its spin-offs serves a specific purpose within the context
of a particular property or brand. For video games, main entries
feature gameplay, a story and characters that are consistent with
a property's primary image and are usually sequenced using a
number to denote its place in either a chronological timeline or
in the order it was released. In Square Enix's *Final Fantasy* series,
the main entries are *Final Fantasy*, *Final Fantasy II*, and so forth,
all the way up to *Final Fantasy XV*. Meanwhile, a side story or
spin-off may carry the brand name, but will be different somehow,
perhaps featuring a different gameplay style or a separate, though
marginally related, plot. Typically, there is no number attached to
a side story or spin-off, with a subtitle often taking its place. In the
Final Fantasy series, *Dissidia: Final Fantasy* is considered a spin-off

because it is a fighting game rather than an RPG. In a film series like *Star Wars*, Episodes *I* through *IX* are main entries, whereas the 2016 film *Rogue One: A Star Wars Story* is a stylistically distinct side story featuring a new cast largely unrelated to the Skywalkers or the Jedi of the other films.

Yet with the *Resident Evil* series, the distinction between main game and side story is somewhat more complicated. One could not be faulted for believing that the game known today as *Resident Evil 3: Nemesis* can stand triumphantly alongside its fellow-numbered brethren because it, too, possesses a number. However, hidden beneath the number three lies the story of a project that was born out of the most modest of expectations; one that was not originally meant to be either a true sequel to *Resident Evil 2* or a third entry in the what fans today commonly refer to as the "mainline" *Resident Evil* series. Instead, *Resident Evil 3: Nemesis* was originally conceived as a spin-off title called *Resident Evil 1.9*. It was born out of the state of the game industry in the late 1990s.

The original *Resident Evil* was released early in PlayStation's lifecycle and helped establish Sony's success over its competitors, while *Resident Evil 2* was released at the height of that system's generation, enjoying record sales that transformed *Resident Evil* into a household name. Hideki Kamiya was therefore chosen to direct the next *Resident Evil* game, which would ostensibly be *Resident Evil 3*. However, the gaming landscape changed dramatically in November 1998, eleven months after the launch of *Resident Evil 2*, with the release of the Sega Dreamcast. A new generation had already begun. But Sony had plans of its own, with its much-hyped and technologically superior PlayStation 2 due to arrive in late 1999. Kamiya took great interest in the new-generation PlayStation and wanted to develop the next *Resident Evil* game for it. "I think *Resident Evil 2* represents everything I would have been able to achieve for a survival horror game on PlayStation," Kamiya explains. "My vision for the next game was to make something brand new and more provoking. As a result, I decided to make *Resident Evil 3* for PlayStation 2." But with new game consoles come new challenges: Kamiya's team would need more time than ever to develop a new game for the PlayStation 2 hardware, on top of figuring out how to evolve the game style.

It so happened that Sony was not able to launch PlayStation 2 until March 2000, more than two years after the release of *Resident Evil 2*. Because of this delay, Yoshiki Okamoto and Shinji Mikami needed to figure out other ways to keep the *Resident Evil* brand active. The industry was very competitive, and other publishers were already looking into releasing their own horror games. Square had released *Parasite Eve* for PlayStation a mere two months after *Resident Evil 2*. Square's horror game was lauded for its high quality and sold over a million units in Japan. Konami was also underway with its own new horror game called *Silent Hill*, released in January 1999, also for PlayStation and to great fanfare. Capcom was the market leader for the horror genre, but a long absence put it at risk of being usurped by its competitors. "Capcom couldn't afford to wait for PlayStation 2 to launch," Mikami explains. "The company wanted to release a spin-off title during the interim transition from PlayStation to PlayStation 2." As a result, Okamoto commissioned the development of not just one, but *five* different *Resident Evil* games between the spring and summer of 1998. One of those was *Resident Evil 1.9*.

DIALING UP THE ACTION: *RESIDENT EVIL 3: NEMESIS*

Resident Evil 1.9 would prove to be a very different project from both *Resident Evil* and *Resident Evil 2*. Intended as a less important and prestigious spin-off, it also had a smaller budget and team than its predecessors. Executive producer Yoshiki Okamoto aimed to have its development completed within approximately one year, targeting a summer 1999 launch. As a result of its more limited resources, *Resident Evil 1.9* would lack the bells and whistles of the first two games, instead being shorter and leaner, focusing very specifically on action.

Shinji Mikami chose Kazuhiro Aoyama to direct *Resident Evil 1.9*. Aoyama joined Capcom in April 1995, just months after the port city of Kobe was afflicted by the devastation of the Great Hanshin earthquake. The disaster killed approximately 6,500 people and left many more without adequate housing, including many who worked at Capcom in nearby Osaka. "In Japan, newly graduated employees often live in company housing to help save money. As a result of the earthquake, some of Capcom's new hires in 1995 lost their homes or couldn't find alternative accommodation due to shortages. So, some of us were asked to share rooms while the situation sorted itself out," Aoyama recalls when looking back at his first year at Capcom. He worked on both *Resident Evil* and *Resident Evil 2* as a system planner, which saw him involved in "hidden" elements such as enemy- and weapon-damage values, movement speed, and other components related to gameplay balancing (a term used by developers to describe the process of ensuring a game has an appropriate difficulty level for a general audience, as well as being free of programming glitches that can hinder the player). As a result, Aoyama became very knowledgeable about the inner workings of the *Resident Evil* gameplay system, and Mikami felt that Aoyama could direct a new game that took the existing mold in a different direction without veering into the total revamp that Hideki Kamiya was aiming for on his own project. Creative differences between Aoyama and Kamiya also seemed to play a role in Mikami's decision. "I think Mikami-san felt my tastes were too different from Kamiya-san's, so he put me on my own project instead," Aoyama explains. It is interesting to note that Aoyama, whose early career experiences were partially influenced by a natural disaster, would go on to direct a game about a disaster-struck city.

Aoyama had some ideas he wanted to bring to the table for the first ever *Resident Evil* spin-off, but, even before that, he needed a writer for the game. At the time, Noboru Sugimura was working on other, more important, *Resident Evil* stories at Flagship, so Mikami hired a young writer named Yasuhisa Kawamura to pen the scenario for *Resident Evil 1.9*. Kawamura had begun his career as an apprentice for manga illustrator Yukito Kishiro, although he saw very little success from the endeavor. At the behest of his older sibling, Kawamura applied for a scenario-writer position at Capcom, coming into contact with Mikami and Aoyama for the first time. By his own admission, Kawamura is highly passionate about his ideas to the degree that he will speak about them at length, which he felt may have given Mikami the wrong impression, seeing as job interviews are usually succinct affairs. In a 2016 interview with Eurogamer, Kawamura recounted how he nearly failed the interview, saying, "I looked back at how I behaved after my interview, and I assumed that I was disqualified. Later I found out I was offered the position." It turns out Mikami shared an interest with Kawamura in the form of a martial art called *kenpo*, which helped cinch Mikami's decision to bring the young writer onto Capcom's most prestigious game series.[1]

Once on board, Kawamura and Aoyama got to work on hashing out the setting of *Resident Evil 1.9*. The story would focus on three different characters who worked as hired mercenaries for the Umbrella Corporation, and the setting would be the streets of Raccoon City a day before *Resident Evil 2*, hence the use of "1.9." This meant the game would also serve as a prequel, thus giving gamers a detailed look at the zombie apocalypse that befell Raccoon City before Leon and Claire arrived.

On the gameplay side, with a smaller budget and fewer resources at its disposal, Aoyama's team did not have the luxury of creating a brand-new engine or doing anything overly ambitious to advance the formula. So, in order to keep costs down and save time, the team decided to reuse the *Resident Evil 2* graphics engine, along with a number of its assets. The pre-rendered backgrounds were back, as were most of the controls, and the core gameplay of puzzle-solving, door-unlocking and zombie-killing remained intact. Even a few locations from the Raccoon City Police Department were reused, in the guise of points of continuity with *Resident Evil 2* while offering an Easter egg to the presumably hardcore *Resident Evil* fans, who were more likely to play a spin-off title than the more casual contingent.

The *Resident Evil 1.9* team only had enough time and resources to create a single scenario, rather than the two featured in the previous games, and the actual length of the scenario would be shorter. Meanwhile, unlike *Resident Evil* and *Resident Evil 2*, the low budget meant there would be no CG cut-scenes in the title.

To offset the game's leaner, more compact experience, Aoyama opted to make minor yet notable alterations to the gameplay to keep things fresh, while not deviating too far from the established formula. The game was taken in a more action-oriented direction than its predecessors, a reflection of Aoyama's preferences. Aoyama had also directed "The Fourth Survivor", the action-focused mini-game in *Resident Evil 2*, and *Resident Evil 1.9* offered a way for him to take things a step further. For the first time ever, players could create different types of ammunition by mixing various types of gunpowder. Zombies now moved faster and more aggressively. In response to the more advanced enemies, players could, with the right timing, trigger a dodge maneuver to avoid being attacked or to tackle enemies and push them away. The characters also ran a little faster than in *Resident Evil 2*, and a feature enabling an automatic 180-degree turn was added to make navigation through the worlds smoother. Meanwhile, some of the item locations and password solutions were randomized and given multiple solutions that would differ from play-through to play-through.

Kawamura also came up with the idea of the so-called "Live Selection" feature, in which players must select one of two different options that occur at a number of fixed points throughout the game. These options result in different scenes that alter the story, and though this is mostly in only minor ways, the Live Selection feature nonetheless sets the game apart from every other *Resident Evil*. "These new additions were intended to give the game more replay value," Aoyama explains. "The idea was for players to be able to complete the game in just one play-through, like an arcade game." By having randomized elements and slightly different cut-scenes, players would be encouraged to go back and play through the game a second, third, fourth, even eighth time (unlocking every secret in the game requires players to beat it at least eight times).

The most notable element of the game was the creature known as Nemesis, the primary antagonist. Japanese gamers often refer to him as "The Pursuer" or "The Stalker." Originally intended to be an amoeba-type creature like the one from the 1958 film *The Blob*, Nemesis could outrun the character, behave more aggressively than any previous enemy in the series, and scream in a disturbing, monstrous voice. He also defied some established *Resident Evil* tropes: unlike other enemies, Nemesis could walk through certain doors to pursue the player, countering expectations that going through a door meant access to a safe haven. Also, though not invincible, Nemesis possessed immense strength, and under the right circumstances could instantly kill the player, resulting in an untimely Game Over.

While the first two games featured an array of different boss fights, the leaner nature of *Resident Evil 1.9* meant the team didn't have much wiggle room for creating multiple bosses. As an alternative, Nemesis was given a pervasive presence throughout the game, appearing many times during the adventure. Some appearances are pre-scripted while others are randomized from session to session – another means to enhance the game's replay value. Aside from Nemesis, there is only one other boss, the Grave Digger, an oversized worm, bringing the total number of bosses to a whopping two, whereas the game's predecessors contained far more.

Because *Resident Evil 1.9* was intended as a spin-off, Aoyama and Kawamura did not originally intend for it to include any of the characters from the first two games, instead giving it a smaller number of brand-new characters. Early development documents show illustrations only for the characters that eventually became Carlos Oliveira, Nicholai Ginovaef and Mikhail Victor, all of whom were Umbrella mercenaries. However, in the middle of development the team was presented with an unexpected change. As a result of an alteration to the story of another *Resident Evil* game in development at the same time, Kawamura amended the setting so that Jill Valentine, co-star of the first game, would reprise her role. Kawamura explained to website Project Umbrella that "the story was initially supposed to just be an escape chronicle from an infected Raccoon City, but after discussions with [Mikami] and [Aoyama], it was decided that instead of introducing a new character, Jill Valentine will play the role of the main character."[2] Given Jill's popularity among *Resident Evil* fans, the change immediately added more legitimacy to this spin-off. She would become a defining element in the game's identity, along with Nemesis, but the most impactful change to the game was yet to come.

FROM SPIN-OFF TO FULL-FLEDGED SEQUEL

The development of *Resident Evil 1.9* was for the most part free of the issues that plagued the first two games. Kazuhiro Aoyama's vision was to make a *Resident Evil* spin-off that was orthodox in some senses, and unique in others. Thanks to the familiarity of the *Resident Evil 2* graphics and gameplay engine, combined with a focused vision, the game was never in any danger of being cancelled or rebooted. However, in summer 1999, just when its development was supposed to have been wrapping up, *Resident Evil 1.9* would see very substantial changes completely uncharacteristic of the first two games.

As development progressed, Yasuhisa Kawamura hashed out the story so that, in addition to being a direct prequel to *Resident Evil 2* in the first half, the game would also be a direct sequel in the second half. The project's name thus became *Resident Evil 1.9 + 2.1*, which was used in development materials during the second half of the project. In early 1999, the team settled on final names: *Biohazard: Last Escape* for the Japanese release and *Resident Evil: Nemesis* for North America and Europe. Capcom felt that the subtitles better reflected the game's content, both the "Nemesis" and "Last Escape" subtitles referencing two different but related themes within the game's story. The former refers to the game's iconic villain, while the latter subtitle, used in Asian countries, refers to the protagonist's "last escape" from the zombie-infested Raccoon City. The Japanese and Western versions were given different subtitles because Capcom's localizers were afraid that "Last Escape" did not sound like an appealing or natural buzzword, while "Nemesis" was not a name commonly used for the antagonist in Japanese at the time.

Then came the bombshell Aoyama was not expecting. In June 1999, a mere three months prior to the game's scheduled September release, an even more drastic change occurred. Executive producer Yoshiki Okamoto called Shinji Mikami and Aoyama into a meeting to discuss the possibility of expanding the scope of *Resident Evil: Nemesis* to match that of a main-entry title instead. The discussions took three days, and in the end, Okamoto decided to add the number three to the game's title. The game thus became *Biohazard 3: Last Escape* in Japan and *Resident Evil 3: Nemesis* in the West. Aoyama recalls being caught completely off guard by the change: "This game was supposed to be a spin-off, so I adhered to that framework during development. I was not expecting it to become *3* at all." Mikami, who had very little active involvement in the game's creative elements but oversaw the project from a distance, further explains: "The basic idea for *3* was to make an indie *Resident Evil* game." Mikami's interpretation of "indie" refers to underground rock bands whose music tends to be different and unconventional from the mainstream, rather than "indie games" developed by independent teams without the support of a publisher. "Aoyama's game was supposed to target underground hardcore fans of *Resident Evil* who didn't care if the game was weird or quirky," Mikami elaborated. A number in the title implied that the game would be a main entry, and Aoyama and Mikami feared that *Resident Evil 3: Nemesis* was both too short and too different from what fans expected *Resident Evil* to be. If Capcom was not careful, the move could backfire, especially when measured against the immense commercial success and critical acclaim of *Resident Evil 2*.

Regardless, it was too late to reboot the game, and the team had only about two months, over the summer, to add enough content to extend the game's playability. "Okamoto-san requested that more content be added to lengthen the game's playtime," Aoyama explains. In particular, the game was originally intended to end at an earlier point, but a number of extra areas were added to Raccoon City Park and the Dead Factory, while other locations were also expanded. The game's content did not dramatically change as a result of these additions, but it did make the game a little bit longer than it was originally intended to be; Aoyama estimates that the game gained about thirty minutes of extra playtime. It was the best the team could do with only two months of development time available. Anything more would have risked a delay, which Capcom wanted to avoid, given that there were other *Resident Evil* games scheduled for release later in 1999 and early 2000 as well. According to Aoyama, the game also got a last-minute budget increase to allow the team to include CG cut-scene videos. Capcom hoped that the modest additions made to *Resident Evil 3: Nemesis* would help alleviate fears that the company was releasing a *Resident Evil* sequel that offered considerably less content than its predecessors.

Aoyama has one theory about why Capcom chose to transform his spin-off into a full *Resident Evil* sequel. "If I remember correctly, Capcom wanted to become a publicly listed company during the fiscal year 1999. Capcom needed a hit title to gain investor confidence. They thought that a new, numbered *Resident Evil* game could help achieve that." Kawamura offers more insight, claiming that the factors were beyond the direct control of his team. Hideki Kamiya's team had been simultaneously developing "*Resident Evil* 3" for PlayStation 2, but the project's progress was stalled, due to large directional changes. Kawamura says, "Kamiya-san's team was forced to go back to the drawing board to design for the PlayStation 2. This meant that fans on the PlayStation would have to wait several years for the next sequel, a scenario that Capcom wanted to avoid. On the other hand, it would've been unacceptable for a game designed by Kamiya-san to be any less than perfect in quality, and besides, it would be unthinkable to rush the development on a brand-new hardware like the

PlayStation 2."³ After Aoyama's project adopted the number 3, Kamiya's game subsequently became *Resident Evil 4*. Aoyama also says that, due to the changes and delay seen with *Resident Evil 3*, some of the budget originally assigned to Kamiya's game was transferred to *Resident Evil 3: Nemesis*, which made it possible for the game to include those CG cut-scene videos.

Resident Evil 3: Nemesis was finally released on September 22, 1999, in Japan. While the first two games had been released in Japan and North America almost simultaneously, the release of *Resident Evil 3: Nemesis* in North America was pushed to November in order to give more breathing room to *Dino Crisis*, which was released in August. Co-directed by Mikami, *Dino Crisis* was essentially a *Resident Evil* clone, with dinosaurs instead of zombies. The European PAL version was not released until much later, in March 2000, because the game's European publisher, Eidos Interactive, apparently wanted to avoid interfering with sales of *Tomb Raider III*, which had launched in November.

The game became a commercial and critical success for Capcom. In Japan, it followed in the footsteps of *Resident Evil 2* by selling over 1 million copies in its first week. It also enjoyed success elsewhere, selling over 2 million units in the US and Europe. "*Resident Evil 3: Nemesis* was probably Capcom's most profitable *Resident Evil* game at the time," says Mikami. "We expected to sell only 1.4 million copies, but instead sold 1.8 million. It's unbelievable!" Final sales of the PlayStation game are at 3.5 million.⁴ This is lower than the 4.9 million copies of *Resident Evil 2* sold, but when taking into account its shorter development time, its lower budget and the fact it was originally planned as a spin-off, the results were quite strong as a whole. Okamoto's move to transform the game into a numbered mainline entry was, in the end, very well calculated. The title was well liked by most game fans, achieving a respectable 88.21 per cent score out of 100 on GameRankings.[5]

Resident Evil 3: Nemesis also left a footprint in gaming pop culture in ways no other game in the series has. Thanks to her tube-top outfit and tough persona, Jill Valentine became a representative of female video game characters, placing her in the same category as Lara Croft from *Tomb Raider*, Chun-Li from *Street Fighter*, Samus from *Metroid* and even Princess Peach from the *Mario* series. Nemesis, too, became an icon, and is fondly remembered for his aggressiveness and terrifying personality, appearing in several "best of" lists for enemies and characters. He went on to appear in a number of future *Resident Evil* releases, as well as in crossover titles such as *Marvel vs. Capcom 3: Fate of the Universe* and *Project X Zone 2*. There is a very high probability that someone attending a video game, anime or comic book convention will run into at least one person cosplaying Jill and another playing Nemesis.

Aoyama's game is also the only one in the series to see its content reproduced in another form of mainstream media: cinema. The year 2002 saw the release of the first live-action *Resident Evil* film, which was directed by Paul W. S. Anderson and starred Milla Jovovich. It was successful enough for Sony and film production studio Screen Gems to immediately pursue a sequel, which was released in 2004 under the title *Resident Evil: Apocalypse*. The second film was a fairly close adaptation of the game, featuring the same general story, setting, characters and enemies as *Resident Evil 3: Nemesis*, with a number of minor additions to suit the separate universe of the live-action films. *Resident Evil: Apocalypse* grossed $129 million worldwide on a budget of $45 million.[6]

Commenting on the game's legacy, Aoyama says, "I'm truly happy at the response to the game over the past twenty years. I never imagined it would have this sort of impact on gaming culture. I'm grateful for that."

WHAT'S IN A NUMBER? REFLECTIONS FROM KAZUHIRO AOYAMA

In 2016, the *Resident Evil* series turned twenty. At San Diego Comic-Con the same year, Capcom USA created a short video celebrating the series' history. *Resident Evil 3: Nemesis* was featured in the montage alongside the first two games and most of the entries that came after. *Resident Evil CODE: Veronica*, the entry that came directly after *Resident Evil 3: Nemesis*, was conspicuously absent, despite the former having a story that was in many ways more vital to the *Resident Evil* lore. Capcom USA justified this by explaining that the video was only meant to include "numbered titles," as if a number served as a prerequisite for being classified as a "mainline" *Resident Evil*. What's in a number, anyway? In this case, someone probably forgot that numbers are not everything in the *Resident Evil* series.

"I really wish I could've done more." Those are Kazuhiro Aoyama's words when I ask him to reflect on his role as director of *Resident Evil 3: Nemesis*. He has harbored this exact sentiment for nearly two decades without change, regardless of the game's commercial success, critical praise and legacy in video game pop culture. He wishes he could have had more time and money to make a game that would have been, in his eyes, actually worthy of that coveted mainline status. Aoyama admits that his game was not as revolutionary as *Resident Evil* or as legendary as *Resident Evil 2*, but "that was never the intention," he explains, reminding us that *Resident Evil 3: Nemesis* was not originally supposed to have a number in its title.

In our initial conversation, Aoyama sounds very humble as he reflects on his past as a game creator. He makes *Resident Evil 3: Nemesis* sound like a beautiful accident instead of a deliberately crafted piece of art. However, that would be misunderstanding his true feelings. It is true that there were plenty of factors around the game's development that were simply beyond his control. He only had the smaller budget Capcom was willing to allocate for his project, but from the sidelines observed the better treatment that other teams, such as Hideki Kamiya's, were receiving. The fact that the game gained its number, and therefore its main-entry status, was entirely due to the volition of his boss, Yoshiki Okamoto; Aoyama did not personally agree with it.

In a follow-up conversation, Aoyama emphasizes that developing video games is more than just about the creators; it is about the players as well. "While Mikami and Kamiya may emphasize the role of creators in completing production of a game, I think it's vital for creators and players to have an equal and positive relationship," Aoyama says. "Without that, the game cannot be realized as a full-blown product." Aoyama's view is that, despite Capcom's initial low expectations for *Resident Evil 3: Nemesis*, *Resident Evil* fans' positive response to the title ultimately legitimized it. Aoyama personally loathes putting profit before quality, and the hurdles he faced with the production of *Resident Evil 3: Nemesis* – particularly the requests from his superiors – only motivated him to strive to achieve more.

Indeed, the success of *Resident Evil 3: Nemesis* leaves a legacy that goes beyond its humble beginnings. Aoyama directed only one game, but its legacy is greater than anything that 99 per cent of creators out there can ever hope to achieve. While he continues to stress that his relationship with players is part of his creative process, Aoyama certainly has plenty to be proud of as a creator.

After *Resident Evil 3: Nemesis*, Aoyama moved on to other teams at Capcom. He would never work on another *Resident Evil* again. He directed another PlayStation title, the Japan-only point-and-click adventure game *Fushigi Deka*, then returned to his roots as a system planner, joining the team developing *Onimusha: Warlords*, another *Resident Evil*-inspired series, this time featuring samurai warriors in feudal Japan. He next joined the *Dino Crisis 3* team, again as a system planner.

Aoyama remained at Capcom until 2004, when large-scale organizational changes at the company took place due to the protracted development of *Resident Evil 4*. For personal reasons, Aoyama decided to move to Ishikawa Prefecture on the west coast of Japan – a more peaceful, affordable and relaxing locale than Tokyo or Osaka. He currently works at another game developer, where he performs many of the same tasks that he did as a system planner for *Resident Evil*, albeit in very different genres, such as pachinko games. Despite not having been involved in *Resident Evil* since 1999, he still harbors fond memories of working at Capcom. When, out of simple curiosity, I ask Aoyama if he would like to work on a new *Resident Evil* game, he replies simply, with a stern look on his face: "If there's an opportunity, why not?"

CHAPTER 4: READY TO RUMBLE

CENSORSHIP DRAMA: *RESIDENT EVIL: DIRECTOR'S CUT*

The protracted development of *Resident Evil 2* had negative financial repercussions for Capcom. When *Resident Evil 1.5* was cancelled and subsequently rebooted, the company was now down one hit title for 1997. To fill the gap, executive producer Yoshiki Okamoto decided to pull a page out of the now-classic Capcom playbook: re-releasing a game with newly added content. *Street Fighter II* had become its own sub-series by this point, due to its infamously high number of incarnations, spanning from *Street Fighter II Turbo: Hyper Fighting* to *Street Fighter II: Champion Edition* all the way to *Super Street Fighter II: The New Challengers* (the latest *Street Fighter II* re-release hit in 2017, so still only the beginning). Each version was more or less similar to another, although it would feature new characters, stages and/or audio to set it apart from previous ones. *Resident Evil* would be no different in this regard.

Enter *Resident Evil: Director's Cut*, which was green-lit for PlayStation in spring 1997. Hiroyuki Kobayashi, a programmer for the original version, was placed in charge of the re-release, with Mikami taking a supervisory role. The team looked into the reception of the original to see what sort of alterations could be made. According to Kazuhiro Aoyama, Capcom received a considerable amount of Japan-based consumer feedback complaining that the game was too difficult, so the team decided to augment the original with new difficulty modes, including "Beginner," tailored to casual players. On the other hand, the original *Resident Evil* had developed a hardcore audience consisting of players who would try to beat the game as quickly as possible (known as a "speed run"), without using firearms ("no-weapon run"), and/or without taking any damage ("no-damage run"). To give those fans a reason to purchase the re-release, Kobayashi's team added "Arrange" mode, which was more difficult than the original and also relocated items, changed how some rooms looked and even offered new costumes for the protagonists. In the modern era, speed runs, no-damage or no-weapon runs and the like have transformed into a specialized segment of gaming, and players often stream their sessions on YouTube or Twitch for people to observe, which game publishers such as Capcom see as a form of "influencer" PR. *Resident Evil: Director's Cut* is significant in that it was Capcom's first attempt to target a hardcore subset of customers who enjoyed *Resident Evil*, and it's a venture that continues to pay dividends more than two decades later.

For gamers in the West, *Resident Evil: Director's Cut* was a topic of particular interest because, in the run-up to its September 1997 release, Capcom marketed the game as "uncut" and "uncensored." With the original release, there had been several key differences between the Japanese and Western versions. Most notably, in the Japanese game the recorded cut-scenes were slightly longer and rendered in full color, while the Western game included black-and-white video, with the more violent segments removed entirely. A scene showing Chris Redfield lighting and smoking a cigarette was also removed from the Western version, as youth anti-smoking initiatives throughout North America and Europe made such depictions in video games a sensitive issue.

Although violence, profanity, and nudity in video games will surprise few people today, the environment was different in the 1990s, when gaming demographics skewed younger and the impact of violent games and movies on youth was a hot topic. Nintendo had been at the forefront of video game censorship since 1988, and even issued official guidelines on imagery that would not be allowed in first- or third-party games released for its systems. Sega and Sony were less stringent than Nintendo; when Acclaim's *Mortal Kombat* was released, in 1992, the Sega Genesis version featured blood spewing from characters after they were hit, while the Super NES version had the visuals changed – via a palette-color swap from red to gray – to depict sweat instead.[1] The growing popularity of *Mortal Kombat* led even the US Congress to hotly debate violence in video games in the early 1990s, and as recently as 2005 certain states, such as California, entertained the idea of prohibiting the sale of Mature-rated (M) games to minors (generally those below the age of eighteen).[2]

Meanwhile, the amount of grotesque imagery in *Resident Evil* was so groundbreaking for a mid-1990s title that the game opens with a disclaimer that would become a *Resident Evil* staple: "This game contains scenes of explicit violence and gore." Japan also confronted the topic, as Aoyama remembers. "After *Resident Evil* was released, Capcom received complaints from parents who thought the game was too violent for their children," Aoyama says. "I don't think anyone's ever publicly admitted this, so it's just a theory, but it is believed that CERO, Japan's game-ratings agency, was established partly because of *Resident Evil*." CERO, which stands for Computer Entertainment Rating Organization, was established in 2002 and is Japan's equivalent to ESRB (Entertainment Software Rating Board) in North America and PEGI (Pan European Game Information) in Europe. Virtually all commercial games are rated through these agencies, and the *Resident Evil* series is generally given a "Mature" rating. While *Resident Evil* never attracted the same level of controversy as *Mortal Kombat*, Capcom USA were right to be cautious given that attitudes had evolved with the release of PlayStation.

As a result, when Capcom announced that *Resident Evil: Director's Cut* would restore the cut-scenes to their intended state, as seen in the Japanese version, Western gamers had good reason to be excited. There was no YouTube or high-speed broadband internet at the time, nor was importing a Japanese copy of the game practical for 99 per cent of players.

However, as soon as Western buyers booted up their shiny new copy of *Resident Evil: Director's Cut*, they were greeted with the same censored videos as the original. This was in spite of the game's packaging advertising "uncensored" cut-scenes. The game was guilty of false advertising, and a considerable portion of Capcom's customers were upset. According to Capcom USA, the cut-scenes were initially intended to be uncensored, but due to miscommunication during the game's certification process with Sony, the censored videos remained in the final product. To placate angry fans, Capcom USA uploaded the uncensored videos onto its official website. To this day, no version of the original *Resident Evil* released in the West contains the uncensored introduction video.

Perhaps the ultimate incentive for fans to pick up *Resident Evil: Director's Cut* was the demo of *Resident Evil 2* that was included for free. The demo featured Leon S. Kennedy and gave players a glimpse of the early parts of the game, including the streets of Raccoon City and the police station. Those who did not care for the new difficulty modes or the censorship drama (which was a non-issue in Japan) found a sneak peek of *Resident Evil 2* to be enticing enough to purchase the re-release of the first game.

Despite the censored-video controversy in the West, *Resident Evil: Director's Cut* was a very successful re-release, selling 1.13 million copies worldwide. This helped Capcom offset the loss caused by the delay of *Resident Evil 2,* while giving fans something else to play while they waited for the sequel. In terms of marketability, *Resident Evil: Director's Cut* effectively replaced the original game, which was subsequently discontinued. This meant that many players first got into the *Resident Evil* series through *Director's Cut*, rather than the original version. Sales of both versions combined are at 3.88 million, thus outselling all other Capcom games released up to that point except for *Street Fighter II* and *Street Fighter II Turbo* for Super NES.

RESIDENT RUMBLES: *RESIDENT EVIL: DIRECTOR'S CUT DUALSHOCK VER.* AND *RESIDENT EVIL 2: DUALSHOCK VER.*

When Nintendo 64 launched in June 1996, one of its most lauded new features was the analog stick included with its unconventional three-pronged controller. Allowing for more fluid movement than the D-Pad, the analog stick, like the control sticks featured on arcade boards, made controlling 3D games like *Super Mario 64* a more intuitive experience. In contrast, the Saturn and PlayStation controllers initially only had traditional D-Pads. Nintendo then released the so-called "Rumble Pak" accessory, which was first bundled with rail-shooter *Star Fox 64* in April 1997. The Rumble Pak attached to the bottom of the Nintendo 64 controller and allowed gamers to feel vibrations emitted from the accessory in response to occurrences in gameplay. In *Star Fox 64*, when an enemy plane is shot down, the Rumble Pak will vibrate as if the player is experiencing the crash. For the time, vibration served as a differentiator between Nintendo and its 32-bit competitors.

Not wanting to be outdone by its rival, Sony developed a new controller for PlayStation called the DualShock. The original PlayStation controller was a minor evolution over Nintendo's Super NES game pad, adopting the same basic layout but adding a second pair of shoulder buttons (R1 and R2), plus handles for improved comfort. The DualShock, however, was a more significant advancement, keeping the basic template of the original controller but adding two analog sticks and dual-motor rumble-vibration feedback. Unlike the Rumble Pak, the DualShock carried its vibration functionality inside the controller, so there was no need to purchase an extra accessory. The DualShock became standard with newly sold PlayStation consoles beginning in 1998.

Games now had to be programmed to work with the DualShock's analog sticks and vibration, and games developed previously, such as *Resident Evil* and *Resident Evil 2*, could not utilize either the analog sticks or the vibration functionality. Executive producer Yoshiki Okamoto believed that the *Resident Evil* series would benefit from supporting the DualShock, so he green-lit re-releases of the first two games to include the necessary updates. This meant PlayStation would see its third incarnation of the original game in as many years. But for Capcom, this was just par for the course: after all, they released three versions of *Street Fighter II* on the Super NES. The re-releases were titled *Resident Evil: Director's Cut DualShock Ver.* and *Resident Evil 2: DualShock Ver.*, and the team effortlessly programmed the new vibration functionality and analog control into the games. Players could now experience the sensation of rumble when shooting weapons or getting bitten by zombies, and could use the analog stick to move the characters or navigate menus, although the tank controls were retained.

Although they were relatively minor projects, Okamoto felt that the re-releases should still contain additional content not included in previous versions, rather than simply adding in DualShock functionality. In early 1998, Okamoto had pushed for a collaboration with a Japanese composer named Mamoru Samuragochi for another game. Purported to be deaf, Samuragochi had become moderately famous by the late 1990s for his work composing for TV shows, and Okamoto thought it would be interesting to have Capcom associated with him, in a way that was similar to how famous scriptwriter Noboru Sugimura was brought onboard for *Resident Evil 2*. Samuragochi's name carried enough weight for the new soundtrack to generate attention on its own, even if nothing else in the game was added. Okamoto's hunch would prove correct, though not in the way he had expected.

Samuragochi was commissioned to produce a soundtrack for the *Resident Evil* re-release, but his work turned out to be completely distinct from the original music. In contrast to the electro-synth compositions in the game's previous versions, Samuragochi aimed for a more grandiose, symphonic sound reminiscent of Japanese horror films from the 1960s and 1970s. Unfortunately, a number of the tracks were universally derided by players not only for being worse than the tracks they were replacing, but for being ill-suited to the game itself. One particular track, commonly referred to as "Mansion Basement" due to the room it plays in, has become infamous for representing Samuragochi's whole soundtrack: while the original conveys a sense of mystery and tension, Samuragochi's version is comparatively unstructured, sounding like a random parade of synth trumpets. The track attempts to portray a sense of dread, but because it comprises multiple stems of dull, almost monotone rhythms, it comes off as sarcastic and decidedly not frightening. Kazuhiro Aoyama, who nominally directed the re-releases, recalls sitting down with Shinji Mikami to listen to the newly delivered tracks. "Mikami-san and I listened and laughed at the tracks as we listened to them. Mikami-san thought they were a poor fit. I think Okamoto-san listened to the tracks as well, but he insisted we include them since we already went through all the trouble to get them made," Aoyama explains.

Perhaps "Mansion Basement" was more of a speed bump than a defining moment in Samuragochi's career. He went on to compose the music for Capcom's *Onimusha: Warlords*, in 2001, which turned out to be a well-made and memorable soundtrack that captured the mood of the game perfectly. He became even more famous after his work with Capcom; in 2003, he released "Symphony No. 1: 'Hiroshima'," which became one of the most defining pieces of his career. In 2008, the city of Hiroshima, where he is from, bestowed upon him an award celebrating his artistry. Samuragochi was dubbed "Japan's Beethoven," and became a household name in Japan's music scene.[3]

However, in 2014 it was revealed that for a period of eighteen years Samuragochi had been taking credit for music that was actually composed by a ghostwriter named Takashi Niigaki. The other bombshell was that Samuragochi might not have been completely deaf.[4] The public rightfully found the revelations shocking, and the issue became a celebrity scandal. Aoyama, however, was not remotely surprised, having become suspicious of Samuragochi's claims sixteen years earlier. As the director of this re-release, Aoyama had worked directly with Samuragochi, and recalls a phone call they shared. "I spoke to Samuragochi-san on the phone once, to discuss the music for *Resident Evil*. From my vantage point, it seemed like he could hear exactly what I was saying to him. I wondered how he could possibly be deaf!" Aoyama admits. Samuragochi's revelation was so profound that when, in December 2018, Capcom re-released *Onimusha: Warlords* for PlayStation 4, Xbox One, Nintendo Switch and PC, it decided to replace Samuragochi's compositions (in reality, Niigaki's compositions) with an entirely new soundtrack made up of music by several different composers.

Aside from the new soundtrack, the other major addition to the 1998 *Resident Evil* re-release was the so-called "*Biohazard* Complete Disc," which contained save files for each *Resident Evil* game, with infinite ammunition and alternate costumes as well as footage of *Resident Evil 1.5* before it was cancelled. Intended as a bonus reward for fans who had bought previous *Resident Evil* games, the disc was never offered for sale outside Japan.

Released in August 1998, *Resident Evil: Director's Cut DualShock Ver.* sold only modestly in Japan and, for reasons unknown, it was never released in PAL territories. However, the game was considerably more successful in North America, where Capcom USA released it for $19.99 under Sony's Greatest Hits budget-price game line-up, which was reserved for games that had sold at least 250,000 units.[5] New games tended to retail for $39.99 and higher, so Capcom USA had, new soundtrack aside, introduced an improved version of the game with a lower barrier to entry. According to Capcom, *Resident Evil: Director's Cut DualShock Ver.* even outsold the vanilla *Resident Evil: Director's Cut* in total, worldwide, despite the lack of release in Europe and the lower Japanese sales, with 1.2 million sold compared to 1.13 million for the first re-release. This would be the third and final version of the first *Resident Evil* to be released on PlayStation.

The DualShock-enabled versions of *Resident Evil* and *Resident Evil 2* were released on the same day. Given that the original *Resident Evil 2* had been released only seven months earlier, the changes made for this re-release were more modest. The most notable addition is "Extreme Battle Mode," a mini-game in which players must find four bombs before they can blow up all of Raccoon City. Chris Redfield makes a cameo as a playable character, along with his sister Claire, plus Leon and Ada.

As with the initial version of *Resident Evil: Director's Cut*, Capcom included new difficulty modes in *Resident Evil 2: DualShock Ver.* as a means to expand the game's consumer appeal. The team added a "Rookie" difficulty mode, which gave Leon and Claire overpowered weapons that make the game far too easy. According to Aoyama, the mode was intended for both novice players and those who wanted to casually enjoy the game. The Japanese version also added a so-called "USA Version," which incorporated the higher-difficulty mode of the North American release. "We made the overseas versions of *Resident Evil* games more difficult in order to curb game rentals," Aoyama admits. In Japan, video game rentals had been prohibited by law since 1984,[6] while used-game sales would not be allowed until 2002,[7] thus giving less incentive for Capcom to make the Japanese versions of their games more difficult. For Japanese gamers, the inclusion of a USA Version mode made for an exotic, if niche, sales point. *Resident Evil 2: DualShock Ver.* enjoyed modest sales worldwide, effectively replacing the original version, which was discontinued following the re-release.

CHAPTER 5: THE HISTORY OF *RESIDENT EVIL* ON SEGA

THE CONSOLE WAR

For gaming enthusiasts, the console war is serious business. People who grew up in the early 1990s might have engaged in passionate discussions (or even fought) over which 16-bit console was better; whether it was Sega Genesis or Super NES. The competition extended to gaming mascots, as well: gamers have probably pitted the Mario Brothers against Sonic the Hedgehog at some point in their lives, conjuring imaginary scenarios of Mario duking it out with Sonic and wondering who would actually win. (The world would have to wait until 2008 for this dream battle to take place, when *Super Smash Bros. Brawl* for Wii was released.) The console war eventually moved into the so-called "32-bit era," which was comprised of Sega Saturn, released in November 1994, and

PlayStation, released by Sony one week later, in December. Both Saturn and PlayStation popularized console games featuring 3D graphics, which was previously a high-tech privilege seen only in arcades and PCs. Nintendo would not join Sega and Sony until June 1996, when Nintendo 64 was released. The advanced 3D capabilities of these systems were what made the survival horror genre and *Resident Evil* a possibility for the first time.

The console war may have made for interesting schoolyard banter for the average gamer, but for executives working throughout the industry they were extremely serious business. Nintendo and Sega, the main first-party developers, were fiercely defensive of their success and pulled no stops to ensure they maintained their dominance. During the original NES era, Nintendo developed a reputation as an overly selective and inflexible software licenser intent on conveying a family-friendly image. Sega aimed for an older demographic, targeting teenagers with its more mature, cooler-looking games, such as *Sonic* and *Streets of Rage*. Sony eventually released its own mascot title in the form of *Crash Bandicoot*, in 1996.

Third parties, including Capcom, fell right into the middle of this competitive environment. When deciding which platform to develop a new game for, a game company had to make both technical and commercial considerations. Should the next *Street Fighter* be developed for Nintendo, Sega, or perhaps both? In the specific case of *Street Fighter II*, the fighting gameplay happened to be sensitive to a console's processing speeds, which influenced how fast the gameplay could run. Genesis, with its speedy processor (which Sega marketed in the 1990s under the non-technical term "blast processing"), could run the game faster than Super NES, but Nintendo's system was more popular globally. Capcom was also influenced by how much technical and marketing support the first parties were willing to provide for any given project. *Street Fighter II* eventually went to both Super NES and Genesis (and several other systems, as well). Some games stayed exclusive to certain platforms, but many more did not. Capcom was, at its core, a multiplatform game publisher that did not specifically favor one first party over another. "Capcom has always maintained a platform-agnostic stance and has created games for all hardware manufacturers," explains Yoshiki Okamoto, who was instrumental in deciding which platforms would get Capcom's support. Other companies, like Square, generally stuck to one manufacturer in the 1990s, but these instances were the exception rather than the rule.

By 1996, Nintendo, Sega and Sony were engaged in an intense competition hitherto unseen in the game industry. Sony took an early sales lead worldwide, thanks to certain miscalculations made by both Sega and Nintendo. Priced at $399 during its launch, the Saturn system was $100 more expensive than PlayStation and more difficult for developers to program 3D games for. Nintendo, meanwhile, opted to stick to high-price, low-capacity cartridges, which made its games less feature-rich and more expensive than the CD games on the other two. *Resident Evil*, in becoming a million-seller soon after its March 1996 launch, was an early major victory for Sony. But both Sega and Nintendo wanted their own piece of the pie, effectively bringing the *Resident Evil* series into the console war from day one.

RESIDENT EVIL JOURNEYS TO SATURN

The rivalry between PlayStation and Saturn is legendary, in part because the competition was ultimately between the different philosophies of their manufacturers. Although they were both 32-bit consoles with CD drives, the systems' similarities probably ended there. Saturn was originally designed with a unique architecture that offers advanced, 2D games while also supporting 3D. PlayStation, on the other hand, was designed primarily for polygonal 3D games and had a reputation for being the easier of the two to develop for, thanks to its more orthodox architecture. Because Saturn and PlayStation had very different architectures, porting games between them was a time-consuming endeavor. While multiplatform games are a dime a dozen today, thanks to development middleware such as Unreal Engine, which runs on different platforms, they were far less common in the 1990s.

In spring 1996, Sega took immediate notice of the success of *Resident Evil* and quickly approached Capcom about creating a version for its Saturn. Although the game was originally developed only for PlayStation, Capcom had thought about creating the game for other platforms as well. "The team looked into a Saturn version early on, but we could only do so on PlayStation due to lack of resources at the time," Kazuhiro Aoyama explains. Capcom had previously released 2D fighting games on Saturn, but for *Resident Evil*, differences between Sega's and Sony's hardware, coupled with the team's inexperience in developing 3D games, precluded the possibility of developing simultaneously for both 32-bit consoles. At the time, PlayStation, Saturn, Nintendo 64 and PC systems each required specialized approaches when developing software for them, which meant that ports to other systems were likely to be exclusive, dedicated pipelines.

Capcom accepted Sega's overture anyway. But mindful of its lack of experience with developing 3D games for Saturn (they had previously released only 2D fighters and platformers), Capcom decided to outsource the Saturn version to Nextech, a Japanese development studio partly owned by Sega. The Saturn version took about a year to develop and was released in Japan on July 25, 1997. The North American release followed in August the same year, and the PAL version in October. The port generally featured noticeably inferior audio and visuals than the PlayStation original, but it contained all of the content seen in the original version, plus a few extra features unique to Saturn. Most notable is "Battle Game," an action-oriented mini-game set in a series of randomly arranged rooms taken from the main game. Players have to kill every enemy before progressing to the next room. Additionally, in the main adventure there's a new enemy, the quick, lethal and amphibious creature known as the Tick, which resembles the Hunter but has brownish-red skin instead. Chris's story now includes an extra boss battle, with a second, gold-colored Tyrant in the underground laboratory, which pops out of its storage tube as Chris attempts to leave.

This version was more than adequate for any player who owned only a Saturn in 1997, despite the technical downgrades. However, *Resident Evil* on Saturn did not sell nearly as well as the PlayStation original. Exact figures for the West are not available, but in Japan the game sold approximately 148,000 copies in 1997, less than 10 per cent of the 1.19 million copies achieved on PlayStation.[1] The Saturn version barely moved the needle, partly due to the fact that Sega's 32-bit platform was nowhere near as popular as PlayStation, but also because the brand new *Resident Evil 2* for PlayStation was only six months away (due for release in late 1997 before Capcom settled on the eventual January 1998 date) by the time the Saturn version launched. Despite soft sales, the Saturn port is a notable demonstration of Capcom's early commitment to making *Resident Evil* a platform-agnostic franchise and of its willingness to overcome technical hurdles to bring the series to other consoles. Longer-term, it was just the beginning of a four-year-long partnership between Capcom and Sega with the aim of bringing more *Resident Evil* games to Sega platforms.

Still aware of the commercial opportunities from working with Sega, Capcom decided to green-light *Resident Evil 2* for Saturn while the game was still in its *1.5* incarnation. However, this meant that when Okamoto and Mikami opted to restart its development, the Saturn port was also delayed. In addition, the final version of *Resident Evil 2* had graphics that were more detailed than those of *Resident Evil 1.5*, which was already an improvement over the first *Resident Evil*. This led to problems when developing the final version of *Resident Evil 2* for Saturn. Despite Capcom's best efforts, the Saturn hardware was not powerful enough to produce a version of the game that met Capcom's standards. "We tried to port the game to Saturn, but it only would've been possible if we made downgrades to the game. We wanted to avoid that," Mikami explained.[2] In 2018, director Hideki Kamiya explained through Twitter that Saturn's notoriously limited 3D-object-rendering capabilities made it unable to handle the game's larger zombie count.[3] Indeed, part of what made *Resident Evil 2* such an improvement over the original was its smarter enemy AI, increased enemy count and larger environments. Unwilling to stray from maintaining high standards for *Resident Evil*, Okamoto and Mikami decided to cancel the Saturn port of *Resident Evil 2*.

A NEW DREAM FOR SEGA

The cancellation of the Saturn port of *Resident Evil 2* was a considerable loss for Sega fans. Having gotten a taste of the series through a port of the first game, they were now left in the dark for the much-hyped sequel. Sega had one less hit title for its lagging system, making its position in the console war ever more precarious. Conversely, cancelling the port was a victory for Sony, who would be able to hold *Resident Evil 2* exclusively through its year of release. Although the original *Resident Evil* was nearly two years old by 1998, it maintained consistent sales since its release, while most games' sales slowed down within months of launching. When *Resident Evil: Director's Cut* was released, in September 1997, the original game saw renewed sales, and when *Resident Evil 2* hit PlayStation in January 1998, it broke various sales records in the US and Japan. Losing the next *Resident Evil* was a setback for Sega and one of the final nails in Saturn's coffin.

The decision to cancel the Saturn port did not end Capcom's desire to bring *Resident Evil* to Sega hardware: Capcom was still a platform-agnostic publisher and a close partner of Sega's. But even though Capcom (like other game companies) was sure to achieve its best commercial results with platform-exclusive content, the idea of an original, Saturn-exclusive *Resident Evil* in place of a port was a tough sell in 1998. While the system remained marginally competitive in Japan, Sega officially announced its intention to withdraw Saturn from the North American market, beginning in March 1998, a stunning reversal of its fortunes since the previous console generation, when Genesis/Mega Drive had proven to be a fierce competitor to Super NES. There are several issues that contributed to Saturn's underwhelming performance. When they both launched in North America, in 1995, PlayStation retailed for $100 less than Saturn. Sega also infamously stealth-launched Saturn in North America in only select retailers, preventing it from reaching wider distribution channels early on.[4] Meanwhile, Square had decided to release *Final Fantasy VII* exclusively for PlayStation. Square's premier RPG franchise was so popular in Japan that it all but guaranteed PlayStation's dominance there, which eventually caused a ripple effect worldwide (one that *Resident Evil* would ultimately benefit from, as well). Even if Saturn could handle a port of *Resident Evil 2* or an entirely new game, there were doubts whether the inevitable lower sales could justify the resources needed to make it happen.

Down but not out, Sega was eager to move on from Saturn's failure. On May 12, 1998, Sega officially lifted the curtain on Dreamcast. Its latest console, which could render 3 million polygons per second, was a 128-bit system capable of more advanced 3D graphics than PlayStation or Nintendo 64. It was scheduled for launch in November 1998 in Japan and in autumn 1999 in the West. With Dreamcast, Sega was intent on starting a new generation of console at a time when PlayStation and Nintendo 64 were nowhere near the end of their lifecycles. Sega hoped that a head start would grant it an early lead over Sony's upcoming PlayStation 2, which at the time was tentatively slated for a 1999 release. With Nintendo 64 barely two years old, its successor was also a long way off. Faced with mounting financial losses, a successful Dreamcast was Sega's only chance for survival as a game system manufacturer.[5]

In early 1998, Yoshiki Okamoto still saw potential in developing an exclusive *Resident Evil* game for Sega. This time, however, it would be for Dreamcast rather than Saturn. As one of the most popular new franchises at the time, Capcom's support would bolster Sega's console early on. Thanks to Dreamcast's more advanced capabilities, Capcom would be able to create a better-looking, potentially more ambitious next-generation *Resident Evil*, allowing the product to stay cutting-edge against competitors such as Konami and Square, who were working on their own horror games. The new game would also serve as an unofficial apology to Sega fans for cancelling *Resident Evil 2* on Saturn.

However, there were two hurdles. First, Capcom did not have the capacity to develop yet another new *Resident Evil* in-house, given all the other games already in development at the time. Also, the company's software engineers were unfamiliar with the new Dreamcast hardware. To support Capcom, Sega agreed to have Tokyo-based Nextech, the studio that previously ported *Resident Evil* to Saturn, develop the Dreamcast *Resident Evil*.

Capcom management green-lit the Dreamcast *Resident Evil* in spring 1998. The public learned of its existence for the first time in October that same year, when Sega held a press conference to unveil a line-up of upcoming Dreamcast games. The console was due to launch the following month in Japan, so, to generate interest, Sega and Capcom worked together at the event to show off their *Resident Evil* title. When the trailer broadcast, those in attendance were amazed. The trailer, which featured Claire Redfield and a slew of enemies, both familiar and unfamiliar, in a dark, mysterious location, was still early in development, but featured graphics clearly better than those of *Resident Evil 2*. Gone were the pre-rendered graphics employed as a compromise against the limitations of the 32-bit era, having been replaced by a more detailed, fully polygonal engine. The title of the game was *Resident Evil CODE: Veronica*, which Capcom billed as a true sequel to *Resident Evil 2*, continuing the story of Claire Redfield and her search for Chris.

Despite being a continuation of *Resident Evil 2*, the absence of the number 3 in the title was not lost on audiences and game fans. The reason for going with a subtitle rather than a number essentially came down to console-war politics. "The idea was to keep numbered games on Sony and use different names for games made for Sega and Nintendo," Okamoto explains. A project called *Resident Evil 3* (distinct from the game released in September 1999 as *Resident Evil 3: Nemesis*) was already in development for PlayStation 2 by Hideki Kamiya's team. But because Kamiya had grand ambitions to develop a completely new experience, his game would not be able to come out until after *Resident Evil CODE: Veronica*. As far as Okamoto was concerned, the lack of a number did not equate to a lack of legitimacy or prestige: *Resident Evil CODE: Veronica* was the next mainline *Resident Evil*, and fans would need to buy a Sega Dreamcast to play it.[*]

---

[*] At this point, Capcom had only recently green-lit Aoyama's *Resident Evil 1.9* for PlayStation, which was not intended as a mainline game until it was renamed *Resident Evil 3: Nemesis* in June 1999; Kamiya's *Resident Evil 3* was subsequently renamed *Resident Evil 4*.

NEXT-GENERATION *RESIDENT EVIL*

With Nextech in charge of developing *Resident Evil CODE: Veronica*, executive producer Yoshiki Okamoto made sure that key Capcom talent was onboard. Shinji Mikami was to oversee the project as producer, while Noboru Sugimura was asked to pen the story at Flagship, something he had already done even before *Resident Evil 2* was completed. Interestingly, while the initial trailer for *Resident Evil CODE: Veronica* featured Claire Redfield, Sugimura originally intended for Jill Valentine to be the protagonist. However, plans changed after Hideki Kamiya, without Sugimura's permission, altered Claire's final line in *Resident Evil 2* to allude to her objective to continue searching for her brother, Chris. This meant that fans would expect a follow-up to that cliffhanger. Seeking to avoid a plot hole, Sugimura decided to change the starring character from Jill to Claire. Kamiya recalls Sugimura yelling at him for being irresponsible, but as it turned out, his decision would provide an opening for Jill's successful appearance in *Resident Evil 3: Nemesis* instead.

As an outsourced yet vital title in the series, *Resident Evil CODE: Veronica* required a capable director who could maintain the franchise's high standards. For that, Mikami chose Hiroki Kato, a veteran who had worked on *Resident Evil* as a system planner. Hailing from Oita Prefecture in southern Japan, Kato became interested in both video and board games as a young child. "I didn't just enjoy playing games; I enjoyed creating them, too," Kato recalls. "I created my own original board games and formed rules that players needed to follow while playing. I tested the viability of these rules when playing with my friends." After graduating university, Kato felt that video game development would be an interesting career path, leading him to join Capcom in 1994. As with Kamiya and Aoyama, Kato began with job training and then assistance with quality assurance for miscellaneous titles before being assigned to *Resident Evil*. As one of its system planners, Kato designed the game's garden and underground tunnel stages. Afterwards, Kato worked on the Saturn port of *Resident Evil*, followed by the Saturn port of *Resident Evil 2* until its cancellation. When Mikami was working on the original *Resident Evil* on PlayStation, he took notice of Kato's focus on rules and logic in games. Given the importance of *Resident Evil CODE: Veronica* to Capcom in the new console generation, Mikami believed Kato could utilize his skills to craft interesting and compelling game concepts.

With Capcom funding and overseeing *Resident Evil CODE: Veronica* and Nextech undertaking all the development, Kato split his time between the former's headquarters in Osaka and the latter's base in Tokyo. Development for *Resident Evil* a little over two years earlier had been a slog requiring countless hours of overtime, so Kato could not help but compare Nextech to Capcom in terms of work–life balance, stating, "At Capcom, we stayed in the office long past standard working hours to meet our deadlines. We often couldn't go home in the evening. But because Nextech was a separate company from Capcom, policies were different. Nextech was more obedient to labor law and encouraged its employees to go home on time." Although he was away from home for most of production, Kato acknowledges that working on *Resident Evil CODE: Veronica* was less intense than working on the original game, in spite of his greater responsibility now that he was a director. When asked about why Mikami chose him to direct, Kato self-deprecatingly jokes, "I think it's because everyone hated me! The game was developed outside Capcom, so I wouldn't be at headquarters that often!" Of course, the truth was that Mikami liked him a lot. Aoyama speculates: "I think between me, Kamiya and Kato, Mikami-san seemed to adore Kato the most."

Resident Evil CODE: Veronica was to pick up after the ending of *Resident Evil 2* and offer both Claire and Chris Redfield, as co-protagonists, so Kato decided to bring back the Zapping System, but with his own unique take on it. Instead of the concurrent Zapping System used in *Resident Evil 2* with Leon and Claire, Kato wanted *Resident Evil CODE: Veronica* to feature a chronological Zapping System, in which the two protagonists' stories occurred one right after the other instead of simultaneously. The Redfields would explore many of the same environments, but these changed

Hiroki Kato

shape and form according to developments in the story. For example, an explosion eventually deals structural damage to the island where the game begins, sealing off or destroying certain doors and walls, while opening up others. Claire explores the island first, but Chris will arrive later on, after Claire escapes. They will explore many of the same rooms at different times, and in locations visited by both Redfields, players can opt to ignore certain items while playing as Claire then have Chris pick them up later, or choose to take the items as Claire and leave nothing for Chris. This presents players with the choice of making the game easier earlier on as Claire and harder later, as Chris, or vice versa. Kato explains that this style came in response to the Zapping System in *Resident Evil 2*, which he felt did not go far enough in differentiating between Leon's and Claire's scenarios. "I didn't think it'd be interesting for Claire and Chris to explore the same exact areas without any changes to them, so that's why they change dramatically in Chris's game," he says. "Kamiya prefers to have the scenarios cross over using events in the story, while I prefer for the scenarios to cross over via the actual gameplay." However, in a departure from all of its predecessors, the game has exactly one ending, limiting its replay value.

Resident Evil CODE: Veronica is notorious among series fans for having an unusually high number of so-called "chokepoints" – situations in which a player's resources are insufficient to complete the game, possibly forcing them to start over. Most of the game's boss fights require a specific weapon to win, and without any real warning, players may be rendered unable to acquire a crucial weapon such as the Magnum. The only remedy for these chokepoints is to start from a previous save point or restart the game entirely, from the very beginning. And then there is the number of booby traps that can instantly kill players, such as the puzzle requiring Claire to manipulate a falling slab of concrete with just the right timing, in order to acquire a keycard inexplicably encased in a crystal ball. Such chokepoints and booby traps have frustrated first-time players of *Resident Evil CODE: Veronica* since its release, and with gameplay time also considerably longer than in the game's predecessors, these chokepoints can be even more aggravating for some players as they potentially mean having to repeat long segments of the game. They can be attributed to Kato's own design preferences and are rooted in his childhood hobby of crafting board game rules designed to outsmart players. It should therefore come as no surprise that Kato was also the one who designed the rolling-boulder traps in *Resident Evil*. "I have an affinity for booby traps in my games," Kato explains. "People actually complained about them to me during development, but I really like it when players have to think hard in order to figure out how to beat the game."

From a technological perspective, Dreamcast's advanced capabilities allowed for the presentation of *Resident Evil CODE: Veronica* to visibly stand out from its 32-bit predecessors. The game was the first mainline *Resident Evil* that eschewed pre-rendered backdrops in favor of a fully polygonal engine. Thus, the game added a sense of interactivity and of cohesion between the characters and the environments that were not feasible with the pre-rendered predecessors. One notable feature is camera panning; in certain rooms, the camera moves so that it follows the character. Capcom previously employed this technique in the fully 3D 1999 game *Dino Crisis*, while Konami used it in *Silent Hill*, but this was the first time it was used in *Resident Evil*. Another improvement was the game's new lighting system, which is evident from the very beginning of the game: Claire, who begins the game inside a pitch-black jail cell on an unknown penal island, uses a lighter to illuminate the room, turning it from pitch dark to brightly illuminated in one second. *Silent Hill* had previously used the contrast of brightness and darkness, but the implementation was more rudimentary in Konami's title. *Resident Evil CODE: Veronica* looked more beautiful than Konami's game thanks to the more advanced Dreamcast hardware, offering a clear contrast between light and dark.

Coinciding with the better graphics is a greater emphasis on cinematic presentation. *Resident Evil CODE: Veronica* employs the same CG cut-scene technology as *Resident Evil 2* and *Resident Evil 3: Nemesis*, but features more detailed visuals, improved art design and better animations. The game also features cut-scenes using the in-game graphics engine. These cut-scenes are more detailed than their 32-bit equivalents; they make use of a panning camera, zoom in on facial expressions and are generally longer. *Resident Evil CODE: Veronica* achieves a more cinematic feel, which was simply impossible on PlayStation without the use of CG.

The game has an equally impressive soundtrack. Composed primarily by Takeshi Miura, with additional compositions by Sanae Kasahara and Hijiri Anze, the music is comprised of memorable and thematic melodies that fit the game. The soundtrack is also notable for having vocals accompany the background music during the "Berceuse" lullaby (no relation to the Frédéric Chopin lullaby of the same name), a first for the series.

In contrast to the improved visuals and music, innovations in the gameplay are more subdued. The gameplay and pacing are fundamentally similar to *Resident Evil 2*, which results in the game lacking certain features introduced in the earlier *Resident Evil 3: Nemesis*, such as the dodge maneuver. Back in 2000, this disparity led some gamers to wonder why *Resident Evil CODE: Veronica*, despite being the newer and shinier next-generation *Resident Evil* title, had the less advanced gameplay of the two. Aoyama offers one answer, stating, "*Resident Evil CODE: Veronica* was always intended to be a traditional *Resident Evil* experience, while *Resident Evil 3: Nemesis* was originally intended as an action-oriented spin-off with gameplay not intended for a mainline game." The aspects of gameplay that actually are improved in *Resident Evil CODE: Veronica* are more rooted in its enhanced graphics and AI. Players can now wield two weapons and shoot two enemies at the same time; there are larger, multi-floor rooms throughout the game that have no loading times within them; and, for the first time in a mainline title, players can equip a sniper rifle and aim it in first-person view. There is also more interactivity with the environments, as enemies can be pushed against walls or over railings. In spite of these improvements, however, *Resident Evil CODE: Veronica* does not fundamentally stray too far from what was, at the time of its release, a four-year-old gameplay formula.

THE CODE IS VERONICA

The plot of *Resident Evil CODE: Veronica* picks up where *Resident Evil 2* left off. Three months after Raccoon City's sterilization, Claire continues her search for Chris, but is captured and taken to Rockfort Island, which soon after is bombed by unknown forces, causing the island to become infected with the T-virus, thus populating it with zombies. Claire meets fellow prisoner and Leonardo DiCaprio-lookalike Steve Burnside, with whom she attempts to escape the clutches of Umbrella Corporation base commander and psychopath Alfred Ashford and his twin sister, Alexia. Later, the landscape shifts to an Umbrella base in Antarctica. Chris eventually arrives, to discover the existence of a new bioweapon created by Alexia, the T-Veronica Virus. Even more profound is his discovery of Albert Wesker, who not only has survived the events of the first game, but now possesses superhuman strength. Wesker, the perpetrator behind the attack on Rockfort Island, is after Alexia's T-Veronica Virus, but decides to take the opportunity to gain revenge against Chris for his interference during the "Mansion Incident" (the in-game term used to describe the events of the first game). The story thus transforms into a convoluted, three-way struggle between Chris, Claire and Steve at one angle, the Ashfords at another angle and Wesker at a third. The two Redfields eventually reunite and defeat the Ashfords, although Steve is killed by the T-Veronica Virus, making him the first protagonist in the series to die.

The meaning and significance of the game's subtitle finally comes to light at the very end: "Veronica" is the name of the Ashfords' oldest documented ancestor, the namesake of the T-Veronica Virus, and the final access code to the Antarctic base's sterilization mechanism.

The game ends with a CG cut-scene showing Claire and Chris flying away from the Antarctic Umbrella base just before it explodes. Chris, with his unwavering determination, tells Claire that they "must defeat Umbrella once and for all." For years, many players interpreted the ending to mean that the next game would finally feature an epic showdown with Umbrella.

Beyond its shiny new graphics and high-fidelity sound, perhaps the farthest leap *Resident Evil CODE: Veronica* offered from its predecessors is in the game's plot. *Resident Evil* and *Resident Evil 3: Nemesis* featured straightforward and largely self-contained storylines with clearly defined beginnings and endings. Meanwhile, *Resident Evil 2* brought Sugimura onboard and expanded the franchise's scope by incorporating literary themes into its plot, though at the same time the game was not overly complex. *Resident Evil CODE: Veronica*, in contrast, takes the approach of *Resident Evil 2* and turns things up a notch, with a more complex and dramatic plot. This was possible due to a combination of longer gameplay, higher budget, and the ever-evolving importance of story and narrative in the greater realm of video games. While *Resident Evil 2* had already improved on its predecessor in this regard, other games, such as *Final Fantasy VII* and Konami's *Metal Gear Solid* – directed by video gaming's most prolific auteur, Hideo Kojima – had pushed the boundaries of video game stories even further. Those games proved that cut-scenes and dialogue could now be longer, deeper and more elaborate. As a cinematic game property, new games in the *Resident Evil* series needed to keep up with competitors. In crafting the plot of *Resident Evil CODE: Veronica*, Sugimura was not only improving on his own previous work, but also keeping up with rising standards seen throughout the rest of the game industry.

One of the central themes Sugimura employs is the importance of family. While *Resident Evil 2* introduced the concept to the series with the Birkins and Redfields, it never hits the peaks seen in

Resident Evil CODE: Veronica. There are no fewer than three distinct familial threads in the game: Claire with her brother Chris, twins Alfred and Alexia with their father Alexander Ashford, and Steve Burnside with his unnamed father. However, while the Redfields enjoy a family reunion, the Ashfords experience something decidedly more twisted and unconventional. Alexia decides to inject herself with the T-Veronica Virus after her father fails to be a viable test subject. Alfred, who is emotionally close to his sister, laments that Alexia's infection will require fifteen years of cryogenic sleep before the virus takes effect. Alfred is thus driven to madness from loneliness, which he can only cope with by crossdressing and impersonating his sister. This clearly draws inspiration from the plot of Alfred Hitchcock's classic horror film, *Psycho*.

Meanwhile, Steve, who has been imprisoned by Umbrella as a consequence of his father's renegade dealings, is forced to confront his father after he has become a zombie in one of the most emotional (if awkwardly voiced) scenes in the entire series. An injured Claire is ambushed by Steve's zombified father; Steve, wielding two automatic weapons, hesitates. Steve's father nearly bites Claire before Steve finally comes to his senses and unloads all of his submachine gun ammunition on his father, saving Claire but putting his father down permanently. Steve begins to sob uncontrollably and blames his father's recklessness and stupidity. This emotional scene is not the first of its kind in the series – in *Resident Evil 3: Nemesis*, Carlos is put in a similar situation when he is forced to put down a fellow soldier infected with the T-virus – but it is certainly the most significant.

Resident Evil CODE: Veronica improves its portrayal of villains as well. Alfred plays a larger and more sinister role as an antagonist than either Albert Wesker, Chief Brian Irons or Nicholai Ginovaef from the first three games. Compared to its treatment of William Birkin, who is portrayed in *Resident Evil 2* as a paranoid scientist, the game takes a deeper look at Alexia Ashford, who is shown to be psychotic, manipulative and cunning.

While *Resident Evil CODE: Veronica* will never win an award for its voice-acting, it takes large leaps beyond its predecessors with regards to its characterization and storyline. It made its mark at launch because of its technical advancements over its predecessors, but naturally over time its graphics have been surpassed by those of its successors. Even though few people in 2020 would consider *Resident Evil CODE: Veronica* to be a visually appealing game, the plot makes it one of the most relevant and pivotal entries in the series.

X MARKS THE PLOT

Resident Evil CODE: Veronica was originally scheduled for a December 1999 release, but in the autumn of that year, Capcom decided on an early 2000 release instead. The delay was ostensibly due to the need for a last-minute developmental polish, but the decision may have been more commercially motivated. Sega launched Dreamcast in North America on September 9, 1999, so its user base was likely too small to support sales of a new *Resident Evil*. Moreover, both *Dino Crisis* and *Resident Evil 3: Nemesis* surpassed Capcom's modest expectations, so it made sense for Capcom to ride out the success of those two survival horror games a few more months.

To make up for the delay, Capcom released a port of *Resident Evil 2* on Dreamcast in Japan in late December, bundled with a demo of *Resident Evil CODE: Veronica*. This "Trial Edition" allowed players to experience an early portion of the game, with a slightly modified ending made to serve as a conclusion to the demo. In North America and PAL territories, the Trial Edition never saw the light of day because the Dreamcast port of *Resident Evil 2* was not released there until late 2000, nine months after *Resident Evil CODE: Veronica* had already been launched.

Resident Evil CODE: Veronica was finally released in Japan on February 3, 2000, and the following month in North America. The game was a hit with critics. The Western video game press praised the game's visuals, story, gameplay and music, with most remarking on the improvements made possible with Dreamcast's more powerful hardware. As of the time of writing, on GameRankings *Resident Evil CODE: Veronica* has an average score of 93.79.[6] It is also widely considered to be one of the best Dreamcast games, even among such highly regarded hits as *Soulcalibur*, *Phantasy Star Online*, *Space Channel 5*, *Jet Grind Radio* and *Shenmue*. Shinji Mikami and Yoshiki Okamoto have also spoken very highly of the game's quality in recent years, the former stating that *Resident Evil CODE: Veronica* deserved a number in its title instead of *Resident Evil 3: Nemesis*.

Although a critical success, the game's commercial performance was more of a mixed bag. Initial sales of *Resident Evil CODE: Veronica* were lower than the PlayStation entries, eventually selling 1.14 million units worldwide. Although this made it one of the best-selling Dreamcast games ever, the figure was considerably lower than those of *Resident Evil 2* (4.9 million) and *Resident Evil 3:*

Nemesis (3.5 million). However, Hiroki Kato says that the game still made a profit for Capcom and that the company's incentive-based bonus system worked in his favor following its release. Okamoto also mentioned that the game saw decent sales. Yet given that the *Resident Evil* series was one of the most popular game franchises in 2000, it is highly likely Capcom had expected more from *Resident Evil CODE: Veronica* than either Kato or Okamoto are willing to admit. The company poured in a considerable amount of financial resource to ensure the game was the industry's equivalent of a Hollywood blockbuster. At one point, Capcom purportedly hoped to sell the game to a third of Dreamcast owners, which they later refined to a forecast of 1 million copies in Japan alone. However, despite Sega's efforts, Dreamcast proved to be far less popular than PlayStation, even when accounting for Dreamcast's much later release date, selling only 1.2 million units as opposed to a whopping 16.68 million PlayStation systems in Japan by the end of 1999. Even if Capcom had been able to sell a copy of *Resident Evil CODE: Veronica* to every single Japanese Dreamcast owner at the time (a feat unheard of in video game history), sales would still be lower than for *Resident Evil 3: Nemesis* – never mind *Resident Evil 2*, which was a double-platinum hit in Japan.

Aside from Sega's commercial struggles with Dreamcast, Capcom's branding approach for *Resident Evil CODE: Veronica,* and for the series as a whole through to early 2000, may have also contributed to the game's muted sales. Although the game was a direct sequel to *Resident Evil 2*, the lack of a number in the game's title may have made it look less prestigious than the numbered *Resident Evil 3: Nemesis*. Meanwhile, Kamiya's *Resident Evil 4* was in development for PlayStation 2, while Nintendo 64 was scheduled to receive its own exclusive game, *Resident Evil Zero*. And with *Dino Crisis* and *Resident Evil 3: Nemesis* still recent releases, Capcom's survival horror fanbase may have been content with their original PlayStations. With the much-hyped PlayStation 2 scheduled to hit in March 2000, there seemed to be little room in the crowded market for the Dreamcast to succeed.

But Capcom was not quite done with *Resident Evil* on Dreamcast. The company released a port of *Resident Evil 3: Nemesis* worldwide in November 2000, which meant that, between Saturn and Dreamcast, Sega-only console owners could finally play through all four main *Resident Evil* entries. Capcom also had further plans for *Resident Evil CODE: Veronica*. In the original *Resident Evil*, Albert Wesker dies in every possible ending, making his resurrection as a superhuman in *Resident Evil CODE: Veronica* a perplexing plot development. It turns out that even before the release of the Dreamcast version, Capcom had been planning to re-release the game with additional cut-scene footage that would explain Wesker's role in the game. "Of course, we wanted to include the additional Wesker scenes with the original release, but we did not have time to do so," Kato explains.

Capcom publicly announced this expanded Dreamcast version in November 2000, and revealed at the same time that the game would also be ported to PlayStation 2. Titled *Biohazard CODE: Veronica – Complete Edition* in Japan, the re-release would include nine minutes of additional footage featuring Wesker, including an expanded-ending cut-scene. The gameplay would remain identical to the original, with a tiny number of minor cosmetic changes made to the visuals, notably Steve's hairstyle. The game was scheduled to be released for both platforms simultaneously on

March 22, 2001, the fifth anniversary of the series. In spring 2001, Capcom revealed the game's Western title: *Resident Evil CODE: Veronica X*.

In addition to the extra cut-scenes in *Resident Evil CODE: Veronica X*, Capcom would further contextualize Wesker's background through a DVD mockumentary called *Wesker's Report*, available with pre-orders of the game. Written by Kato, the short film, made out of footage pieced together from the four *Resident Evil* games and narrated by Wesker himself, describes his history with the Umbrella Corporation, the STARS, Ada Wong and a special virus he received from William Birkin that allowed for his superhuman resurrection. *Wesker's Report* was notable for having a number of inconsistencies and contradictions compared to the story in the games themselves. Kato has offered up two explanations. "I wrote *Wesker's Report* while pretty intoxicated," he mused over dinner in 2007. Over a decade later, in a more formal setting, he offers further insight: "I was not involved in the development of either *Resident Evil 2* or *Resident Evil 3: Nemesis*, and I had a tight deadline to write the script, so I ended up playing through both games very quickly and integrated their plots into *Wesker's Report* from memory."

THE DREAM IS OVER

On January 31, 2001, in a groundbreaking announcement, Sega made public its decision to cease development and manufacture of Dreamcast and all new game hardware, instead transitioning to the production of software as a third-party developer for its former rival platforms PlayStation 2, Nintendo GameCube and Game Boy, as well as Microsoft's upcoming Xbox. This announcement marked the end of Sega's iconic era as a first-party hardware manufacturer. The presence of *Resident Evil* on Dreamcast was partly intended to ensure the platform's competitiveness in the console war, but the tremendous sales momentum of PlayStation, the industry's expectations for a Nintendo rebound with GameCube, and Microsoft's deep pockets and vast resources, made it difficult for Sega to compete. Faced with consistent financial losses and the threat of bankruptcy, Sega's former chairman, Isao Okawa, was compelled to inject 85 billion yen ($692 million at the time) into his company to keep it from collapsing.

Despite Dreamcast's premature discontinuation, Capcom followed through on its commitment to release *Resident Evil CODE: Veronica X* for Sega's platform in Japan, alongside the PlayStation 2 port. However, due to the lack of commercial viability, Capcom decided not to release the Dreamcast version in North America and PAL territories, instead opting to focus solely on the PlayStation 2 port. Thanks to the re-release, Capcom was able to offset lower sales for Dreamcast with higher sales for PlayStation 2. *Resident Evil CODE: Veronica X* eventually sold 1.4 million units on PlayStation 2, somewhat more than the 1.14 million units sold on Dreamcast. When counted together, *CODE: Veronica* and *CODE: Veronica X* would represent Capcom's best-selling product in the so-called sixth generation of video game consoles until 2005.

In the four years between the release of *Resident Evil* on Saturn in July 1997 and *Resident Evil CODE: Veronica X* on the Japanese Dreamcast in March 2001, Capcom had managed to create an association between Sega and the game that was distinct from the association it had with PlayStation. The contrast is remarkable: on PlayStation, the franchise benefitted from the platform's popularity, with record-breaking sales of numbered entries; on Sega's platforms, *Resident Evil* was always following on the heels of the PlayStation releases, with late ports and a non-numbered new entry. *Resident Evil CODE: Veronica* was an effort to transfer some of the popularity of the PlayStation games over to Dreamcast, with mixed results. Despite the stronger historical association with PlayStation, it was actually the Sega family of hardware that initially hosted the first four mainline *Resident Evil* games (that is, until *Resident Evil CODE: Veronica X* was released for PlayStation 2 in March 2001, which put Sega and PlayStation hardware at parity until late 2005).

One may wonder if the series could have seen additional *Resident Evil* sequels on Dreamcast after *CODE: Veronica X*, had the system enjoyed a more successful commercial existence, but none of the creators interviewed for this book had ever heard plans for such a development.

HIROKI KATO, NOT A FARMER AT ALL

Hiroki Kato's career as a director would span exactly one game. Following *Resident Evil CODE: Veronica*, he went on to write the story for *Resident Evil: Gaiden*, a non-canonical handheld game released for Game Boy Color in November 2001. *Resident Evil: Gaiden* would be the last *Resident Evil* title involving Kato that would see a commercial release.

Kato next worked as a planner on *Dead Phoenix*, a game developed by Capcom's Production Studio 4 and announced in November 2002. *Dead Phoenix* was to take place in a fantasy-inspired world inhabited by dragons. Given the prominence of shooting in the trailer, observers noted its thematic similarity to Sega's *Panzer Dragoon* rail-shooter series, although Kato clarifies that their gameplay styles were very different as *Dead Phoenix* was not itself a rail-shooter. "The game was more akin to simulation games like *Nobunaga's Ambition*," Kato explains. Unfortunately, *Dead Phoenix* was cancelled sometime in 2003 due to difficulties with the title's development. According to Kato, GameCube lacked the system memory necessary to store all gameplay data, specifically the high number of events that were to occur simultaneously.

Following the cancellation of *Dead Phoenix*, Kato moved on to writing the story of an action game called *Under the Skin* (*Meiwaku Seijin: Panic Maker* in Japan) for PlayStation 2, which was released in September 2004. A more comical and lighthearted game than his previous endeavors, *Under the Skin* was ultimately a minor title for Capcom. Kato next joined Capcom subsidiary Clover Studio, where he was the lead designer and storywriter for *God Hand*, a 3D brawler for PlayStation 2 directed by Shinji Mikami and released in October 2006.

Kato left Capcom following the closure of Clover Studio in October 2006, and joined Seeds Inc., which eventually merged with Odd Games to form PlatinumGames Inc. There, Kato worked on the Sega-published title *Vanquish*, another Mikami-directed third-person shooter, released in October 2010. After *Vanquish*, Kato departed PlatinumGames to pursue a new career outside of the video game industry – in a 2014 interview with the website Polygon, Shinji Mikami reported that Kato had become a farmer, of all things.[7] However, when Kato was questioned in 2017 about his drastic career change, he was shocked to learn of it, having never read the Polygon interview, and put it down to a misunderstanding by Mikami or a miscommunication with the website's interpreter. In actuality, after leaving PlatinumGames, Kato began his own consultancy for companies looking to expand their customer reach. He admits consulting for clients in the agriculture industry, which occasionally required him to undertake farming tasks, but confirms he has certainly not become a farmer. When asked about his motivations to change careers, Kato cites work–life balance as a primary motivator. "I want to prioritize spending time with my son," he says. "As a consultant, I can do that because I get to decide my own work hours." Given the endless nights and weekends Kato had to endure for *Resident Evil*, his new priorities make plenty of sense.

Kato's consultancy appears to be a drastic departure from his previous work but he says there is in fact a logical connection between his previous career as a game creator and his current career as a consultant. "Many e-commerce sites have no idea how to build their customer–user base. They think making a social networking page is enough, but it actually is not that simple. You need to make your presence look compelling to consumers," Kato explains. "Games are no different in this regard. You need to figure out what to do to create an interesting game. That is the job of the designer." In that sense, one can look back to Kato's childhood to see where these inclinations originate. He needed to make the rules of his board games fun and challenging if he wanted his friends to continue playing with him. Hopefully, his consultations are free of booby traps and chokepoints, however.

Kato is happy with his life and his consultancy is proving successful. Presently, he has no intention to return to the game industry; busy with his family and current career, he has done little to keep up with trends and developments in the game industry, becoming disconnected to the extent that when he was told in 2017 that *Resident Evil 7* had been released ten months earlier, his response was: "There's a *Resident Evil 7*? I had no idea!"

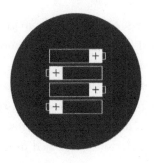

CHAPTER 6: POCKET-SIZED SURVIVAL HORROR

GOING PORTABLE: *RESIDENT EVIL 2* ON GAME.COM

Video game hardware has traditionally been categorized into four segments: arcades, home consoles such as PlayStation, handheld systems like Game Boy and personal computers. Mobile phones joined the fray from the late 1990s, having evolved into the segment known today as "mobile gaming." Capcom, ever the agnostic publisher, has long supported handheld platforms in addition to home consoles, even if the technologically inferior capabilities of a handheld system would, in theory, prevent it from receiving certain games. In 1995, a version of Capcom's then best-selling game, *Street Fighter II*, was created for the monochrome 1989 Game Boy, despite it having only two face buttons and a much slower processor than the series demanded. Handheld entries made more sense for other Capcom products, such as *Mega Man*, which received several entries on Game Boy of comparable quality to its NES cousins.

Despite being inherently unsuited to a handheld, with its 3D design and use of polygons, Capcom was open to the idea of bringing *Resident Evil* to handheld platforms relatively early in the history of the series. By 1998, Sega had dropped out of the race after its Game Gear and Nomad portables failed, leaving Nintendo a virtual monopoly with Game Boy, thanks to the incredible popularity of the *Pokémon* franchise. However, few could have predicted that it would be the obscure system Game.com, from Tiger Electronics, that would be home to the first-ever handheld *Resident Evil*. Released in September 1997, Game.com had been outdated out of the gate, with technical capabilities on par, or worse, than that of Game Boy, which had been released eight years earlier.

The first portable entry in the series was a product called *Resident Evil 2*. The game was released by Tiger sometime in late 1998, under license from Capcom. However, the game is not a port of the PlayStation title released earlier that year. Instead, it is more of a "demake," an informal term used in the game industry to refer to a game that has been remade for an older, technologically less-capable platform. A demake might have the same story and setting as the original game, but with different (usually worse) graphics or gameplay to accommodate for the inferior technology. Like the Game Boy version of *Street Fighter II*, *Resident Evil 2* on Game.com can be classified as a demake.

The basic premise of the *Resident Evil 2 demake* is inherited from the console version: the story still takes place in the Raccoon

City Police Department and stars Leon S. Kennedy. However, to conform to the Game.com's monochrome screen, the visuals have been reinterpreted in black-and-white dot-pixel 2D, while the game employs a specific visual scrolling technique to approximate the look of 3D environments. Except for the introduction video, there is no background music whatsoever, with the only audio being repetitive chiptune sound effects for gunshots, footsteps, zombies' moans and the sound of them chewing on Leon. Completely missing from the port are Leon's B scenario and all references to Claire Redfield, Ada Wong, the Birkins and the rest of the supporting cast. Due to data storage limitations, there are no cut-scenes aside from the introduction video.

For all the effort Tiger put into reproducing *Resident Evil 2*, the results were lackluster as the developers made no attempt to properly tailor the *Resident Evil* experience for a 2D handheld. It is missing elements that make *Resident Evil* and *Resident Evil 2* unique and enjoyable experiences, like scare factor, an actual plot, voiced cut-scenes, catchy music and beautiful graphics. The demake is also visually unappealing, suffers from slow and sluggish performance, has only minimal interactivity with the environments and ends abruptly, following a boss fight with William Birkin without any explanation or resolution to the story. Experienced players can finish the game in under thirty minutes. Even when accounting for the leaner nature of handheld games, this version of *Resident Evil 2* offers nothing of interest either to the series' fans or handheld gaming enthusiasts.

Details regarding the development of the demake are scarce, if not non-existent; once the game has been completed, it shows no ending credits, and there is no information on where it was developed or by whom, although some theorize that it was produced within Tiger Electronics itself. Nobody interviewed for this book has admitted to being involved in the development; most did not even know about the existence of the demake or Game.com itself. The device was never released in Japan, and was discontinued in the US by 2000 due to poor sales. In the following years, Capcom would forge ahead with its own plans to bring the *Resident Evil* series to the far more popular Game Boy Color, an upgraded, color-screen iteration released in 1998. However, it is a stretch to argue that *Resident Evil 2* on Game.com was the humble start of Capcom's grand plan to bring the series to gamers' pockets. With no one to account for its existence and contextualize its development, this demake remains an enigma that leaves virtually no *Resident Evil* legacy.

RESIDENT EVIL ON GAME BOY COLOR

In 1999, United Kingdom-based studio HotGen sought to recreate the original *Resident Evil* for Game Boy Color. A quasi-successor to the original black-and-white Game Boy, Game Boy Color was released by Nintendo in October 1998 and, as its name suggests, allowed for colored pixels for its games while offering backwards compatibility with nearly the entire Game Boy catalog. Thanks to the emergence of the Pokémon franchise in February 1996, handheld gaming had skyrocketed in popularity, and Game Boy and Game Boy Color counted among the highest-selling game hardware in the late 1990s.

Like the Tiger Game.com, both Game Boy and Game Boy Color were 2D video game systems whose capabilities, roughly speaking, were close to that of the 8-bit NES. Despite these limitations, it made some commercial sense to bring *Resident Evil* to Game Boy Color. HotGen presented Capcom with a tech demo that showed it was indeed a possibility, albeit with several liberties taken with the game's content. Capcom was convinced and the project was green-lit. The game would be a demake of the original, tailored to the limited capabilities of the Game Boy Color.

Resident Evil on Game Boy Color was to feature the core content of the PlayStation original. Throughout 1999, Capcom and HotGen released screenshots that showed recognizable elements of the Spencer Estate, such as the pre-rendered camera angles of the claustrophobic mansion hallways, the zombies, Chris Redfield, Jill Valentine and even some dialogue. All of this was to be squeezed into a 4MB Game Boy Color cartridge and playable with only two face buttons and a D-Pad. There was virtually no chance the Game Boy Color rendition would be anywhere near as good as the original, but it didn't need to be. HotGen's efforts should be commended, given the limitations of the Game Boy Color. In a January 2000 interview with website IGN, HotGen founder and then CEO, the late Fergus McGovern, explained, "We have still managed to keep all the locations and puzzle elements totally authentic, and all the locations use the same viewpoint and are identical to the PlayStation version."[1] The port had been intended for release the same month but was delayed for quality reasons. In the month prior, Capcom had publicized their game line-up for 2000, which did not contain *Resident Evil*. Capcom told IGN that development needed more time due to the challenging communication barrier between its UK developer and Japanese publisher.[2]

Despite HotGen's best efforts, *Resident Evil* on Game Boy Color was not meant to be. Despite development being around 90 per cent complete, Capcom officially cancelled the port on March 22, 2000, ironically the fourth anniversary of the original game. Capcom stated, "We were not confident that the product would have made both consumers and Capcom happy."[3] Elliot Curtis, who worked as an artist on the then upcoming *Resident Evil: Gaiden* (the game that would ultimately become the successor to this project), recalls how the project got pulled: "I don't know if there's any juicy gossip about it; it just wasn't very playable, so Capcom cancelled it. Happens all the time. We had seen the first attempt..." Curtis laughs, then continues: "It was the perfect example of how not to make a handheld game. You have to design a game differently for handhelds."

More than a decade later, in 2012, two similar prototypes of the scrapped game were leaked and subsequently distributed over the internet. They are playable through Game Boy Color emulators on modern PCs, although they are missing the last few minutes of the game and some crucial death animations for zombies and boss enemies that were never completed, due to the game's cancellation. In a detailed analysis of the leaked prototype, Matt Gander of website Games Asylum attributed the missing zombie animations to "the Game Boy Color's constraints – having to render and draw different 2D sprites for each of the static camera angles used may have been an issue, and one that also restricted character movement. It could however have simply been the case that the animation was unfinished."[4] The prototype contained the same dialogue as the original, while the gameplay and story unfolded in much the same way. Chris and Jill are both playable, and Wesker,

Barry and Rebecca are also present as supporting characters, just as in the original. As of 2020, the leaked prototype is the only way to experience the cancelled game in any capacity.

RESIDENT EVIL: GAIDEN

Despite the setbacks with *Resident Evil 2* on Game.com and the demake of *Resident Evil* on Game Boy Color, Capcom was still eager to give handhelds another go. For its third attempt, Capcom explored the possibility of creating a completely original handheld game, rather than taking an existing console title and shoehorning it into a far less capable system with questionable results. This led to the creation of *Resident Evil: Gaiden* for Game Boy Color. As hardcore gamers may have learned through Koei Tecmo's *Ninja Gaiden* series, the Japanese word *gaiden* translates roughly to "side story," implying that *Resident Evil: Gaiden* would have an original plot that could be related to the rest of the series, but with a different gameplay approach.

In 2001, Capcom chose to outsource development of the project to the small, UK-based development studio M4. The company was a partnership between its founder Tim Hull, who was to be the producer for *Resident Evil: Gaiden*, and James Cox, who would program the game's engine. The two had previously worked together at another UK developer, Bits Studios, which produced licensed games in the 1990s. The studio had developed specific tools that could streamline the development of Game Boy Color titles, making M4 a suitable fit for Capcom's most ambitious handheld *Resident Evil* yet.[5]

The product that became *Resident Evil: Gaiden* actually began as a handheld rendition of another Capcom franchise, *Dino Crisis*, of which M4 had created a prototype at the behest of publisher Virgin Interactive. Capcom had previously inked a European game publishing deal with this arm of the Virgin Group, the UK conglomerate founded by Sir Richard Branson: since the 1980s, Virgin Interactive had been publishing Japanese and North American-developed games throughout the European market, including some of Capcom's *Resident Evil* titles. Virgin Interactive now hoped to deepen its relationship with Capcom through the development of original titles, so the publisher commissioned production of the handheld *Dino Crisis* prototype. "As I recall, we produced a very impressive demo for a [Game Boy Color] version of *Dino Crisis*," says Elliot Curtis in a 2011 retrospective by NowGamer. "*Resident Evil* was already in development as an over-ambitious port from the PlayStation version. This was scrapped and Capcom asked us to do a bespoke game with our *Dino Crisis* engine."

The prototype employed an overhead-exploration view, similar to 8-bit titles such as the MSX *Metal Gear* and, perhaps coincidentally, Capcom's *Sweet Home*, which inspired *Resident Evil* in the first place. As in the console versions of the *Resident Evil* and *Dino Crisis* series, players would explore environments – in this case a luxury cruise ship – looking for keys and other items to unlock new paths. The major divergence from its console cousins comes from the combat mechanics; when a monster appears, the game shifts to first-person view, and players have to defeat the enemy before returning to the overhead view. Seeing its template as a suitable fit, Capcom requested that the prototype be converted from a *Dino Crisis* game to what would become *Resident Evil: Gaiden*.

Capcom had very little direct involvement with *Resident Evil: Gaiden*. Shinji Mikami served as a content advisor, which in practice meant offering the developers at M4 advice for improving the game's quality. According to Curtis, it was Mikami who recommended implementing a so-called "slider" into the game's first-person combat. The slider is essentially a dot that moves ("slides") horizontally across the Game Boy Color's screen, symbolizing a gun's crosshairs. Players must press the A button when the slider overlaps with the designated target point in order to shoot the enemy. The slider moves at different speeds depending on the enemy being confronted. However, other than the slider, Mikami was very hands-off with the game, leaving the rest of development to the team at M4.

Meanwhile, Hiroki Kato was assigned to craft the plot of *Resident Evil: Gaiden*, although his involvement ended there. "I wrote the story and handed it off to the developer, but that was all I ended up doing," Kato remembers. "I do not remember interacting with the development team directly. *Resident Evil: Gaiden* needed a plot, so I just wrote one." The story features Leon S. Kennedy teaming up with Barry Burton as they infiltrate a luxury cruise ship in search of BOWs. Ultimately, the plot is inconsequential to the series lore and has never been referenced in another title. In fact, in 2003 Kato modified *Wesker's Report* for a port of *Resident Evil CODE: Veronica* to incorporate elements of *Resident Evil: Gaiden*, hinting at some level of relevance, but this was never followed up in revisions that came after. The scene depicts Leon as having been kidnapped or killed by a BOW, but this has never been referenced in any other *Resident Evil* game.

In a series first, *Resident Evil: Gaiden* was released in Europe before being launched in any other territory, on December 14, 2001. It was released in Japan on March 29, 2002, and in North America a couple of months later, on June 3. The game failed to garner any notable sales or attention in any region. Both fans and gaming media criticized the game for various reasons, ranging from its large departure from the standard *Resident Evil* formula to its lack of scares and tension, as well as its basic and irrelevant story.

Game Boy Color's limited capabilities and low budget restricted what M4 could realistically do to bring a credible *Resident Evil* to a handheld device, and in March 2001 Game Boy Advance had been released. It offered 2D visuals whose sophistication came close to that of Super NES, so consumer attention had begun to turn away from Game Boy Color even before *Resident Evil: Gaiden* was launched. M4 pushed to move the game over to Game Boy Advance, with the developers revealing that they had created a prototype with improved visuals, but Capcom and Virgin Interactive decided to stick to their original plans, seeing a revamp of the visuals as a costly and time-consuming process that, when combined with the high cost and low margin of Game Boy cartridges, in the end could not be justified. It was perhaps for the best; amidst the numerous potential complaints one may have about *Resident Evil: Gaiden*, the graphics were arguably one of the better aspects of the game, if not the best. M4 became defunct in 2002 after failing to secure funding for future games.

To its credit, *Resident Evil: Gaiden* is noteworthy in some respects. It was the first *Resident Evil* game to employ the idea of shifting perspectives from third-person exploration to first-person combat, an idea that would reappear in future games. It was also the first of a still-growing number of *Resident Evil* games to take place on ships. However, it is undeniable that *Resident Evil: Gaiden* was yet another failure in Capcom's many-year attempt to bring *Resident Evil* to handhelds, following *Resident Evil 2* on Game.com and the cancelled Game Boy Color version of the original *Resident Evil*. In baseball, the saying goes: "Three strikes, you're out!" Similarly, following the release of *Resident Evil: Gaiden* (and with the exception of very minor spin-offs released exclusively for Japanese mobile phones), Capcom finally put to rest the idea of bringing *Resident Evil* to underpowered 2D handhelds.

CHAPTER 7: GOING
FIRST-PERSON: THE
SURVIVOR SUBSERIES

RESIDENT EVIL: SURVIVOR

Resident Evil made its grand entrance on PlayStation in March 1996, ushering in the survival horror genre, as gamers know it today. *Resident Evil 2* and *Resident Evil 3: Nemesis* followed, and despite their different scales and varied development histories, the three games form one of the most iconic trilogies to grace PlayStation, the system which gives *Resident Evil* its distinct identity as a game franchise. In the first game, players embark on a journey where they experience the beginnings of the Raccoon City story; by the third game, they see how it all ends. *Resident Evil 3: Nemesis* (1999) should have concluded the PlayStation trilogy on the highest of notes, like a triumphant hero in the most perfect fairy tale ever. But it turns out that one more *Resident Evil* would be released for PlayStation the following year: an obscure, first-person offshoot known as *Resident Evil: Survivor* (titled *Biohazard: Gun Survivor* in Japan). *Resident Evil* was now a tetralogy on PlayStation.

Details about the development of *Resident Evil: Survivor* are scarce, particularly compared to the well-documented history of the first three *Resident Evil* games. It is difficult to track down anyone intimately involved with the game's creative direction, as very few of the core *Resident Evil* team were involved. Noboru Sugimura is credited with having penned the story at Flagship, and Tatsuya Minami, who worked on the original game's Sega Saturn port, is credited as producer, but others, such as Shinji Mikami, had no involvement in the game's development whatsoever. "From what I can remember, the idea behind *Resident Evil: Survivor* was to test the franchise's suitability with other genres," Kazuhiro Aoyama says, confirming that he, too, had no involvement with the game. Notably, Sega had created its own first-person zombie-shooter franchise, *The House of the Dead*, for arcades, Saturn and Dreamcast. While different in tone from *Resident Evil*, *The House of the Dead* and *The House of the Dead II* showed the potential in expanding the zombie concept to other genres. This seems to have gotten some minds at Capcom thinking about a first-person *Resident Evil* game.

Part of the enigma surrounding *Resident Evil: Survivor* lies in the company that developed the game; released in Japan on January 27, 2000, this was officially the first non-port *Resident Evil* game developed externally (though it was closely followed by *Resident Evil CODE: Veronica* for Dreamcast, also outsourced, which was released one week later, on February 3). The developer, Kyoto-based Tose Co., Ltd., is particularly secretive about the role it plays in the development of games published by its clients. In a 2015 interview with Polygon, Tose's head of overseas marketing, Koji Morosawa, explained that the company is "contractually barred" from discussing what it has worked on.[1] The game's credits lead nowhere; the staff list is comprised of a mishmash of names that do not appear in any other *Resident Evil* games and colorful aliases like "Heybay-Hiradiera." Today, there is almost no remaining evidence of the game's marketing cycle, which would have begun in late 1999, besides a single fifteen-second Japanese commercial.[2] Based on the paucity of useful information, one might think that *Resident Evil: Survivor* is not worth remembering. However, that would be far from the truth; for a number of reasons, the game does in fact carry a unique significance in the history of the series.

The general premise of *Resident Evil: Survivor* is similar enough to the other games. The protagonist, an agent suffering from amnesia, infiltrates the Umbrella-owned Sheena Island, which is rumored to be the literal breeding ground for the monsters seen in the main series. The game also features zombies, Hunters, Lickers, Tyrants, keys, passwords and other *Resident Evil* staple elements. However, as a spin-off with an original cast, the story is only sparingly connected to the main series, although the few links that do exist are of interest to dedicated fans of the lore. Some files give additional context to events of other *Resident Evil* games, thanks to the involvement of Sugimura, who often emphasized the importance building a connected universe within the series. At the end of the game, the agent manages to remember his real name, Ark Thompson, which means he's an acquaintance of Leon S.

Kennedy. The story is later referenced briefly in *Resident Evil Zero*, but other than these minor connections, *Resident Evil: Survivor* holds only a fleeting relevance within the entire series.

The main distinguishing element for *Resident Evil: Survivor* is that it plays entirely from a first-person perspective and is powered by a fully polygonal 3D engine instead of the pre-rendered fixed camera angles that defined the first three games. The game also eschews the exploration and puzzle-solving elements in favor of a much greater focus on shooting enemies. Ark's handgun even comes with unlimited ammunition, where the series had previously made a name for itself in ammo conservation. In what is perhaps a throwback to Capcom's origins as an arcade game developer, players are required to make it to the end of the entire game without quitting in the middle. As in more traditional entries, players can save their progress using typewriters, but unlike those games, this only saves the weapons they acquired; if players turn the PlayStation off, they must start all over again from the beginning next time they play. *Resident Evil: Survivor* is not terribly long, however – most players can beat it in under two hours – but it has multiple branching paths throughout the adventure to incentivize replays. *Resident Evil: Survivor* is thus the first true deviation from the third-person exploration-focused formula introduced in the 1996 original.

Most fans consider *Resident Evil: Survivor* to be a subpar and problematic game. Its production values are comparatively lacking, evidenced by the game's underwhelming graphics and lack of production polish. Although this was the first and only fully polygonal *Resident Evil* on PlayStation, the character models lack detail, the frame rate and animation are erratic, and there is little variety to the gameplay except to shoot enemies, who have very unsatisfying reactions to bullets. The liberal recycling of enemy models from *Resident Evil* and *Resident Evil 2* was another sore demonstration of the game's low budget.

The game's voice-acting was also a major step back from the progress Capcom had made since 1996. Somehow, despite four years of advancement since the original *Resident Evil* rocked gamers' ears with its unforgettable dialogue, *Resident Evil: Survivor* managed to contain voiceovers every bit as terrible as the original yet without the requisite lines to give the game the same unintentionally iconic status in this regard. In particular, there is a line delivered by an elderly British woman, the antagonist's mother, which might just be the most unnaturally voiced line in the entire series. The list of voice actors in the credits is one of the few verifiable parts of the game's development team, indicating that recording had been done by native English speakers living in Tokyo, just as the 1996 original had been.

One additional element made *Resident Evil: Survivor* a unique experience: it was compatible with the GunCon, a PlayStation peripheral manufactured by Namco (now Bandai Namco). The GunCon is a toy gun that uses infrared technology to allow gamers to point and shoot at an enemy on the screen, in lieu of using the analog stick or D-Pad to navigate a crosshair, which can be cumbersome and unwieldy in comparison. Sega's *The House of the Dead* franchise had already popularized the idea of a lightgun-compatible first-person zombie-shooter, and both the Saturn and Dreamcast entries had compatible lightgun accessories. However, while the Japanese and PAL versions of the title supported the GunCon, Capcom USA ultimately removed its compatibility from the North American version. Furthermore, while the Japanese version was released in January 2000 and the PAL version in March, the North American release wasn't until August 30, one of the longest gaps between a Japanese and North American release seen in the series so far.

Capcom has never officially explained its rationale for delaying the North American release or removing GunCon support, but one popular theory is that it was due to the Columbine High School massacre, which occurred in Littleton, Colorado on April 20, 1999. This event brought the debate of gun control to the forefront of US national politics that year and some blamed violent video games, such as *Resident Evil*, for corrupting the minds of youth and contributing to the incident.[3] *Resident Evil: Survivor* came during a very sensitive period in US history, and in light of the game's general lack of quality, eschewing GunCon support was probably the appropriate decision; the GunCon would not have improved the experience anywhere near enough to offset the controversy it could have invited otherwise. However, even the shooting does not explain why the game took unusually long to release in North America. It is also likely that *Resident Evil CODE: Veronica*, which was due for release in March 2000, was viewed by Capcom as a more prestigious title, which deserved the bulk of the US branch's attention.

It is worth remembering that the developers of the first *Resident Evil* initially experimented with a first-person concept but abandoned the idea early on due to the difficulty of developing such a title for PlayStation. *Resident Evil: Survivor* thus symbolically brings things full circle, giving a clue as to what might have been, had the original game gone in its initial intended direction.

What is even more remarkable, however, is the ultimate lesson Capcom took from *Resident Evil: Survivor*. Not every game that a publisher releases will be a successful endeavor; the game industry was born out of, and continues to grow, as a result of constant creative experimentation, and some games will inevitably fail and be forgotten. By most counts, *Resident Evil: Survivor* should have been one of those games. Instead, it was merely the beginning of a behind-the-scenes push to marry the *Resident Evil* franchise with the first-person shooter genre. In the years ahead, Capcom would release a number of first-person *Resident Evil* games, altering the landscape of the franchise and slowly but surely transforming the first-person perspective into one of its most indispensable elements. In this sense, *Resident Evil: Survivor* marked a turning point in the history of the franchise, dislodging it from its identity as a third-person game with fixed camera angles, even if, ironically, *Survivor*'s actual production history continues to be shrouded in mystery.

FIRE ZONE: *RESIDENT EVIL: SURVIVOR 2 – CODE: VERONICA*

Following the release of *Resident Evil: Survivor* in early 2000, Capcom was interested in creating another first-person *Resident Evil* game. The first game had been a collaboration between Capcom and Tose, with the final results a mixed bag in terms of quality. For the second attempt, Capcom decided to partner with a fellow Japanese publisher with a more credible background in the genre. In February 2001, Capcom announced it was collaborating with Namco to develop a first-person shooter titled *Biohazard:*

Fire Zone for the arcade in Japan only (no Western release was ever announced). Namco was known for the *Time Crisis* franchise, a series of on-rails arcade shooters.

In April 2001, the collaboration was renamed *Gun Survivor 2: Biohazard – CODE: Veronica* in Japan (and eventually *Resident Evil: Survivor 2 – CODE: Veronica* in the West), indicating the game's connections with both *Resident Evil CODE: Veronica* and *Resident Evil: Survivor.* The game was initially scheduled for release in July 2001 in Japan. As well as Capcom and Namco, Sega subsidiaries Nextech and SIMS were also involved. From Capcom, Tatsuya Minami acted as the game's producer, continuing the role from the original *Resident Evil: Survivor.* Shinji Mikami acted as a supervisor, while the game's creative co-director was Yasuhiro Seto. Namco was in charge of developing and manufacturing the arcade board; among its directors was Akihiro Ishihara, who later became known for the *Idolmaster* series. Nextech, the original developer of *Resident Evil CODE: Veronica*, was in charge of cut-scenes, while SIMS was in charge of programming the game.

Survivor 2 is an even more dramatic departure from the *Resident Evil* formula than its predecessor. Instead of an original story, setting and cast, it reuses the setting and characters of *CODE: Veronica*. The game revisits Rockfort Island and Umbrella's Antarctic base, rearranging each place to fit the pace and flow of the arcade-style first-person-shooter gameplay. The game's cut-scenes feature only subtitles, with no voice-acting whatsoever. Technically, the game can be considered a canonical entry because the events are actually a manifest of a dream Claire is having directly at the end of *Resident Evil CODE: Veronica*, but in practice, the story is irrelevant and inconsequential to *Resident Evil* lore.

Running on Sega's Dreamcast-based NAOMI arcade board, the game employs a graphics engine identical to the one used in *Resident Evil CODE: Veronica*. The first-person viewpoint is based on the option featured in its mini-game, "Battle Game". One or two players can control either Claire Redfield or Steve Burnside in single or co-op mode, and players encounter hordes of zombies, Hunters, Lickers and other enemies from the original *CODE: Veronica*. Unlike *Resident Evil: Survivor*, which had almost no time limits in gameplay, the levels in *Resident Evil: Survivor 2 – CODE: Veronica* are timed; players only have a few minutes to complete the stage. If the timer runs out, Nemesis from the third game appears and begins chasing the players; one hit from Nemesis will kill the player instantly. Each level concludes with a fight against a boss from *CODE: Veronica*.

Survivor 2 was housed in an oversized arcade cabinet with two monitors side by side, two model submachine-gun-shaped controllers mounted onto a protruding stand, and a banner above the monitors featuring the game's logo and artwork of the Tyrant and Claire. The model submachine gun controls differed from other arcade shooters by Sega or Namco in that the guns had to be moved left or right to control the characters. Unlike the first-person Battle Game in *CODE: Veronica*, which retained the traditional series' auto-aim controls, *Survivor 2* is closer to the original *Survivor* in that it allows players to aim a crosshair at any location on the screen.

Capcom announced a home console port of *Survivor 2* for PlayStation 2 in mid-2001. This version is compatible with Namco's GunCon 2 accessory, allowing PlayStation 2 owners to play the game in a similar way to the arcade original. However, instead of physically moving the GunCon 2 to steer the characters, as in the arcade game, the GunCon 2's side buttons and D-Pad are used to move the characters left or right. The PlayStation 2 port also adds extra modes, as well as the option to select Chris Redfield and Rodrigo Juan Raval. The PlayStation 2 port launched in Japan on November 8, 2001, both as a stand-alone disc and as a bundle with the GunCon 2. It sold approximately 32,000 copies in its first week,[4] a number that more than likely recouped Capcom's low-cost investment. A PAL release followed in February 2002, but the game was never announced for, or released in, North America. Capcom USA provided no official explanation for the lack of a North American release.

The English localization in the PAL version is riddled with strange dialogue that manages to sink lower than even some of the worst lines in the original *Resident Evil*, without the benefit of having become part of pop culture. One example is when Steve says, "If I wasn't here, you would have been cleared," which would have been better translated as, "If I weren't around, you wouldn't have made it." There are also several mistranslations, such as the use of the term "Fast Aid Spray" instead of "First Aid Spray."* Typographical errors throughout further dampen the already low quality of the game's localization. As with other video games with poor localizations, the root causes are likely some combination of mismanaged schedules, a low budget and non-existent

---

* In Japanese, the term for "First Aid Spray" is literally "Emergency Spray." In Japanese, "emergency" contains the Chinese character for "urgent," which appears to be where the translation "Fast" comes from. Also, the English words "First" and "Fast" are spelled and pronounced identically in Japanese, which may have also contributed to the mistranslation.

quality control. Both Minami and Mikami had very little active involvement with the game, which may have contributed to its various shortcomings.

GUN SHOT: *RESIDENT EVIL: DEAD AIM*

Resident Evil: Survivor 2 – CODE: Veronica sold well enough for Capcom that the company decided to continue the *Survivor* series. The company green-lit the production of not one, but two sequels: the first was *Dino Stalker*, which is known in Japan as *Gun Survivor 3: Dino Crisis*. As the Japanese title implies, the game is a successor to the first two games, but instead takes place within the *Dino Crisis* universe. Capcom decided to remove the "Survivor" branding from the Western release in order to disassociate *Dino Stalker* from the negativity of the first two *Survivor* titles. Although *Dino Stalker* had higher production values than its predecessors, thanks to its original graphics assets, full voice-acting and original plot, it was released worldwide in summer 2002 for PlayStation 2 to middling reviews and low sales. The *Gun Survivor* idea was failing to catch on with consumers, despite Capcom's repeated efforts. *Dino Stalker* soon became a forgotten game.

The other first-person title that got the go-ahead would bring the *Survivor* brand back to the *Resident Evil* universe. Announced in autumn 2002 for PlayStation 2, this fourth game was titled *Gun Survivor 4: Biohazard: Heroes Never Die* in Asia and *Resident Evil: Dead Aim* elsewhere. As with *Dino Stalker*, the "Survivor" name was replaced in order to allow *Resident Evil: Dead Aim* to better stand on its own. Produced once again by Tatsuya Minami, the game would feature an original story with a new cast, much like the first game. Capcom collaborated with Cavia, a Japanese third-party developer, on the game's production. *Resident Evil: Dead Aim* was to be compatible with the GunCon 2 accessory or a standard DualShock 2 controller.

While not directly tied to the main *Resident Evil* games, *Resident Evil: Dead Aim* – whose writers included Noboru Sugimura – finally brought the chronology beyond 1998 (except for *Resident Evil: Gaiden*, which is not part of the canon). Taking place in September 2002, *Resident Evil: Dead Aim* features Bruce McGivern, a US government agent attempting to thwart a plot by a French ex-Umbrella scientist, Morpheus Duvall, to unleash the T-virus against the world. Aiding Bruce is Fong Ling, a Chinese Government operative with the same objective. The game initially takes place on a cruise liner before shifting to an unnamed island containing an Umbrella facility, where the existence of a new bioweapon that combines the T-virus and G-virus is uncovered.

Employing a fully polygonal engine, the graphics were a notable improvement over *Resident Evil CODE: Veronica*, offering greater textural detail and superior particle effects like fire and lightning. Also, players could rotate the camera in circles, giving them the ability to explore the environments more closely. Meanwhile, traditional elements that were missing from *Survivor* or *Survivor 2*, such as Item Boxes and typewriters, returned in *Dead Aim*.

But the biggest departure of *Resident Evil: Dead Aim* from its predecessors is its combined use of both first- and third-person viewpoints. Although both *Resident Evil CODE: Veronica* and *Resident Evil: Gaiden* technically did this earlier, *Resident Evil: Dead Aim* is the first game whose entire premise revolves around shifting between third- and first-person. *Resident Evil CODE: Veronica* restricted the first-person viewpoint to two minor boss fights and a mini-game, while *Resident Evil: Gaiden* played differently from other titles in the series. *Resident Evil: Dead Aim* has quite a bit in common with the traditional formula – players explore environments in third-person, just like earlier *Resident Evil* games – but when the time comes to fight against the game's large number of enemies, such as zombies, Hunters and a variety of Tyrant-like creatures, players aim their weapon, which automatically shifts the perspective from third- to first-person. This clever combination of viewpoints actually functions well and makes for a solid gameplay experience, one that's certainly an improvement on the previous *Survivor* games.

Resident Evil: Dead Aim was released in Japan on February 13, 2003, and in the summer elsewhere, including North America. Unlike *Resident Evil: Survivor*, which eschewed lightgun support in the North American release, *Dead* Aim retained compatibility with the GunCon 2 in all territories. In Japan, its ending music track and marketing promotion were tied in with rock band Rize, but despite these efforts the game did not garner notable sales or attention anywhere, with only 40,000 copies sold in Japan in 2003, the fewest of the four *Survivor* titles. The game was somewhat more successful on a critical basis, with GameSpot's review noting *Dead Aim*'s improvements over the other *Survivor* games, stating, "Though not a *Resident Evil* game in the traditional sense, it does capture the pacing and the tone of the series fairly well, and it's generally the best *Survivor* game released to date."[5] *Resident Evil: Dead Aim* would be Capcom's final *Survivor* game. Despite its passable quality, the game has never appeared on another platform and its ties to past and future *Resident Evil* games are few and far between.

It is fascinating how much time Capcom invested in the idea of a first-person *Resident Evil* sub-brand, given the constant negative feedback that began with *Resident Evil: Survivor*. In summer 2003, Capcom finally retired the *Survivor* name for good, opting to focus its efforts on creating *Resident Evil* sub-brands for other burgeoning genres, such as online multiplayer. Fans now remember the *Survivor* series as that experimental first-person derivative of the otherwise third-person *Resident Evil* series.

CHAPTER 8: THE HISTORY OF *RESIDENT EVIL* ON NINTENDO

FAMILY-FRIENDLY AND CAPACITY-CONSTRAINED: THE NINTENDO PROBLEM

While Capcom was able to take the *Resident Evil* franchise to Sega hardware not long after its debut on Sony's PlayStation, it took considerably longer to reach Nintendo platforms. There were two barriers confronting Capcom here: the first was the issue of Nintendo's corporate image. In the 1990s, Nintendo actively promoted a family-friendly image and, as a matter of policy, the company behind *Mario*, *Zelda* and *Donkey Kong* was unwelcoming to third-party video games depicting realistic violence or sexual imagery. It was only after Sega began making inroads in North America and Europe with Genesis/Mega Drive that Nintendo slowly began to reconsider its stance. By the time *Resident Evil* launched, in March 1996, Nintendo was no longer actively preventing third parties from releasing mature content on its platforms. However, Nintendo itself did not begin developing or publishing mature content until the late 1990s, giving the company a pervasive reputation among gamers that Nintendo games were only for children. *Resident Evil*, with its scenes of explicit violence and gore, may have looked like a bad match-up for a Nintendo platform.

The second and more difficult issue was technological. While Sony and Sega opted to use the high-capacity, low-cost CD-ROM for PlayStation and Saturn respectively, Nintendo was hostile to the format, instead favoring the traditional cartridge. For Nintendo, the CD was too risky: games would have loading times that could hurt the customer experience, and even more devastating would be the relative ease with which games could be pirated – with the CD-ROM being a general-purpose format used for music, video and data storage, consumers had easy access to blank discs and could simply borrow or rent a game or music CD and copy it. Piracy of CD-based games did eventually become a severe issue for the industry, particularly on PlayStation. (Anecdotally speaking, a small but not insignificant number of this author's childhood friends possessed pirated copies of the *Resident Evil* games on PlayStation, among other titles.) While Sony's platform employed security features to make pirated content unplayable, hackers were able to bypass anti-piracy measures with so-called "mod-chips," "boot discs" or other similar hacks. It is difficult to pinpoint exactly how much effect piracy has had on Capcom, Sony and the rest of the industry – there is no consensus on whether piracy has been a net negative at all in sales terms – but Nintendo's concerns regarding the vulnerability of CDs were well-founded.

Afraid of widespread piracy, Nintendo opted to use cartridges for its next system, even though they were far more expensive to manufacture and had considerably less storage space than CDs. Launched on June 23, 1996, in Japan, just a few months after the release of *Resident Evil*, Nintendo 64 was Nintendo's official successor to Super NES and the company's answer to PlayStation and Saturn. The name refers to the system's 64-bit tech specs. To the average Joe, the 64 made the system appear twice as powerful as the 32-bit PlayStation and Saturn, though it was similar in general capabilities. From a technological standpoint, there was little stopping Nintendo 64 from having games with visuals similar to the *Resident Evil* series. But Nintendo's decision to use cartridges on Nintendo 64 would preclude such games and franchises, and ultimately become its undoing in the war against PlayStation.

In February 1996, Square made the ultimate bombshell announcement of that generation: *Final Fantasy VII* was scheduled for release exclusively on PlayStation. Square had been an ardent supporter of Nintendo since the 8-bit era, and the *Final Fantasy* series was a staple of both NES and Super NES.[1] Role-playing games formed the most popular genre in Japan, and *Final Fantasy*, along with *Dragon Quest*, was a top-level franchise rivaled only by the likes of the *Super Mario* series. Among Capcom franchises, only *Street Fighter* came close. Square's decision was a clear victory for Sony, setting the stage for its usurping of Nintendo's position as the market leader. Combined with Sony's efforts to broaden gamer demographics with content more palatable to older audiences, Sony eventually surpassed Nintendo's market share and never looked back; by the end of their lifetimes, PlayStation had outsold Nintendo 64 nearly three to one. Capcom, as with other third parties, was a clear beneficiary of Square's switch of allegiances. After *Final Fantasy VII* launched in January 1997, Sony recorded its best year of PlayStation sales in Japan, with over 5 million sold.[2] *Resident Evil 2*, which launched in late January 1998 and became an instant million-seller, benefitted from PlayStation's meteoric rise the year before, one of the reasons it nearly doubled the sales of its predecessor.

Given the demographic mismatch and technological limitations, it was not unreasonable to think *Resident Evil* was a poor fit for Nintendo. For the first few years of the series' existence, the option to make a port was not even available to Capcom, even if they had wanted it because there was no way the standard cartridge could hold all the data of either *Resident Evil* or *Resident Evil 2*, which comprised voice-overs, pre-rendered backgrounds, full soundtracks and full video. However, Yoshiki Okamoto respected Nintendo as much as he did Sega and believed that Capcom should release software for all platforms, including Nintendo 64, Game Boy and PlayStation.

Nintendo, meanwhile, attempted to address Nintendo 64's severe storage-capacity constraints. The company was developing 64DD, a disk drive that would attach to the bottom of the Nintendo 64 hardware and allow the system to be used with a magnetic disk (not to be confused with a compact disc) that could hold up to 64MB of data, far more than the 4MB that cartridges could hold. Less expensive to manufacture than cartridges, and supposedly better protected from mass piracy than CDs, the 64DD's magnetic disk was Nintendo's attempt to reach an acceptable equilibrium on price and security, but the company was ultimately unsuccessful. Although an improvement over cartridges, the 64MB of capacity offered by the magnetic disk was still far less than that of a CD, which holds nearly ten times as much data. The 64DD also faced the same problem that Sega encountered years earlier with its Genesis/Mega Drive add-ons, the Sega CD and 32X: adoption of the peripherals would be wide enough among players to justify long-term support of games that required them. The 64DD was initially announced in 1995, even before Nintendo 64 itself came out, but a lack of acceptable game software ultimately pushed the release all the way back to December 1999, when it was launched in Japan to virtually no consumer interest. It was never released elsewhere and was soon forgotten. Ironically, thanks to advancements in their technology, capacity for Nintendo 64 cartridges managed to grow to the same 64MB as the 64DD's magnetic disks, rendering the accessory entirely redundant.

In the end, Capcom did not release any games for 64DD, but existence of the peripheral meant the company could for the first time seriously entertain the possibility of *Resident Evil* on Nintendo. In early 1997, Okamoto asked members of the *Resident Evil* team to research the feasibility of developing either a port or a new *Resident Evil* game for Nintendo 64 or 64DD. In an interview with the magazine *Dengeki Nintendo 64* in May, Okamoto also divulged for the first time the concept of a "*Resident Evil* game with ninja".[3] Some believed this to be a Nintendo 64 title, but he was actually referring to a different project, called *Sengoku Biohazard*, which eventually became *Onimusha: Warlords*.[4] This game never went into development for Nintendo 64, as rumors at the time alleged, having begun development for the original PlayStation before moving over to PlayStation 2.

Capcom eventually found two viable paths to bring the series to Nintendo's cartridge-based console. By October, it learned of data-compression techniques and algorithms available on Nintendo 64 that could bring a full-fledged soundtrack, full video and voice-acting to the system, in spite of its cartridges. Initially unwilling to green-light a new game, Okamoto instead chose *Resident Evil 2* as a test case, giving the project twelve months to be completed. The PlayStation version was nearly complete at this point and ready for its January 1998 launch, while the Saturn port was to be cancelled shortly after. The original *Resident Evil* might have been an easier game to port, owing to its smaller data footprint, but Okamoto believed it was too old at this point to be commercially viable. If the *Resident Evil 2* conversion went well, then Okamoto could better justify dedicating resources to an exclusive Nintendo 64 entry.

RESIDENT EVIL 2 ON NINTENDO 64

Compared to most other video game ports, *Resident Evil 2* on Nintendo 64 has a fairly colorful development history. In late 1997, Capcom enlisted San Diego-based developer Angel Studios to handle the conversion. The studio was given a $1 million budget, which at the time was a significant sum for a belated port. While many ports are, simplistically speaking, a matter of converting code created for one platform to run on another, Angel Studios carried the additional responsibility of resizing all of the data in *Resident Evil 2*, originally a two-disc PlayStation game, to fit inside a single Nintendo 64 cartridge; the maximum size Capcom could use was the recently released 64MB variant. Such data includes hundreds of background images, over fifteen minutes of CG cut-scenes, an extensive soundtrack and around twenty minutes of voice-acting. John Linneman, a technical analyst for video games at *Eurogamer's* technology-focused media outlet Digital Foundry, says, "On the face of it, a [Nintendo 64] conversion of *Resident Evil 2* shouldn't be a problem … the action consists of fairly simple 3D characters and objects overlaid on a series of pre-rendered 2D backdrops."[5] Unsurprisingly, the data-compression process proved to be time-consuming and expensive. The nine-person team at Angel Studios underwent months of trial and error to see which techniques worked and which did not, attempting to find ways to reduce the data size of every last asset in the original code to fit inside that cartridge. In a July 2000 post-mortem for video game technology website *Gamasutra*, former Angel Studios programmer Todd Meynink explains how his team "relentlessly tried everything, often multiple times" in a cycle of trial and error that involved returning to failed approaches in hope of a different outcome. The result, Meynink says, was "an industry first – high-quality video on a cartridge-based console."[6] Regarding the compression process, Meynink adds, "Audio and video received most of the attention and were pushed and squeezed until they fit." Linneman considers the audio to be the most impressive result among all the different elements. It required Angel Studios to seek outside assistance from development studio Factor 5, the German–American pioneer in video game technology known for hits including *Star Wars: Rogue Squadron* on Nintendo 64. Composer Chris Huelsbeck, who worked at Factor 5, had to design a tool that could convert the original PlayStation audio to run on the Nintendo 64's specs.

Resident Evil 2 for Nintendo 64 launched in North America on October 31, 1999, and elsewhere, including Japan, in early

2000. Although Meynink admits that the team completed the conversion behind schedule, the end result was nothing short of magnificent. In particular, the Nintendo 64 conversion maintains virtual parity with the visuals of the original. Although Linneman observes differences in certain visual elements between the two versions, he says, "It's tremendous to see just how close Angel Studios got in replicating the PlayStation experience for owners of the Nintendo system." Moreover, when played on a Nintendo 64 containing Nintendo's Expansion Pak RAM accessory, the resolution of certain backgrounds increases, improving their image quality further.

Although the Nintendo 64 version's audio and CG cut-scenes suffer from noticeably high compression in comparison to other incarnations, the game's entire script, almost every CG video and the soundtrack all made the transition to cartridge. Angel Studios even managed to implement a number of minor additions to the gameplay and story. Players could, for the first time in series history, select a control scheme that allowed players to guide the character in the direction they pushed the analog stick. The team also added a violence adjuster, a blood-color setting, cheat codes for infinite ammo and health, and extra files that provided clues to the plots of other *Resident Evil* games, including those that had yet to be released. These additional files were intended to give Nintendo 64 owners some background on other, earlier titles that are unavailable on the console, such as *Resident Evil 3: Nemesis* and *CODE: Veronica*.

Capcom and Angel Studios aimed to sell 1 million copies of *Resident Evil 2* on Nintendo 64, a goal that would ultimately go unmet. Perhaps Capcom was too optimistic: *Resident Evil 2* on

PlayStation was nearly two years old at this point and had already sold nearly 5 million copies on its own; *Resident Evil 3: Nemesis* was released in North America within days of the Nintendo 64 port; while *Resident Evil CODE: Veronica* hit Dreamcast less than half a year later. Ultimately, *Resident Evil 2* arrived on Nintendo 64 at a busy time for the franchise, diverting Capcom's marketing resources away from it and onto other, newer games.

However, beyond the mild commercial underperformance lies a showpiece for Nintendo 64. Capcom, Angel Studios and Factor 5 proved, with ingenuity and tenacity, that cinematic experiences that were once the exclusive realm of disc-based platforms could find another home, on Nintendo 64's tiny cartridges. Much like Saturn, Nintendo 64 received only one *Resident Evil* game, but in many ways, it is certainly a port for the history books; one still discussed and admired nearly two decades later.

ZERO CAPACITY REMAINING: *RESIDENT EVIL ZERO* ON NINTENDO 64

Porting *Resident Evil 2* to Nintendo 64 may have proved to be an expensive and time-consuming process, but it was evidence that Nintendo's cartridge-based platform could handle a fully featured *Resident Evil* game. As such, Yoshiki Okamoto decided to go ahead with plans for a *Resident Evil* exclusively for a Nintendo platform. With Shinji Mikami's Production Studio 4 preoccupied with both *Resident Evil 3: Nemesis* and *Resident Evil 4*, Capcom assigned the Nintendo 64 project to Production Studio 3, which was headed by producer Tatsuya Minami. For the role of director,

Mikami chose Koji Oda, who had previously worked on the original *Resident Evil* as system planner for the camera angles early on in that game's development. Noboru Sugimura of Flagship was in charge of writing the story. As with *Resident Evil CODE: Veronica* on Dreamcast, Capcom's lack of experience in developing a 3D title for Nintendo 64 meant the company needed to seek outside expertise for the project, and so they enlisted Tose for programming and development.

Capcom needed to strike a balance between creating a new game that carried the legitimacy of other titles in the series, without disadvantaging PlayStation owners who did not own a Nintendo 64. Therefore, Oda and Sugimura decided to go back in time to just one day before the events of the original *Resident Evil*. Sugimura's story would expand on the scope of the original game by providing background context to the Mansion Incident, as seen through the eyes of STARS Bravo Team member Rebecca Chambers. By going with the premise of a prequel, this new game would have plenty of connections to the rest of the plot, without it being necessary to know the overall story in the same way it would be for a true sequel like *Resident Evil CODE: Veronica*. Likewise, Nintendo 64 owners could jump right into their first *Resident Evil* game and enjoy the plot without necessarily having to play another entry. Fittingly, Capcom chose to name the title *Resident Evil Zero*.

As a cartridge-based system, Nintendo 64 presented Production Studio 3 and Tose with unique challenges not seen with other *Resident Evil* games. As with the port of *Resident Evil 2*, the lack of capacity on Nintendo 64 cartridges meant that the team could not just indiscriminately add CG cut-scenes, pre-rendered backgrounds and voice-acting, all of which were defining traits of the Sony and Sega *Resident Evil* games. There would be no second disc to fall back on, should Production Studio 3's ambitions grow too large.

On the flip side, the cartridge gave way to a new benefit that would uniquely shape the gameplay of *Resident Evil Zero*: its lack of loading times. One of the most notable drawbacks of disc-based platforms like PlayStation, Saturn, and even Dreamcast, is the time needed for those systems to completely load data from the disc into the console's memory. In the early disc-based *Resident Evil* games, Capcom mitigated the loading times by inserting the now-iconic door-opening sequences between rooms, diverting player attention away from the unappealing idea of watching a black loading screen. Although the developers now had the option of removing the sequences entirely, they decided to include them in *Resident Evil Zero*, feeling that they helped the game maintain its sense of tension.

Instead, the team decided to use Nintendo 64's data-loading speed to make alterations to the gameplay formula. While the core premise was identical to other games in the series, Production Studio 3 decided to introduce simultaneous dual protagonists with *Resident Evil Zero*. Aside from Rebecca, who would serve to connect the story to the original *Resident Evil*, the game would also tell the story of Billy Coen, an ex-Marine who is being transported to a location near Raccoon City for execution, having been accused of murdering twenty-three people during a mission. Billy manages to escape when his escort vehicle encounters a BOW. He meets Rebecca on a luxury train that has stopped in the middle of Raccoon Forest and, after some initial distrust, the two decide to cooperate in order to escape. Unlike the trope in which *Resident Evil* characters decide to split up to cover more ground, the game keeps Rebecca and Billy together, similar to an RPG. Thanks to the lack of loading times, the engine allows players to switch between the two characters on the fly. This dynamic essentially meant *Resident Evil Zero* would be impossible on PlayStation or Saturn without a serious compromise in the player experience. Minami explains: "The concept was to create a *Resident Evil* that could be stored on a cartridge. The big point is that at that time [PlayStation] was the main platform, but if you have two characters and switch between them, you have to load each time you switch. But if you use Nintendo 64, there's no need for loading because of the cartridge."[7] The other notable change in this title is the removal of the series staple of Item Boxes in favor of being able to drop and pick up items in any room at any time. This was another benefit of Nintendo 64 cartridges, one that Oda says was discovered after the team conducted various experiments with capacity limitations.[8]

Development of *Resident Evil Zero* continued into 1999. By this point, the artists had drawn a considerable amount of early-stage backgrounds, while the team produced a number of sound effects and recorded voice-overs for both Rebecca and Billy. Sugimura also completed the script at this time. Oda recalls that there was a competitive nature between the teams of *Resident Evil Zero* and *Resident Evil CODE: Veronica*, which benefitted from the more technologically capable Dreamcast. In a "Developer Diary" video recorded for a 2016 re-release of *Resident Evil Zero*, Oda explains: "From the very beginning, super-detailed graphics and story-driven CG cut-scenes have been hallmarks of the *RE* series... *Resident Evil CODE: Veronica*, which had reached the peak of its production cycle, took advantage of the large CD-ROM size, so if we made *Resident Evil Zero* in the same way, with the same visual style, it could have paled in comparison to other games in the series."⁹

Capcom publicly unveiled the existence of *Resident Evil Zero* for Nintendo 64 in January 1999.¹⁰ Both fans and the video game media welcomed the announcement with curiosity and intrigue, as the idea of a *Resident Evil* on Nintendo 64 had been difficult to imagine up to that point, given that the port of *Resident Evil 2* had not yet been released. Capcom exhibited the game at the Spring 2000 Tokyo Game Show, the only time Capcom officially demoed *Resident Evil Zero* to the public. In the demo, players controlled Rebecca inside a mysterious luxury train populated with zombies. She encounters Billy and fellow STARS member Edward Dewey, and they share fully voiced cut-scenes together. While ultimately an early prototype demo, *Resident Evil Zero* seemed to show plenty of promise as a Nintendo 64 exclusive, the engine, animations and sound effects resembling the quality of *Resident Evil 2*. Capcom did not have a concrete release date, however, instead offering a vague time period of either late 2000 or early 2001.

But despite a solid reception at the Tokyo Game Show, Capcom was unable to ignore other trends happening in the video game industry at the time. The market was in a state of transition. Sales of Nintendo 64 were dwindling as the console generation transitioned to next-gen hardware. Sega was still in the market with Dreamcast, while Sony had released PlayStation 2 earlier that month, with impressive sales. Nintendo itself was underway with a successor to Nintendo 64, codenamed "Dolphin," which it was initially planning to release in late 2000. This would have been around the same time as, or perhaps even earlier than, *Resident Evil Zero* on Nintendo 64.

According to Oda, development could have proceeded despite the challenges posed by cartridge-capacity constraints. However, Okamoto saw little viability in continuing development of *Resident Evil Zero* for Nintendo 64. The final game would have been difficult to market for the dying platform, and had it come out, it would have had visuals inferior to games such as *Resident Evil CODE: Veronica*. Okamoto and Capcom's other management decided shortly after the Spring 2000 Tokyo Game Show that *Resident Evil Zero* would have to be switched to another platform. Given that the game was designed to target Nintendo fans, the choice was clear: development of *Resident Evil Zero* would be shifted over to Dolphin as a next-generation title.

THE *BIOHAZARD* STRATEGY PRESENTATION

On September 13, 2001, Capcom invited the video game press to the Akasaka Prince Hotel in Tokyo for an announcement on a new, upcoming game. The event turned out to be related to the *Resident Evil* series, and it was called the "*Biohazard* Strategy Presentation." It was here that Capcom dropped one of the most provocative and significant announcements in video game history. Taking the stage, producer Shinji Mikami announced that, going forward, the *Resident Evil* series would be developed exclusively for GameCube, which was the final name for Dolphin and the next-generation successor to Nintendo 64. Along with Capcom's new policy came the announcement of an unprecedented six games, all for GameCube, which was due to release in Japan the following day, and in November in North America.

The first was the original *Resident Evil*. However, this was not just a port of the original PlayStation game; this was a new version of the game featuring completely remade graphics that took advantage of GameCube's capabilities. The pre-rendered graphics were stunning by any measure, exhibiting a level of realistic detail that made the relatively recent *Resident Evil CODE: Veronica* look antiquated in comparison. Not only was this remake of *Resident Evil* already at an advanced stage of development, but Capcom also announced a concrete release date of March 22, 2002, in Japan. This was just six months away and coincided with the series' sixth anniversary. The wait would be quite short in comparison to past *Resident Evil* games.

Next, Mikami confirmed that *Resident Evil Zero* for GameCube was still in development. Development had begun on Nintendo 64 in spring 1998, and the team had made progress through to 2000, but Capcom's management had decided to move the title to GameCube due to the storage limitations of Nintendo 64 cartridges and the more favorable commercial viability offered by GameCube. Capcom did not have any footage of *Resident Evil Zero* to show at the event, but Mikami mentioned that the game would come out sometime after the remake.

The most significant revelation came when Mikami further announced that *Resident Evil 4* was still in development and that, like *Resident Evil Zero*, it would now be developed exclusively for GameCube. Capcom had begun development of *Resident Evil 4* back in 1998 for PlayStation 2, as *Resident Evil 3*, which was being directed by Hideki Kamiya. When *Resident Evil 3: Nemesis* materialized in 1999, Kamiya's game was subsequently renamed *Resident Evil 4* before becoming a new title called *Devil May Cry*, which was released for PlayStation 2 in August 2001. Once *Devil May Cry* became its own product, Capcom had intended to start over with *Resident Evil 4*, again on PlayStation 2. Now, Mikami was telling audiences that the game would be released exclusively on GameCube.

To top things off, Mikami also announced the development of GameCube versions of *Resident Evil 2*, *Resident Evil 3: Nemesis* and *Resident Evil CODE: Veronica*. The video game press initially assumed that these three games would be complete remakes in the vein of the original. However, later that month, Mikami clarified in an interview that the games would only be ports of the original PlayStation or Dreamcast versions, without a cosmetic makeover or any new content whatsoever. He explained that the time and resources necessary for remaking three more games would push back the release of *Resident Evil 4* even further. He also admitted that the ports were intended only to give GameCube fans access to the entire series in advance of *Resident Evil 4*; he wanted GameCube owners to experience every mainline game to date on one console, which he partly attributed to complaints from single-console owners when *Resident Evil CODE: Veronica* launched exclusively on Dreamcast.[11] Mikami finished the announcement by mentioning that other Capcom games, aside from *Resident Evil*, were under development for GameCube and that such games would be revealed in the future.

The *Biohazard* Strategy Presentation was a momentous event, not just for Capcom and Nintendo, but for the entire video game industry. Observers compared its impact to Square's groundbreaking announcement, back in 1996, that *Final Fantasy VII* would be exclusive to PlayStation. That decision ultimately contributed to the end of Nintendo's dominance of the global console market and the rise of Sony and the PlayStation brand. While Square made its decision based on the technological capabilities of PlayStation and Nintendo 64, Capcom had an entirely different motive: Mikami's vision for how video games should be made and enjoyed. At some point, Mikami had developed a strong affinity with Nintendo in that regard. He felt that games were about more than just graphics; they needed to be entertaining and meaningful. He believed that Sony, which was a consumer electronics manufacturer, lacked the focus on games that Nintendo was known for.

The conference was also significant due to the attendance of Shigeru Miyamoto, the architect of products like *Donkey Kong*, *Super Mario* and *The Legend of Zelda*. Miyamoto briefly took the stage to announce his support for Mikami's vision and the *Resident Evil* franchise on GameCube. Afterward, the two creators were photographed together shaking hands. Miyamoto's attendance was a notable show of support, given his status as Nintendo's – and indeed gaming's – most iconic creator.

Securing *Resident Evil* was pivotal to the evolution of Nintendo's brand image. As a result of its marketing activities in the 1990s, Nintendo's appeal had become skewed towards a younger demographic, represented by family-friendly franchises like *Mario*, *Zelda* and *Pokémon*. By this point, many adult gamers viewed Nintendo's emphasis on younger content unfavorably, with the majority opting to purchase Sony's more adult-friendly PlayStation. Nintendo's image was further called into question at Space World 2001 trade show, which was held in August, just weeks before the *Biohazard* Strategy Presentation. At the show, Nintendo had unveiled new footage of the game that would eventually become *The Legend of Zelda: The Wind Waker* for GameCube. Unlike the more realistic-looking style they had previously used for *Zelda* games, this latest would utilize cel-shaded, cartoon-like visuals. With the video game market seemingly holding darker, more mature games in higher regard than ever, the new game was met with considerable pushback. As a result, observers viewed Capcom's *Resident Evil* announcement as a counterweight to Nintendo's cartoony *Zelda*. Nintendo hoped that with the full backing of Capcom, GameCube, which was set to launch in Japan the following day, would be appealing to all gamer demographics.

Over the years, observers have speculated whether Nintendo provided financial incentives to Capcom in exchange for having *Resident Evil* exclusively on GameCube. Every former Capcom employee who contributed to the company's decision, including Mikami and Yoshiki Okamoto, has emphatically denied it. "We had a strong relationship with Nintendo even before the GameCube announcement," Okamoto explains. "We collaborated on the two Game Boy Color games, *The Legend of Zelda: Oracle of Seasons* and *The Legend of Zelda: Oracle of Ages*." Mikami says that the decision was born out of a genuine affinity with Nintendo: "Game creators are not really unscrupulous people. We make games from our hearts. This is true for me, for Kamiya, Aoyama and Kato, as well. I made the decision because I believed in Nintendo's vision as a game company. We never got any money from Nintendo for it."

OVERTURES FROM MICROSOFT AND A BIRTHDAY
GREETING FROM KEN KUTARAGI

By late 2001, the video game console market had been reshaped
into the competitive landscape that still exists nearly two decades
later. Sega had already bailed out, following the commercial failure
of Dreamcast, while Sony was riding high with PlayStation 2. At
the same time that Nintendo was preparing to launch GameCube,
another formidable opponent was gearing up to join the console
war: Microsoft. The American computer software giant had become
one of the wealthiest companies globally, with a vast financial war
chest that dwarfed its competitors. The company unveiled its Xbox
platform at the Game Developers Conference in March 2000 and
was set to be launched in November 2001. The sixth-generation
console war would thus be a three-way competition between Sony,
Nintendo and Microsoft, all formidable companies with unique
advantages over each other. Xbox was technologically more powerful
than its contemporaries, which Microsoft made sure to highlight in
its marketing. Given Microsoft's prior history with PC games and its
multimedia business, the Xbox brand vision was, and still is, more
closely aligned with PlayStation than Nintendo, and, as a result,
Microsoft, too, would be targeting a more mature demographic.
Therefore, the *Resident Evil* franchise on GameCube would serve as
a counterweight to Xbox as much as it did to PlayStation 2.

One may wonder whether Capcom and Shinji Mikami ever
considered releasing a *Resident Evil* game on Xbox, or if the
platform was ever in the running to get the franchise exclusively,
instead of GameCube. In a 2013 article about Xbox's history in
Japan, Eurogamer discovered that Microsoft's executives made

overtures to Mikami in December 2000, a year prior to the launch of Xbox, as part of an effort to recruit key Japanese developers onto the system.[12] Before its launch, many observers and analysts questioned Microsoft's chances of succeeding in Japan due to its American-centric hardware design and an ingrained presence by local incumbents Sony and Nintendo.

Microsoft certainly made the effort to bring Japanese talent onboard its gaming platform. Kevin Bachus, who was Microsoft's director of third-party relations at the time, traveled to Microsoft's Japan office to meet with Mikami through an interpreter. According to Bachus, Mikami was unimpressed with Microsoft due to its unclear philosophy. "What is your philosophy? Sony says games are entertainment, something larger, fueled by the Emotion Engine. Nintendo says games are toys, created by the legendary Shigeru Miyamoto, perhaps the greatest game developer of all time. What do you feel?" asked an exasperated Mikami.[13]

Bachus, who does not speak Japanese, could only observe quietly as Mikami spoke with Microsoft Japan's representatives. The interpreter had no satisfactory answer for Mikami. Of course, to believe Microsoft was devoid of vision was an unfair assessment, but Bachus would not catch wind of Mikami's specific concerns until it was too late. Despite an attempt to remedy the situation through a Microsoft Japan upper-level executive, Bachus says that Mikami had already committed the *Resident Evil* series to Nintendo's consoles.[14] Despite Mikami's concerns, Xbox received other Capcom games during its lifetime, such as *Steel Battalion* and *Dino Crisis 3*. But, as of 2020, Xbox is the only major home console since 1996 not to have a single *Resident Evil* title ever released or announced for it.

A different story unfolded between Sony and Capcom with regards to the future of the *Resident Evil* series. Sony's then chairman and CEO, Ken Kutaragi, the esteemed "Father of PlayStation," learned of Capcom's announcement and was taken aback. Kutaragi decided to show Capcom exactly how he felt. In October 2001, about a month after the *Biohazard* Strategy Presentation, Kutaragi invited Capcom COO Haruhiro Tsujimoto and Yoshiki Okamoto to a business dinner in Shibuya, Tokyo. It just so happened to fall on Tsujimoto's birthday, which would normally be a cause for celebration. However, the dinner would be anything but; the timing was certainly no coincidence. "Kutaragi-san expressed his displeasure at Capcom's decision to bring *Resident Evil* exclusively to GameCube. He said Sony assisted Capcom in nurturing the *Resident Evil* series," Okamoto recalls of the awkward birthday dinner. "Kutaragi-san thought we had abandoned Sony despite the support they provided us."

One may see Kutaragi's timing as passive-aggressive and his sentiment hypocritical, given that the video game industry is a place where loyalty never lasts forever. After all, Sony's success with PlayStation can be partly attributed to Square's move away from Nintendo. Either way, Kutaragi was certainly displeased and did not hide it. To a certain extent, Okamoto sympathizes with Kutaragi:

I could see where Kutaragi-san was coming from and why he felt the way he did. With the benefit of hindsight, the GameCube decision might not have been the best idea. Yet at the same time, as a company, Capcom has always supported all the console manufacturers, including Sony,

Nintendo and Microsoft. In fact, even after the GameCube deal, Sony still had a majority of our support. We used a 3-2-1 ratio to determine how many games each company would get. For example, if there were six games in development, three would be for Sony, two for Nintendo and one would go to Microsoft.

Indeed, although *Resident Evil* was now a GameCube exclusive, Capcom's PlayStation 2 support remained at the forefront of the company's business strategy. They found success through new products such as *Onimusha* and *Devil May Cry*, which ironically were initially spun off *Resident Evil*. Despite the dinner, Capcom and Sony maintained their relationship without falling into a feud like the infamous one that clouded Nintendo and Square at the time.

Not every *Resident Evil* fan was pleased with the move to GameCube, either. While many fans of Nintendo consoles were eager to dip their toes into the series for the first time, there was also a large segment of PlayStation gamers who felt alienated due to their lack of plans to purchase a GameCube. With Nintendo's system due to be launched the same week as the *Biohazard* Strategy Presentation, it would soon be clear whether Capcom's move had worked out.

BACK TO THE BEGINNING: THE *RESIDENT EVIL* REMAKE

In late 2000, Shinji Mikami made the decision to shift the entire franchise exclusively over to GameCube. Capcom had already moved production of *Resident Evil Zero* away from Nintendo 64 a few months prior, while *Resident Evil 4*, previously in development for PlayStation 2, would be cancelled for that platform and shifted to GameCube as well. Mikami initially decided to augment both those games by approving GameCube ports of *Resident Evil 2*, *Resident Evil 3: Nemesis* and *Resident Evil CODE: Veronica X*. This resulted in a whopping five *Resident Evil* games being green-lit for GameCube nearly a year before the system's launch.

There was one obvious gap remaining: the original *Resident Evil*. Unlike the other re-releases, Mikami wanted to do more than just port it again: "I assigned Hiroki Kato to come up with a proposal for remaking the first *Resident Evil*. I actually wanted Kato to direct the game, but his proposal was far too similar to the original version. Everything would be the same, except for the graphics, which would be redone." Mikami did not favor such an approach, believing that a good remake was needed to upend players' expectations and offer surprises to hardcore fans of the original. "That's when I decided that I had to direct the remake myself," he says.

When software lead engineer Hideaki Motozuka learned that Mikami would assume the director role for the *Resident Evil* remake, he anticipated the road would be long and difficult, as Mikami had high standards and gave great attention to detail.[15] Yet unlike *Resident Evil 2* and *Resident Evil Zero*, there were no major production roadblocks with the *Resident Evil* remake. The only notable challenge came from Production Studio 4's lack of experience of developing for GameCube. Mikami had ambitious visual targets for the remake, wanting the game to look as realistic as possible; this led to the team choosing to return to pre-rendered camera angles, after going fully polygonal with *Resident Evil*

CODE: Veronica. However, GameCube had relatively limited memory bandwidth, making the implementation of highly detailed pre-rendered backgrounds difficult. Fortunately, Nintendo provided Capcom with technical assistance, which helped Mikami overcome such hurdles early on.

The *Resident Evil* remake follows the fundamental premise of the original game very closely. Both generations of the game feature Chris Redfield and Jill Valentine in lead roles, along with the same supporting characters, setting and overall story. But while its core blueprint is respectfully derived from the original, the *Resident Evil* remake goes beyond its reference material by adding new plot points, cut-scenes, areas to explore and gameplay features that modernize the experience. Gone are the original's infamously poor scripts and dialogue-delivery, to be replaced with voice-acting that was, while far from flawless, considerably improved. Virtually every item from the original is found in a different location or serves an alternative purpose. Some rooms will feel familiar to fans of the original, while others have been completely redesigned, now barely resembling their appearance in the original. In some cases, these designs had been intended for the original release but were removed due to time or budget constraints.

The *Resident Evil* remake also contains a number of completely new features. One of the most prominent is the Crimson Head "resurrection" zombie. In the remake, players may notice early on that zombies they have killed, but not decapitated, remain lifeless on the ground even if the player exits the room and returns. This is a departure from the standard *Resident Evil* formula, in which dead enemies usually disappear forever once the player has left the room. In the new game, when the player later returns to the room after some time has passed, the "dead" zombie will complete its transformation into the Crimson Head and suddenly rise to its feet, much faster, stronger and more violent than ever. Players encountering the Crimson Head for the first time are spooked, if not outright frightened.

Another new addition is the "Defense Item," which allows players to avoid being hurt by an enemy if they hold on to the item. A number of extra gameplay modes have also been included, such as "One Dangerous Zombie" and "Invisible Zombie," which offer unique takes on the traditional *Resident Evil* formula for repeat gameplay sessions. "I wanted the remake to be different from the original," says Mikami. "I wanted to design a remake that would trip up players who beat the original time and time again."

Armed with half a decade of experience working on *Resident Evil* games, Mikami decided to place a greater emphasis on story compared to the original. Part of his goal was to address plot points (or retcons) introduced in the sequels, particularly in *Resident Evil CODE: Veronica*, which brought Albert Wesker back from the dead. Mikami also wanted the game to tie in with the upcoming *Resident Evil Zero*, which would take place just one day before the events of the Mansion Incident. The team therefore made various updates, such as new files that mention both William Birkin and Alexia Ashford. Mikami was also conscious that the original's story had been written before Noboru Sugimura joined the series with *Resident Evil 2*, so the remake not only needed to improve the original's connection to its sequels, but needed to be improved for its own sake as well.

The most substantial addition to the remake's story is the tragic tale of Lisa Trevor, who is the victim of a cruel experiment that transformed her into a hunchbacked, shackled, masked and only vaguely humanoid creature with a disturbing feminine shriek. The player encounters her in an entirely new area of the game, a dilapidated cabin located at the end of a single trail leading out from the Spencer Mansion. Initially, players are unable to defeat Lisa even if they have enough ammo, as she is virtually indestructible, so they have no choice but to flee from her. But toward the end of the game, players finally have the option to engage her in a full-fledged boss fight.

While Lisa's shock value will be apparent to any player, including veterans of the original, Mikami also sought to give her a high level of thematic significance. "I wanted players to read the files outlining Lisa's tragic story so that they feel a great deal of sympathy for her. That is why I made it optional for players to actually engage in direct combat with Lisa during the final encounter with her," Mikami explains. During the boss fight, players can perform a specific action to end the encounter, rather than directly attacking her with weapons (and wasting bullets). "I actually prefer if players do *not* kill Lisa," Mikami elaborates. "I want players to feel bad for her and to feel a sense of guilt for attacking an innocent victim like her."

As promised, Capcom released the *Resident Evil* remake for GameCube in Japan on March 22, 2002; it came out in North America the following month and in PAL territories in September (the later PAL launch was due to Nintendo not launching GameCube in those territories until May). The critical reception was very positive, with critics praising the remake for its greater emphasis on horror, its improved gameplay mechanics and its groundbreaking visual design. Many regard the game as a masterpiece and the pinnacle of the classic *Resident Evil* formula. In reviewing the game for IGN, Matt Casamassina stated, "*Resident Evil* is easily the scariest, most atmospheric video game I've ever played. It's the only one I've ever been afraid to play alone. It's a triumph as a stand-alone adventure and a major accomplishment as a remake."[16] When I spoke to Ryan Payton, founder of independent game developer Camouflaj and a fan of the series, he said, "*Resident Evil* is the best remake of any game in history. Its pre-rendered backgrounds still look great and the designers smartly remixed the experience to keep it fresh for veterans." Over a decade after the remake's release, Payton would go on to reference the pacing and environmental layout of the remake when developing his own game, *République*, a stealth-action game initially released for smartphones in 2013. "Initially, I even wanted the backgrounds in *République* to be pre-rendered like the remake, although we ended up using a fully 3D engine for various reasons." The *Resident Evil* remake is one of Mikami's career highlights and an influential, standout title in the *Resident Evil* franchise.

RESIDENT EVIL ZERO: THE LAST TRADITIONAL *RESIDENT EVIL*

While Shinji Mikami and Production Studio 4 were busy remaking the original *Resident Evil*, the team over at Production Studio 3 was hard at work with its own, very different kind of remake: *Resident Evil Zero*. Having begun development for the Nintendo 64 way back in spring 1998, the team had already been on the project for almost three years, which was by far the longest development cycle in the series up to that point. By the time it was cancelled, the Nintendo 64 version was only between 10 and 20 per cent complete. In moving the project over to GameCube, producer Tatsuya Minami, director Koji Oda and the rest of the team decided to retain the design and story of the Nintendo 64 original but to completely recreate the visual assets, using the engine Mikami's team had designed for the *Resident Evil* remake. It was slightly ironic, then, that while the *Resident Evil* remake altered and added to the source material, *Resident Evil Zero* would adhere to the majority of its team's original intentions.

Capcom finally unveiled screenshots of *Resident Evil Zero* on GameCube in May 2002, just two months after the release of the *Resident Evil* remake. Inherited directly from the Nintendo 64 version were the dual-protagonist gameplay, the dynamic of dropping and picking up items in any location, the various settings and the story penned by Noboru Sugimura. The pre-rendered graphics had been completely overhauled, however, matching the style of the remake. *Resident Evil Zero* is perhaps the aesthetic apex of the *Resident Evil* franchise, with visuals more detailed and technically optimized than even the remake. The character models feature high polygon counts and slick, if somewhat robotic, animations. The CG cut-scenes are a notable improvement on previous games', too. The game's increased emphasis on visuals was partly made possible by its high budget, a reflection of Capcom's lofty expectations for the game's commercial success. "I spent a lot of money on the movies," Mikami explained to *Computer and Video Games* magazine. "Actually, company management has scolded me for spending so much money on the movies," he laughed.[17]

The switch to GameCube, being a disc-based platform, ironically brought back the issue of loading times, something that Nintendo

64 cartridges had eliminated. However, Minami explained to *CVG* that Production Studio 3, along with Tose, were able to technically optimize *Resident Evil Zero* and keep loading times to a minimum, even when switching between Rebecca and Billy. The rest of the game, in terms of design aesthetic, would be similar to the *Resident Evil* remake thanks to the common engine and development tools, though the additional development time afforded by its later release date (as well as the increased budget mentioned above) resulted in *Resident Evil Zero* being the better-looking game of the two. Without any major hurdles following the transition to GameCube, Capcom finally released the game in November 2002.

Despite its technological strengths, *Resident Evil Zero* is a divisive game among fans and critics alike, for a number of reasons. Capcom marketed the game as a prequel and companion title to the original *Resident Evil*, yet despite the presence of Rebecca and the other STARS Bravo Team members, many feel *Resident Evil Zero* adds very little to the overall story. The game's primary villain, whom the protagonists initially perceive to be a younger incarnation of Umbrella Corporation co-founder Dr James Marcus, in fact turns out to be a swarm of oversized leeches that Marcus had created in one of his experiments with the T-virus, and which have learned to assume humanoid shape. We discover that they adopt Dr Marcus's form because after he was assassinated, ten years prior the events of this game, one of the leeches fed on his body and brain, thereby taking on his memories. Even by *Resident Evil* standards, the leech plotline seemed to set new boundaries for how absurd villains could be, which some fans disliked.

Players have also criticized *Resident Evil Zero* for its lack of gameplay originality. Some of the game's puzzles and thematic elements resemble those used in previous games. For example, the game requires players to discover a room hidden behind a wall by playing a specific piano piece (a concept taken from *Resident Evil*), uncover a hidden passage behind a painting of the game's antagonist (from *Resident Evil CODE: Veronica*), adjust an electrical panel to the correct voltage (*Resident Evil 2*) and dramatically finish off the final boss with a Magnum (*Resident Evil 3: Nemesis*). This caused *Resident Evil Zero* to exude a subtle, but noticeable, sense of déjà vu.

The gameplay changes were also met with mixed reception. While the ability to drop items anywhere on the game map at any time offered a new layer of convenience to the player, the lack of traditional Item Boxes introduced a different problem: players often needed to backtrack across considerable distances to retrieve previously dropped items that were needed to progress forward. And because Rebecca and Billy each only have six slots to hold items (as opposed to the more common eight or ten slots), item management often became very time-consuming. Moreover, several items, including the game's most powerful weapons and some key items, such as the Hookshot, occupy two item slots, which meant players quickly ran out of space and were often forced to drop items and come back for them later. Some critics believe the frequent and tedious backtracking ultimately hurt the game's pacing. Finally, fans often criticize *Resident Evil Zero* for having few, if any puzzles that stand out for being either clever or original. In reviewing *Resident Evil Zero* for IGN, Matt Casamassina commented, "The remake was essentially an update to a classic game that managed to inspire feelings of nostalgia and still scare the hell out of you. Now, though, we have a completely new outing with the same old problems. In fact, the control is worse and the puzzles are possibly even more stupefied. That's not cool."[18]

While every mainline *Resident Evil* game from the 1996 original to the 2002 remake experienced positive reviews and expanded the boundaries of the series in its own way, the discourse on *Resident Evil Zero* was polarizing. With a Metacritic score of 83, it's far from being a bad game, but the release of *Resident Evil Zero* created a discernible worry, as echoed by Casamassina, that *Resident Evil* was becoming stale and long in the tooth. It turns out that Capcom, including Mikami, tended to agree. "Personally, I never wanted *Resident Evil Zero* to be made," Mikami admits. "*Resident Evil Zero* was developed because Okamoto-san believed that there should be a *Resident Evil* game for Nintendo." While Mikami had very little active involvement in the development, his thoughts on *Resident Evil Zero* are interesting. Even before its release, he had very little personal confidence in the game. As it turns out, *Resident Evil Zero* would, as of 2020, mark the final time Capcom developed and released a mainline *Resident Evil* game centered around the gameplay formula established in the 1996 original.

Change was imminent for the *Resident Evil* series, but before gamers would see any of it, another set of wheels were in motion elsewhere at Capcom as a different studio attempted to bring the series online.

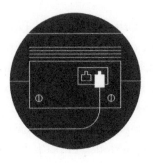

CHAPTER 9: *RESIDENT EVIL* GOES ONLINE

THE RISE OF ONLINE MULTIPLAYER GAMEPLAY

Before *Resident Evil* first spooked game-players around the world, Capcom had become a tour de force among gamers thanks in no small part to *Street Fighter II*. The game's memorable cast of characters, innovative gameplay and unforgettable soundtrack led it to become an indispensable part of 1990s pop culture. *Street Fighter II* was among the best-known games worldwide, rivaling the likes of *Super Mario* and *Sonic the Hedgehog*. What's more, *Street Fighter II* is unique among Capcom's franchises in that its immense popularity is rooted in its competitive multiplayer gameplay, made possible by the inherent social element of arcades. Before the advent of video games, people interacted socially through activities such as sport, but arcades offered a generation of youth in Japan, North America and Europe a new means of socializing. There are countless anecdotes of teenagers going to the local arcade after school and slotting in coin after coin to play *Street Fighter II* against their friends. When ports of *Street Fighter II* later came to home consoles like Super NES and Genesis/Mega Drive, the game's competitive nature remained intact; all players needed was a second controller. Other publishers at the time were also able to popularize multiplayer gaming, a memorable example being Nintendo's *Super Mario Kart*.

Meanwhile, the world was becoming more and more digitally connected, first via PCs and later mobile phones. In time, these would acquire the ability to access the internet. Video game consoles, essentially computers themselves, would also come to use internet connectivity, to enhance their functionality. Internet-enabled games go all the way back to at least the 1980s; a minuscule number of NES and Super NES in Japan featured limited and rudimentary network functionality that allowed owners to purchase additional content, known today as "downloadable content" (DLC). From the 1990s, PC games gained network compatibility to allow for online multiplayer use. The first credible mainstream online gaming service on the console side arrived with Sega Dreamcast, which included a 33.6K dial-up modem that allowed for both DLC and online multiplayer from its 1998 Japanese launch; the 1999 North American launch featured a faster, 56K modem. Although there were technical hurdles with regards to speed and latency on 33.6K and 56K, online multiplayer on Dreamcast was very functional. Sega's online-only *Phantasy Star Online* became one of the most popular Dreamcast games. Meanwhile, even handheld systems flirted with network compatibility as soon as the technology was there; in 2000, Nintendo's *Pokémon Crystal Version* for Game Boy Color could connect to mobile phone networks to add extra quests and items, although it did not offer multiplayer.

From the early 2000s, consumers in Japan, North America and Europe began gaining access to even faster internet speeds, known as broadband, setting the stage for online gaming to penetrate the mainstream by the time PlayStation 2, Xbox and GameCube were released. During this period, Sony, Nintendo and Microsoft each had different approaches to online gaming. Microsoft was the most enthusiastic supporter: the company launched Xbox in November 2001 with a built-in broadband modem and, confident in a broadband-only future, removed the slower 56K altogether, locking out all non-broadband customers. In late 2002, Microsoft introduced Xbox Live, a paid subscription service which, unlike Nintendo and Sony's platforms, meant that Xbox owners needed to pay extra for the privilege of playing any game online. Xbox Live benefitted customers by offering a single network solution that worked with all Xbox games, all centrally managed by Microsoft.

In contrast with Microsoft's Xbox Live, Sony took a more ad hoc approach. The company supported online but did not see it as indispensable to its experience. PlayStation 2 launched without a built-in modem, but the system did offer expansion ports that allowed a modem to be added later. In 2001, Sony released the Network Adapter, which was compatible with both 56K and broadband speeds. In contrast to Xbox Live, Sony, like Sega, did not create its own centralized connection service, leaving each publisher to operate its own services for specific titles, some free and others for a fee. In 2004, as broadband penetration increased and Microsoft saw notable success with Xbox Live, Sony released a slim PlayStation model that included a built-in broadband modem, though the company was still two years away from offering its own centralized service. Until then, the most notable online title for PlayStation 2 was Square's *Final Fantasy XI Online*.

Nintendo was at the opposite end of the spectrum altogether with GameCube. Despite its earlier experimentation with network connectivity in Japan, the company was skeptical of online multiplayer, believing it would never become mainstream. No GameCube game by Nintendo ever featured online gameplay, although, like Sony, Nintendo released 56K and broadband modem add-ons to accommodate third parties that wished to create online content for GameCube. Ultimately, only Sega would take up the mantle, with *Phantasy Star Online Episode I & II* in 2002 and a sequel in 2003 (Sega's games required a monthly fee to play online). With very few exceptions, online gaming was nonexistent on GameCube, and Nintendo would not change its stance until the following generation.

Capcom was far more supportive of online gaming than Nintendo. In fact, among Japanese publishers, it was one of the first to embrace the functionality. It was a natural development, given how instrumental multiplayer was to the brand identity of *Street Fighter II*. In the early 2000s, Capcom operated a network service for Dreamcast in Japan called Matching Service. The company released several ports of arcade games with online gameplay, such as *Super Street Fighter II X*, *Darkstalkers*, *Super Puzzle Fighter II X* and *Street Fighter Alpha 3*. Due to Capcom's unwillingness to develop similar online services in the West, these ports were either never released outside of Japan or were released without online compatibility.

After Dreamcast was discontinued, Capcom next explored online with both PlayStation 2 and Xbox. The company released a cel-shaded car-racing game called *Auto Modellista* in 2002 and an action adventure game called *Monster Hunter* in 2004. *Auto Modellista* was met with consumer indifference and was soon forgotten, but *Monster Hunter* enjoyed more success, sowing the seeds for the explosion of the franchise's popularity later on. On Xbox, Capcom released several fighting games that were compatible with Xbox Live, such as *Capcom vs. SNK 2 EO* and *Marvel vs. Capcom 2: New Age of Heroes*. The *Resident Evil* series, too, would dabble with online gameplay.

YOUR TIMING SUCKS: *RESIDENT EVIL: OUTBREAK*

Capcom green-lit the online *Resident Evil* in 2001 under the working title *Network Biohazard*. Although the mainline *Resident Evil* games became exclusive to GameCube in late 2001, Nintendo's reluctance to support online gaming, coupled with the Xbox's lack of popularity in Japan, meant that online *Resident Evil* was most suitable on PlayStation 2. Capcom's GameCube policy did not preclude spin-offs from appearing on competing platforms, and the benefit of keeping the franchise on PlayStation 2 in some form was very clear.

One of the most prominent members on the *Network Biohazard* project was Noritaka Funamizu, one of the most senior employees of Capcom. He entered the company in 1985 after being invited to join by Yoshiki Okamoto. His early work at Capcom was in designing and planning for arcade games, ranging from *1943: The*

Battle of Midway to numerous *Street Fighter* and "Vs." games. On the console front, he also planned and produced a number of *Mega Man* titles. Later, Funamizu acted as the general producer for *Resident Evil 2*, *Resident Evil 3: Nemesis* and *Resident Evil CODE: Veronica*. He was also producer for the *Zelda* titles *Oracle of Seasons* and *Oracle of Ages* for Game Boy Color, in collaboration with Nintendo. "Initially, it was Shinji Mikami who was supposed to lead development of *Network Biohazard*," says Funamizu. "However, around the same time, Mikami found himself busy with the development of *Resident Evil 4*. Therefore, he asked me if I could take over the project on his behalf. I agreed to do it because I thought the project could be interesting."

Development was placed in the hands of Capcom's Production Studio 1, which primarily developed 2D fighters, although it had also made *Devil May Cry 2* and Capcom's online PlayStation 2 car-

Noritaka Funamizu

racing game, *Auto Modellista*. In the director's seat was Eiichiro Sasaki, who had previously worked on Capcom games such as *Power Stone* and *Tech Romancer*, having joined the company in 1994. The producer working under Funamizu was Tsuyoshi Tanaka.

Marrying the *Resident Evil* formula with online gameplay would not prove to be easy. Unlike the *Street Fighter* series, *Resident Evil* was, up to this point, a single-player experience (the sole exception to this being *Resident Evil: Survivor 2 – CODE: Veronica*). There would therefore need to be changes made to the formula: the gameplay would have to allow for multiple players simultaneously. Ultimately, up to four players were able to participate simultaneously in one online gameplay session, and they could select from a choice of eight original characters, each with a distinct personality and physical abilities. This would allow gamers to choose a character that had a skillset and personality to their individual liking – some characters would be stronger and faster during combat, for example, while others could hold more items or begin the game equipped with a special piece of equipment.

The cast's appearance is also interesting. Like the cast of the original *Resident Evil*, every character in *Network Biohazard* was created as a reflection of the "typical American" – in the eyes of the Japanese developers. Interestingly, some of their faces resemble those of famous Hollywood actors and actresses of the early 2000s. Happy-go-lucky Kevin, a police officer who resembles Tom Cruise, is a strong, well-rounded character. Meanwhile, David is a stoic plumber who resembles Brad Pitt. Cindy, a bar waitress, resembles Cameron Diaz, while Alyssa is a feminist journalist with an uncanny resemblance to Nicole Kidman. Jim, an African American subway employee, is almost a spitting image of Chris Tucker. George looks like Alec Baldwin, while Mark resembles Ving Rhames. The final character, Yoko, however, is modeled on an employee at Capcom Japan. Asked if these uncanny resemblances to Hollywood actors were intentional, Funamizu says, "As far as I know, the team wasn't deliberately trying to model the cast after any particular celebrities' faces. It might just be a coincidence."

To accommodate the relatively short length of most online gameplay sessions, Funamizu's team decided to break the narrative into multiple scenarios that, while taking less time than a typical eight-hour *Resident Evil* adventure, were still long enough to occupy players for a substantial period of time. "Early in development, the team drafted concepts for around twenty scenarios, with each scenario having its own supervisor," Funamizu explains. The team decided to set the game in and around Raccoon City during the events of both *Resident Evil 2* and *Resident Evil 3: Nemesis*, providing a crucial link to the existing series canon. "Although we designed a lot of scenarios at the beginning, we really didn't have enough time to include them all in the final game. We ended up choosing the five best scenarios and fleshing them out."

While previous spin-offs, such as *Resident Evil: Survivor* and *Resident Evil: Gaiden*, were low-budget, outsourced affairs, Capcom was far more ambitious with *Network Biohazard*. "The company saw plenty of potential in the game's success, so we were given a budget that rivaled that of Mikami's GameCube games," Funamizu says. "This allowed us to include high-quality cut-scenes, a full soundtrack and plenty of voice-acting." Indeed, with eight protagonists and five scenarios, the game was slated to have more content than the usual *Resident Evil* title, especially compared to previous spin-offs, which were relatively short games that could be completed very quickly.

The public got its first concrete glimpse of *Network Biohazard* through a teaser trailer shown at Sony's press conference at E3 2002, by which point the game had become known outside of Japan as *Resident Evil Online*. The trailer showed a mix of real-time gameplay featuring the eight playable characters and CG cut-scenes, plus an appearance by the G-virus-infected William Birkin. The fully 3D graphics – utilizing an engine separate from the other *Resident Evil* games – looked quite detailed and considerably more advanced than *Resident Evil CODE: Veronica*, with a capacity to show more playable characters on screen at any one time, and render larger environments. Among the features that set *Resident Evil Online* apart from other *Resident Evil* games was the presence of a viral infection gauge, which would rise as players were attacked by enemies. This effectively instituted a timer into the game, giving players a finite amount of time to complete a scenario. In online mode, players whose viral gauges reached 100 per cent would mutate into a zombie, and for a short duration could control the zombie and attempt to attack their former teammates if they wished. Playing as a zombie was a minor gimmick used in the game's marketing.

In early 2003, Capcom still intended for *Resident Evil Online* to be an online-only title. However, that spring, Capcom changed its mind, announcing that the game would also feature an offline mode. "Originally, we conceived of *Resident Evil Online* as an online-only title, but after careful research and consideration, we decided to allow the game to be played offline as well in order to increase the game's potential sales," Funamizu recalls. At this time, online gaming was still a specific and small niche in gamer demographics, so it made sense to give the game the widest appeal possible. Offline functionality did not alter the gameplay and narrative of the scenarios, but within the framework of multiple characters the online co-op partners would be replaced with AI-controlled versions instead. Capcom also decided to change the name of the game to *Resident Evil: Outbreak*. The term "Outbreak" was a more a neutral subtitle that avoided directly categorizing the game as either online- or offline-enabled, while also referencing the game's setting during the Raccoon City viral outbreak and the characters' viral infection gauge.

Resident Evil: Outbreak was released in Japan on December 11, 2003, several months before its North American release. Its online connectivity was powered by the "Multi-Matching BB" service operated by KDDI, one of Japan's major telecom companies. Subscribing to the service cost ¥945 (approximately $9) per month, a not inconsiderable amount, although the service could also be used with other Capcom titles, such as *Auto Modellista*. The North American localization took three months to release, due to the large amount of text in the game, and in the USA the game's online connectivity was powered by the Sega-operated SNAP (Sega Network Application Package) network service, which had no service fees. As KDDI and Sega's services were operated separately, players in Japan and North America could not play online with each other.

Gamers in PAL regions such as Europe and Australia ended up with rather a raw deal, however. Not only did PAL players have to wait until September 2004 for the game to be launched in their regions, but the PAL localization also completely removed online compatibility from the game, transforming it into an exclusively offline experience. This was ironic considering the game's origins as an online-only game. When asked why the feature had been dropped, the PR department at Capcom's European office attributed the decision to the diversity of languages and internet infrastructure in Europe, explaining that "there are far more technical difficulties bringing an online game to PAL territories than Japan and the US, the most obvious of which are language and service provider issues in each territory. Capcom is working hard to overcome these difficulties."[1]

Resident Evil: Outbreak had a mixed critical reception. Critics and gamers praised its detailed graphics, melodic soundtrack, high replay value and innovations to the gameplay. However, users also noticed crucial issues with the gameplay engine in both online and offline mode. First was the game's loading times: when going between rooms, loading could take as long as forty-five seconds. While technically this was not much longer than loading times in the main series' games, the lack of door-opening animations when transitioning between rooms in *Resident Evil: Outbreak* made the load-times more noticeable and difficult to tolerate. They could be considerably shortened for players using a PlayStation 2 equipped with the system's official hard drive, but in online mode the hard drive's shorter loading times worked only if every player was using the accessory to maintain consistency among all players. However, as the accessory was expensive and compatible with few games, only a minority of players ever used it. When Sony released the slimline PlayStation 2 at the end of 2004, the revision eschewed hard drive compatibility altogether, making the feature even less accessible to owners of *Resident Evil: Outbreak*.

Moreover, the online gameplay was heavily criticized in the North American media for the lack of facility for players to communicate with each other through a headset or using keyboard chat; as a cooperative multiplayer game, *Resident Evil: Outbreak* requires players to understand what all their partners are doing in order to successfully complete a scenario. The game is also considerably more challenging than the mainline *Resident Evil* series, especially at higher difficulty levels, which means that players often need to team up in order to defeat stronger enemies. However, *Resident Evil: Outbreak* only allowed players to communicate via a small number of preset comments that could be uttered – through poorly acted voice-overs – by moving the right analog stick in one of four directions; characters could ask for help, thank other players or ask them to come back or progress forward.

After the game launched, there were soon numerous user anecdotes of the random match-making function creating game sessions that mixed players of highly divergent skill- and knowledge-levels. At times, this made it unnecessarily difficult to complete scenarios, because a player who was unsure of how to progress through the game might inadvertently withhold key items from teammates, who would have no practical way of communicating with, and assisting, the rookie player within the game. Savvier players circumvented this limitation by forming communities on internet message boards, exchanging contact information, setting up private sessions with friends and maintaining communication through the various chat applications of the time, such as AIM (AOL Instant Messenger), or even calling each other on the phone.

Most game developers in the West had recognized the importance of communication in online gaming early on in the life of the technology, making its absence in *Resident Evil: Outbreak* even more of a peculiarity. A member of the game's development team, who asked to remain anonymous, offered some insight, admitting that Capcom simply did not realize how much of an impact voice chat would have: "The lack of voice chat was a conscious decision to limit the communication in that way. The criticism really blindsided [Capcom]. I don't even think they knew [voice chat] was big in the States." He also attributed the omission of communication to the importance of privacy and anonymity in Japan, where Capcom is based. "You go into a Japanese arcade and the machines are facing each other. There's a curtain of anonymity there," he explained. Additionally, the developer recalled how the team feared that voice chat would break the atmosphere of the game, explaining that "they had very specific ideas about things like puzzle-solving. If there are two characters in the room, they wanted you to converse using the limited conversation [presets]. Even today, Japanese games have always been about enjoying the characters designed and predestined." Evidently someone on Capcom's scriptwriting team felt that Kevin's infamous pre-baked phrase "Your timing sucks!" was adequate for communicating displeasure at fellow players.

THE OUTBREAK SPREADS: *RESIDENT EVIL: OUTBREAK: FILE #2*

Despite its imperfections, *Resident Evil: Outbreak* performed better than Capcom had expected it to. In Japan, the game sold 437,779 copies by the end of 2004, making it the best-selling *Resident Evil* game in the country since the 2000 release of *Resident Evil CODE: Veronica* on Dreamcast.[2] The game sold 1.45 million globally, a result that pleased Capcom.

Eager to build on its success, Capcom Production Studio 1 quickly green-lit the development of a successor to *Resident Evil: Outbreak*, though the new game would not be a true sequel. Instead, the game would serve as an expansion pack featuring the same cast, graphics engine and gameplay mechanics, thus allowing Capcom to reuse many assets from the original game. The story would take place across five new Raccoon City scenarios that had been conceived during the *Network Biohazard* phase of the first game but ultimately not selected for the final release. While most of the original's staff members – including director Eiichiro Sasaki and producer Tsuyoshi Tanaka – were onboard for the expansion, Noritaka Funamizu departed Capcom in early 2004, which meant his involvement in the expansion comprised little more than some initial planning work on the five scenarios. Another member of note was Hideaki Itsuno, who worked on the game's "Wild Things" scenario, and who is well-known today as the director of popular Capcom franchises like *Devil May Cry* and *Dragon's Dogma*.

The new game was first announced in *Weekly Famitsu* in April 2004, with a release period set for that autumn, a relatively short time after the original. Capcom chose to name it *Resident Evil: Outbreak: File #2* to underscore its status as an expansion pack complementing the first entry. The basic gameplay, music and visuals were nearly identical, with the eight protagonists returning with minor modifications to their abilities. One key difference is that *Outbreak: File #2* was the first game in the series allowing players to shoot weapons while the character is walking, finally addressing a complaint that had lingered among some critics since 1996. The most positive change, however, came exclusively for gamers in PAL territories: Capcom had been successful in resolving the issues that prevented the first game from having online functionality in Europe, now allowing gamers there to connect. However, as with the first game, the network servers for Japan, North America and PAL territories were operated separately by different companies, so were still unable to connect with each other.

Capcom was also able to shorten loading times compared to the first game, but *Outbreak: File #2* still did not address the need for communication during online play, once again limiting players to the preset commands in lieu of voice chat or keyboard messaging. Once again, fans and critics criticized Capcom's design decision, and they were considerably harsher second time around. On Metacritic, *Resident Evil: Outbreak* commands a decent score of 71, while the expansion has a less desirable score of 58, despite all the improvements it offers. The poor reception ultimately contributed to poor sales. *Outbreak: File #2* was released in Japan in September 2004, with some copies including a demo disc of *Devil May Cry 3* to boost interest. However, the game's first-week sales in Japan came up considerably short of its predecessor's, moving only 89,131 units compared to 208,617 for the first game, in December 2003.[3] The North American localization arrived much later, in April 2005, four months after the release of *Resident Evil 4* on GameCube. *Resident Evil 4* happened to be a revolutionary and well-received game, making *Outbreak: File #2* look stale and uninteresting in comparison. PAL sales fared little better, even with the addition of online play. Ultimately, *Outbreak: File #2* failed to break the crucial 1-million sales mark worldwide.

THE LEGACY OF *OUTBREAK*

Resident Evil: Outbreak and *Resident Evil: Outbreak: File #2* remained connected to their respective network servers for several years after their release. In North America, they were playable online until June 2007. Over in Japan, KDDI operated its servers until the end of June 2011, when it discontinued its Multi-Matching BB service, taking both games offline for good – at least officially, anyway; thanks to tech-savvy members of the video game modding community, the Japanese versions can be played online by connecting them to unofficial servers that imitate the connection environment previously offered by KDDI. These servers are not sanctioned by Capcom or Sony, but, according to users, the experience is virtually identical.

According to Noritaka Funamizu, Capcom had considered releasing more *Resident Evil: Outbreak*-branded games following the release of *Outbreak: File #2*. During the project's *Network Biohazard* phase, the team had drafted at least twenty scenarios, of which ten were used over both *Outbreak* games. There were therefore still at least ten unused storylines that could be used in a new expansion. However, due to underwhelming sales and poor critical reception, further expansions never got off the ground, the possibility of a *Resident Evil Outbreak: File #3* evaporating entirely.

Capcom also considered porting *Resident Evil: Outbreak* to Sony's handheld, the PlayStation Portable (PSP), which was released in December 2004. In theory, the Wi-Fi-equipped PSP would have been an ideal match for *Resident Evil: Outbreak*, given that multiplayer could be handled by players in person rather than over the internet, thus addressing criticisms about the games' lack of communication. PSP was also more powerful than any previous gaming handhelds, with graphical capabilities resembling Dreamcast or early PlayStation 2 games. It would certainly have been able to handle a port of the *Outbreak* titles (though the long loading times would probably have remained an issue). However, *Resident Evil: Outbreak* had some internal competition with *Monster Hunter*, which was released for PlayStation 2 in March 2004. Funamizu had been involved with both *Monster Hunter* and *Resident Evil: Outbreak*, as the two titles were developed at Production Studio 1 and utilized the same engine. Both were part of Capcom's broader strategy to integrate online multiplayer into its franchises. "Capcom was only willing to port either *Resident Evil: Outbreak* or *Monster Hunter* to PSP. For reasons I'm not entirely sure about, the company was unwilling to go ahead and port both games," explains Funamizu, who left Capcom before the final decision was made.

Ultimately, Capcom chose to port *Monster Hunter* to PSP because it believed that it stood a better chance of succeeding. The PlayStation 2 game had been well received in Japan and an expansion pack titled *Monster Hunter G* hit PlayStation 2 in January 2005, further cementing the brand. In the years ahead, *Monster Hunter* would go on to become a sales juggernaut in Japan, selling far more copies than any *Resident Evil* game and putting the *Monster Hunter* franchise both above the *Final Fantasy* series and on par with *Dragon Quest* and *Pokémon*. It experienced its first true worldwide success in 2018 with *Monster Hunter: World*, which reached 10 million sales globally faster than any other Capcom game to date. Therefore, it turned out to be a wise decision to bring *Monster Hunter* to PSP back in 2005, rather than *Resident Evil: Outbreak*.

Compared to the *Monster Hunter* franchise, *Resident Evil: Outbreak* and *Outbreak: File #2* have largely remained consigned to the history books. From 2011 through 2015, Capcom and social game company GREE operated a card game called *Biohazard: Outbreak: Survive*, but aside from the similar name and use of the games' characters, it bore little relation to the PlayStation 2 titles (or the *Survivor* games, for that matter). "Capcom treats the games as if they never existed," Funamizu laments when reflecting on whether *Outbreak* and *File #2* could return in some form. Aside from occasional minor storyline references in other titles like 2017's *Resident Evil 7: Biohazard*, the *Outbreak* titles have been inactive; neither entry has ever been ported to other consoles.

However, to deem both games as insignificant and irrelevant would be an inaccurate assessment. Capcom's first attempt to bring *Resident Evil* online may have been a failed experiment, but *Outbreak* and *Outbreak: File #2* were really just the beginning. They would pave the way for a journey Capcom would make for more than a decade: the careful marrying of *Resident Evil* and online functionality. Capcom was not alone; the entire game industry would double down on its commitment to online connectivity with the start of the next console generation, thanks to increased adoption of broadband internet speeds worldwide. In November 2005, Microsoft launched its next system, Xbox 360, with a revamped Xbox Live service from day one. Then, in November 2006, Sony released PlayStation 3, this time with a built-in broadband modem and internal hard drive, alongside PlayStation Network (PSN), the company's answer to Xbox Live. Nintendo finally got over its disdain for online gameplay, equipping both its DS handheld and Wii console with online connectivity via its

Nintendo Wi-Fi Connection service. The industry had therefore given Capcom a more viable environment to further explore online games. The result: almost every *Resident Evil* game released between 2009 and 2016 offers some form of online multiplayer. And, thankfully, they all offer voice chat.

CHAPTER 10:
FULL MODEL CHANGE

RESIDENT EVIL'S DECLINING POPULARITY

From a creative standpoint, Capcom arguably reached a peak in March 2002 with the *Resident Evil* remake, which was well received and set a widely recognized precedent for remaking a video game the proper way. However, *Resident Evil Zero*, released later that year, was not as critically successful, having been criticized for its lack of originality and its gameplay flaws, questioning the viability of the series' traditional survival horror formula.

Meanwhile, from a commercial standpoint, 2002 was perhaps the series' low point. Both *Resident Evil* and *Resident Evil Zero* saw lower sales than previous games and failed to meet Capcom's expectations. Globally, *Resident Evil* reached just 1.35 million units that year, while *Resident Evil Zero*, despite being an original game, sold even fewer copies at just 1.25 million. This was in contrast to *Resident Evil 2*, which at 4.96 million units had sold more than the two GameCube games put together. The *Resident Evil* series had taken a very noticeable dive in popularity.

It was evident early on that GameCube exclusivity was the primary cause for the underwhelming performance of *Resident Evil* and *Resident Evil Zero*. Following its September 2001 launch, Nintendo's system never gained any momentum against PlayStation 2, which vastly outsold GameCube for the duration of that console generation. Nintendo was in closer competition with Microsoft's Xbox, but even the two systems' combined sales failed to get anywhere near Sony's. Nintendo managed to stay relevant, thanks to its far more successful Game Boy Advance, while Microsoft had other business segments as part of a strong financial foundation. At the end of the generation, in early 2007, the GameCube concluded its run as the last-place console with 21.74 million units sold (even fewer than Nintendo 64); as of 2020, PlayStation 2 has sold a still-unsurpassed 155 million units. Microsoft's Xbox had sold 24 million units by the end of its run in 2006, staging an upset against Nintendo and staying ahead of GameCube for most of the systems' lifespan, despite Xbox selling comparatively few units in Japan.

Observers have attributed GameCube's underwhelming sales to various factors. Some blame the overly child-friendly purple box-and-handle design. Others believe the lack of a DVD player made it less appealing than the other two systems for families looking for diverse entertainment options. The lower capacity of GameCube's mini-DVDs were also an issue: third-party developers, including Capcom, had a more difficult time releasing GameCube ports of titles that were designed around PlayStation 2 and Xbox's 4.7GB DVD. Capcom was able to get around the limitations of the mini-DVD by releasing both *Resident Evil* and *Resident Evil Zero* on two discs, but other publishers were less willing to exhibit the same flexibility due to the higher manufacturing costs.

Another bone of contention was Nintendo's focus on family-friendly titles at the expense of games for adult audiences. Although Mikami's efforts to bring the mainline *Resident Evil* series exclusively to GameCube attempted to address the imbalance in Nintendo's line-up, ultimately most gamers would move on to playing other game franchises or even other *Resident Evil* games on other platforms. Even compared to other Capcom titles, *Resident Evil* and *Resident Evil Zero* sold considerably less than contemporaries such as *Onimusha: Warlords*, *Onimusha 2: Samurai's Destiny* and *Devil May Cry*, which each sold more than 2 million units on PlayStation 2, despite being newer franchises with less initial brand recognition. Another sign that the GameCube move was a mistake came when *Resident Evil: Outbreak* was released for PlayStation 2, in December 2003. Despite being an online-enabled spin-off without a significant story, *Resident Evil: Outbreak* quickly outsold its GameCube counterparts, amassing 1.45 million sales worldwide. Even *Resident Evil CODE: Veronica X* managed to stay ahead of *Resident Evil* and *Resident Evil Zero* with sales of 1.4 million, despite only being a port of a Dreamcast game. The period from 2001 through 2004 also proved to be a breakthrough in the popularity of mature games, as Rockstar's *Grand Theft Auto* and Microsoft's *Halo* franchises sold multiple millions and broke various sales records, making the *Resident Evil* series look almost quaint in comparison.

Had Mikami opted to keep the mainline *Resident Evil* series on PlayStation 2 instead, it is very likely *Resident Evil* and *Resident Evil Zero* would have sold more. Mikami admits that there was little to the technology used in both GameCube games that would have been impossible to replicate on PlayStation 2. "All the games are doing, basically, is displaying pre-rendered backgrounds," he explains. "In fact, some people inside Capcom at the time thought *Onimusha 2: Samurai's Destiny* looked better than the remake," he continues, drawing a comparison between his game and the PlayStation 2 title, released the very same month, which also utilized pre-rendered backgrounds for its visuals. But in any case, as Mikami has always maintained, the decision to go with GameCube stemmed from his creative affinity with Nintendo; it was not because he could not develop for other platforms.

Even if GameCube sales had been to blame for *Resident Evil*'s dramatic decline, it is likely that there would have been a drop, albeit smaller, on PlayStation 2 or Xbox as well. By the time *Resident Evil Zero* was released, there were already various discussions in progress about the viability of the old *Resident Evil* gameplay formula, which had not evolved dramatically since 1996. In reviewing *Devil May Cry* for PlayStation 2 in August 2001, IGN's Doug Perry noted that "While *Resident Evil* long ago reached its height and is now at a development crossroads… *Devil May Cry* blazes past the high-water mark of serious kick-ass action, and reaches right into the limitless sky."[1] While other franchises, even from Capcom, were inspiring critics, *Resident Evil* seemed to edge closer and closer to their indifference. The *Resident Evil* remake was a positive step, but its success arguably depended on the foundations of the 1996 title. Given the ever-advancing video game landscape, the market appeared to be growing tired of the *Resident Evil* series' tank controls, neutered combat mechanics and slow, methodical movement.

It may be that the impact of these criticisms was simply a matter of time. When *Resident Evil 2* topped sales charts and earned critical acclaim way back in 1998, Capcom's management immediately wanted to capitalize on the brand's success. However, Hideki Kamiya already believed he had done everything he could with the formula and wanted to bring innovations to the sequel he was asked to direct. Capcom eventually followed up on *Resident Evil 2* with *Resident Evil 3: Nemesis*, *Resident Evil CODE: Veronica*, the *Resident Evil* remake and *Resident Evil Zero*. While there was creative and technical progression from one game to the next, it was Kamiya's title, the true sequel to *Resident Evil 2*, which was given the go-ahead under the title *Resident Evil 3* before becoming *Resident Evil 4*, that was intended to take the *Resident Evil* formula dramatically forward. The four games that preceded it, as well as the various spin-offs, were considerably more conservative in their evolutions.

Perhaps the changing views on *Resident Evil* were a sign that Capcom had stalled long enough and needed to get going. Mikami certainly felt that way: "It's too bad the *Resident Evil* remake didn't sell," he laments. "But by then, I could also see that we needed to make something new."

STYLISH ACTION: *DEVIL MAY CRY*

After the release of *Resident Evil 2*, Hideki Kamiya had accepted the offer to direct the sequel, *Resident Evil 3*, but now that he had a very successful project under his belt, he was in a position to push the project forward on his own terms. For him, this meant developing for next-generation hardware. By mid-1998, the original PlayStation had been out for more than three years and was on its way to being succeeded by both Sega's Dreamcast and Sony's upcoming PlayStation 2. Kamiya saw this impending console transition as an opportunity to create something more ambitious than before. "With *Resident Evil 2*, I felt that I hit the ceiling on what I could achieve with the first PlayStation," he explains. "Therefore, I decided to create the game for the more powerful PlayStation 2, which would allow me to do more than previously possible."

However, Kamiya was not personally interested in simply creating another *Resident Evil* in the vein of the first two titles, only with prettier graphics. Shinji Mikami agreed that the next game would need to be more groundbreaking. "Go make a new *Resident Evil*," Mikami told Kamiya in 1998. "It doesn't have to be horror-themed." Kamiya was not sure what a new *Resident Evil* would actually entail, but he knew the pre-rendered camera angles used in *Resident Evil 2* would be too limiting to provide a "cool" visual experience. With PlayStation 2's horsepower, Kamiya decided that a *Resident Evil 3* should be developed, with a fully polygonal engine to keep the experience fresh.[2]

Beyond the visuals, Kamiya was interested in shaking up the fabric of the *Resident Evil* universe. He was not a fan of horror, so he looked into ways in which *Resident Evil* could be made into something stylish, which was more to his liking. Kamiya decided that *Resident Evil 3* should go for a gothic aesthetic, and he traveled to Spain and to the UK to scout locations that would inspire the game's stage design.[3] "I envisioned a game in which players control a man with superhuman abilities," Kamiya explains. "The idea was that the protagonist would be infected or implanted with some kind of biotechnology. I wanted the game to have stylish action in it." A superhuman protagonist would have gone beyond the framework of *Resident Evil*, which intentionally limited the movement and combat of its protagonists, but Kamiya prioritized innovation over the status quo. Capcom was certainly not opposed to allowing him to take a few risks, given that other creators were developing more orthodox *Resident Evil* titles. When Kazuhiro Aoyama's *Resident Evil* 1.9 was retitled *Resident Evil 3: Nemesis*, Kamiya's sequel was accordingly renamed *Resident Evil 4*.

Production Studio 4 pressed forward with the game's development. In December 1999, Mikami publicly announced the existence of *Resident Evil* on PlayStation 2 for the first time, referring to Kamiya's still-undisclosed project.[4] Internally at Capcom, Kamiya's project was proceeding smoothly. There was never a threat of a reboot, as had happened with *Resident Evil 1.5*. However, there was a point where Mikami felt that Kamiya had veered a little too far away from the *Resident Evil* formula. "As the project progressed, we realized that the game was no longer a *Resident Evil* game. It had become something different," Kamiya explains. "I consulted with Mikami-san, who agreed that we needed to release the game as something other than *Resident Evil*. That's how *Devil May Cry* was born."

Conceptually, *Devil May Cry* was somewhat similar to *Resident Evil* in that it took place in an isolated location – this time a gothic castle – that the protagonist needed to explore, and the visuals were still dark and spooky, just like the *Resident Evil* series.

However, the protagonist, who was initially intended to be Leon S. Kennedy before being renamed Dante, was fundamentally at odds with the human nature of the *Resident Evil* cast. Dante could run very fast, jump very high, leap off walls and even do mid-air flips. He could switch weapons at will; he brandished two handguns with unlimited ammunition, but also specialized in wielding large swords with demonic magical properties. While *Resident Evil* emphasized ammo conservation and avoiding enemies, *Devil May Cry* required players to amass high numerical scores by killing multiple enemies in rapid succession – another element that contrasts decidedly with *Resident Evil*. Dante's easygoing personality, much like the overall story itself, was also more lighthearted than the *Resident Evil* games, and the soundtrack eschewed soft, ambient melodies in favor of high-beat electro rock. *Devil May Cry* had clearly become its own entity and would never pass for a *Resident Evil* game. In contrast, the *Onimusha* and *Dino Crisis* franchises never strayed this far from their roots as *Resident Evil*-derived titles.

Devil May Cry was released for PlayStation 2 in August 2001 and enjoyed strong sales and a positive reception. It managed to gain traction despite being a new property, thanks in part to a demo of the game that was included with *Resident Evil CODE: Veronica X*. While Mikami took the mainline *Resident Evil* titles to GameCube, the more modern *Devil May Cry* proved to be a viable alternative for PlayStation 2 owners. With sales of over 2 million units, it gave Kamiya yet another hit title to his name. Like Kamiya's *Resident Evil 2*, *Devil May Cry* deviated heavily from its initial conceptualization, but this time Kamiya had given Capcom an entire franchise to explore and develop in the years ahead. It may have been a merry little accident, but it was certainly very beneficial to Capcom.

The flip side, however, was that Capcom was back to square one with *Resident Evil 4* as of mid-2000, which was already later than the company had originally hoped for. Capcom could not afford to wait for Kamiya to finish *Devil May Cry* before recommencing development on the title. Instead, Mikami decided to find a different leader for the project, while maintaining the notion that *Resident Evil 4* would be something completely different from its predecessors – just not as different as *Devil May Cry* had turned out to be.

THE CAPCOM FIVE: *RESIDENT EVIL 4* FINALLY REVEALED

On November 14, 2002, in Tokyo, Capcom held an event called the "GameCube New Game Announcement Meeting," where, as the name implies, the company revealed five upcoming titles that, like *Resident Evil* and *Resident Evil Zero*, would be released exclusively for Nintendo GameCube. Presenting this "Capcom Five" line-up were the company's Shinji Mikami, Hiroyuki Kobayashi, Hideki Kamiya, Hiroki Kato and Hiroshi Shibata, along with Goichi Suda (known more commonly by his nickname "Suda51") of Grasshopper Manufacture, an independent third-party development studio collaborating with Capcom. The group announced the following titles: *PN03*, a 3D shooter directed by Mikami; *Viewtiful Joe*, an anime-inspired 2D platform title directed by Kamiya; *Dead Phoenix*, a flight-action simulator directed by Kato; *Killer7*, a cel-shaded on-rails first-person shooter-adventure hybrid directed by Suda51; and, finally, *Resident Evil 4*, the only game in the line-up that was a sequel rather than an original property. All were being developed at Production Studio 4 under Mikami's supervision, with the exception of *Killer7*, which was being developed at Grasshopper Manufacture as a collaborative effort with Capcom. Early footage of each title was shown, with the respective directors explaining the game concepts and emphasizing their goal to push their creative and artistic boundaries.

Japanese media outlet *Dengeki Online* reported on the event, noting how "up-tempo" the presentation was.[5] The five creators were all dressed in flashy attire atypical of people in the video game industry. Mikami wore a leather jacket and sunglasses (indoors), while Kobayashi had donned an all-white tuxedo almost as if he were attending a wedding. Kato sported a bright reddish-pink patent-leather jacket and black leather pants, while Kamiya was head to toe in leather, wearing a shiny sweater and fingerless gloves. Suda51 also wore a leather jacket. Shibata, the least flashy of the bunch, appeared with a more modest, beige coat, a white shirt and brown, leather business shoes. While attire is rarely a compelling topic with regards to game creators, Mikami and the others were certainly dressed to impress, and exuded an aura of pride and confidence in these new titles. It also was no coincidence that each director's outfit color matched the general aesthetic theme of the game they were creating.

"In recent years, sequels to popular games or ones starring mascots have become mainstream," Mikami told the event attendees. "However, games originated as a business venture and were supposed to be a means in which creators could deliver products they find enjoyable to users. We are announcing five games today because we want everyone to experience what makes games fun. Except for *Resident Evil 4*, every game is an original work. Please look forward to their release."[6] *Weekly Famitsu* magazine observed that Mikami was backing the games up with great confidence. Mikami's words were particularly interesting because they appeared to be a not-so-subtle rebuke to his own work of the last decade, which saw him tied predominantly to *Resident Evil* at the expense of working on original ideas. It was also significant that all five titles were exclusive to GameCube, which was another display of Mikami's solidarity with Nintendo. He still believed that success could be found on GameCube, and that original games were the key to that success.

Even *Resident Evil 4*, the only title in the line-up to come from an existing franchise, appeared to be moving in a completely new direction. The impressive eighty-second reveal-trailer opened with the view of a hallway dominated by large windows and tall drapes blowing inward. The camera moves throughout the trailer, indicating the implementation of a real-time engine. The visuals shift to a deep, spiral staircase straddled by ominous-looking chains before transitioning to what appears to be a mysterious airship-like object kept aloft by an oversized propeller. The phrase "The Cradle of the Progenitor Virus" appears distorted on the screen before the trailer transitions back to the hallway with the drapes, now occupied by a man holding a gun with his right hand as he slowly walks through the corridor. The man, the protagonist, is none other than Leon S. Kennedy. He is seen exploring different areas of the airship, as well as the spiral staircase, where he begins shooting at an unseen creature. "Invading…" the narrator says in a spooky voice; more footage of Leon exploring the staircase, which is revealed to be part of a medieval castle. The trailer finally unveils the entity that has been stalking Leon: a mysterious black swarm that does not seem to react to bullets. "Contamination..." Leon is seen struggling against the black swarm before he finally falls to one knee, clutching his left arm, seemingly enduring a great deal of pain. "Possessed..." The black swarm-creature closes in on the vulnerable Leon before the trailer fades to the *Biohazard 4* logo against a white background. The trailer ends with the game's planned release year: "200X." This meant, literally speaking, that the game could be scheduled for release at any point up to December 31, 2009. Most observers guessed that it would come out in 2004 at the earliest.

The trailer was very well-received, particularly with regard to its atmosphere and visuals; the castle's appearance would have reminded people of the game's predecessor, *Devil May Cry*. The dark and claustrophobic environments looked as though they were shaping up to be a return to form in the horror department, while the fully polygonal engine looked very detailed and realistic for the time, rivaling the aesthetic quality of the pre-rendered GameCube titles. According to Mikami, the concept of "struggle" had always been a key thematic element in the series, and *Resident Evil 4* would take this to the next level, while at the same time breaking away from the mold of the previous games. Mikami reiterated that *Resident Evil 4* was a "full model change," words he had first uttered back in the 2001 "Director's Hazard" interview included with *Wesker's Report*. While *Resident Evil 4* may have seemed out of place among the other Capcom Five games, being a sequel, it was perhaps the most sought-after of the games on show that day. However, Mikami admitted that his own involvement in *Resident Evil 4*'s creative direction was minimal; in the director's seat this time was Shibata, who had previously worked as a background artist for *Resident Evil 3: Nemesis*. While Mikami would oversee development of all games at Production Studio 4, including *Resident Evil 4*, his efforts were for the time being focused on *PN03*, which was scheduled to be released in spring 2003.

DON'T PEE YOUR PANTS

Following its November 2002 reveal, Capcom kept the lid very tight on *Resident Evil 4*, announcing no new information until May 2003, when that year's E3 took place in Los Angeles. Nintendo held its usual press conference, headlined by president Satoru Iwata, where it revealed its upcoming first-party line-up, as well as showing several third-party game trailers. One of those was the highly anticipated *Resident Evil 4*.

The trailer would prove to be a bit unusual. It began ordinarily enough with new footage of the game's environments, but the scenes shifted incredibly quickly before ending on a split-second shot of Leon turning around with a shocked look on his face. The trailer was just ten seconds long, though the game was still slated for a "200X" release. Viewers were understandably puzzled at the short footage, but a few seconds later, the words "Message for E3 Final Cut" appeared on screen, followed by footage of Shinji Mikami – who was absent from the event – sitting in front of a white background and donning his sunglasses. After starting with a greeting in Japanese dubbed over by an English interpreter,

Mikami first addressed a recent unsubstantiated internet rumor regarding his employment status. "Recent rumors would suggest I have been fired, but I assure you, I am still happily working at Capcom." The rumor had stemmed from the recent commercial underperformance of Capcom's GameCube titles, including *PN03*, which had suffered a mediocre reception and low sales. It was certainly an unusual way to open an E3 trailer, but Mikami assured viewers that his inability to attend the show was purely because he was "busy working hard on *Resident Evil 4*." Using his fingers to form the letters V and J, he then told the audience to look forward to the upcoming *Viewtiful Joe*. Next, he gestured a number seven with his arms, telling fans to look forward to *Killer7*. Both games were still on track for a summer 2003 release. "They are so original. They will blow your mind!" Mikami exclaimed. He then returned to the subject of *Resident Evil 4*, which he claimed was "proceeding very smoothly" and would be "scarier than ever before." He finally closed with a line that would become iconic among gamers: "Don't pee your pants!"

The message ended with Mikami pointing straight at the viewer – then the real trailer began playing. Leon was seen exploring the grounds of an estate, walking outside in the rain, holding a flashlight with one hand before lightning flashes. The scenery shifted to indoors. A taxidermal moose head began to spasm as it screamed. Leon wandered into a dining room lit in a supernatural blue hue, his heart beating rapidly. Suddenly, a humanoid figure appeared before him, shrouded in darkness. It wielded a deadly hook in its left hand and appeared to be tethered to an endlessly long chain. This "Hook Man" slowly lumbered toward Leon, who began shooting it, to little effect. Leon fled into another hallway and took aim again; the trailer showed the camera positioning immediately behind Leon's shoulder, which seemed more in line with a first-person shooter than previous *Resident Evil* titles. On the other side of the hall was an open window, the wind blowing the drapes inward. The trailer then showed split-second shots of baby dolls with blades pointing out of their arms. Leon saw the Hook Man walking past the window on the opposite side; he explored more hallways before the Hook Man finally spotted him. Leon attempted to shoot the creature again, but his bullets still seemed to have no effect. The Hook Man attempted to impale Leon, but Leon used his arms to block it. The creature glowed in the same neon-blue color as the rest of the environments, making it seem almost unreal, like a hallucination. Leon broke free and fled once again, aiming for a door that appears to be locked. The Hook Man pursued him and Leon turned around as the camera zoomed in on his face, revealing a look of terror. The trailer ends with the same "200X" screen as the initial quick cut that played before Mikami's message. Internally at Capcom, this trailer came from a build of the game titled "Hallucination."

E3 2003 turned out to be the only time Capcom showed the "Hallucination" build publicly. While fans reacted positively to the direction the game was taking, at Capcom things were not progressing as smoothly as Mikami had claimed in his E3 message. Frustrations were mounting at Production Studio 4. Yasuhisa Kawamura had been assigned to write the scenario for *Resident Evil 4*, following his previous work on the series, on *Resident Evil 3: Nemesis*. In an interview with Project Umbrella, Kawamura, who sought to make the game as frightening as possible, states that his source of inspiration was the film *Lost Souls*, which features hallucinations and a loose killer.[7] It was a decidedly different approach from the science fiction slant of previous *Resident Evil* games. In a 2015 Eurogamer interview, Kawamura explained that Konami's *Silent Hill* and the film *Jacob's Ladder* also served as inspiration. He recalls telling director Hiroshi Shibata, "If we want to pursue pure horror, we need to find an unexplainable concept. Let's create a setting that doesn't revolve around science or reason."[8]

Kawamura's idea for conveying hallucination as a surprise element required specific technical implementations. "You were not supposed to know when Leon's hallucination would happen," he explained to Eurogamer. "Various hidden checkpoints would trigger Leon's fear into hallucination. Depending on the player's behavior, the structure of the stage changed, so we had to create two types of 3D models." However, the team eventually discovered that such an implementation was not so simple in practice, due to the limited memory bandwidth on GameCube. Kawamura explained that creating two models for the entire game would have doubled the design and rendering costs. "Even if we did have the budget, it was almost impossible to cram all of that into the GameCube's memory. We couldn't even add any monsters." As a result, the "Hallucination" build, despite its promising reveal, never progressed much beyond the clip shown in the E3 2003 trailer.

Development of *Resident Evil 4* had hit a severe roadblock. Since 2001, Mikami had advertised a "full model change," and at E3 2003 he vowed that *Resident Evil 4* would be the scariest *Resident Evil* out there. If the team was having trouble implementing the game's single defining feature, that would have implications for its marketing and image. Mikami could hardly claim he had never experienced this situation before; in fact, it was all too familiar. For the second time in five years, the latest *Resident Evil* game was at risk of failing mid-development. But at the same time, there was a crucial difference between what happened with *Resident Evil 2* and what was happening with *Resident Evil 4*. Capcom cancelled the *Resident Evil 1.5* build because Noboru Sugimura believed it lacked originality, enjoyability and a strong conceptual foundation. This time, the team was experiencing the opposite problem: *Resident Evil 4* had a great concept behind it, but the technology was not there to make it happen. While *Resident Evil 2* had simply needed a strong scenario-writer to get the game back on track with the same fundamental gameplay, there appeared to be no viable solution in sight to salvage Kawamura's "Hallucination" concept.

As the head of Production Studio 4, Mikami had to take swift action. *Resident Evil 4* was Capcom's most anticipated game at the time and, in many ways, his reputation as a creator and Capcom's most prolific figure hinged on a successful launch for the game. Mikami had already been battered by the high-profile failure of his GameCube initiative, so the stalled development of *Resident Evil 4* was like rubbing salt into a wound. This time, Mikami decided to cancel the "Hallucination" build and start anew, but rather than retain Shibata and Kawamura, as he had done with Hideki Kamiya for *Resident Evil 2*, he decided to remove them from the project and install himself as the director.

It was a drastic change, especially because just a few months earlier Mikami had touted the virtues of developing original games that were neither sequels nor mascot-based titles. But desperate times call for desperate measures, and Mikami says he made the decision because he literally had no other choice. "I was the only one who could direct *Resident Evil 4*. No one else could, as they were busy with other projects. Kamiya was working on *Okami*, so he wasn't available, either."*

For Kawamura, the change was a personal blow. He told Project Umbrella, "I felt very sorry. You can even say that I was ashamed. While I felt that I put in much effort, refining the idea to the best of my abilities, my mentor Mikami-san had to intervene in the end." Despite that, Kawamura holds no resentment towards Mikami, whom he respects as a mentor, explaining, "When I saw the quality of the finished *Resident Evil 4*, I realized what an amazingly skilled person Shinji Mikami is. The experience I gained from this helps keep me going even to this day. It was an invaluable experience as a game designer." Kawamura departed Capcom shortly after and continued to work in the game industry as a writer on various games, as well as lecturing on game design at local Japanese colleges.[9]

Shibata and Kawamura's "Hallucination" build is now referred to unofficially as *Resident Evil 3.5*, in the same vein as *Resident Evil 1.5*, the cancelled version of *Resident Evil 2*. As with *Resident Evil 1.5*, ideas and various visual assets from *Resident Evil 3.5* found their way into other games in the years ahead, including the final version of *Resident Evil 4*, as well as the PlayStation 2 horror game *Haunting Ground* (*Demento* in Japan), which is a spiritual successor to the *Clock Tower* series. Aside from publicly released trailers and a demo video released with the final *Resident Evil 4*, *Resident Evil*

---

* Kamiya directed the action adventure game *Okami* following the June 2003 release of *Viewtiful Joe*. *Resident Evil 4* marked Mikami's first time directing an original (non-remake) *Resident Evil* game since 1996.

3.5 remains firmly locked inside Capcom, with no playable sample ever leaked to the public.

"THE SHOCKING NEW FACE OF SURVIVAL HORROR"

It was now January 2004. Fourteen months had passed since the initial unveiling of *Resident Evil 4* at the Capcom Five event, and despite the internal reshuffling at Production Studio 4, excitement for the game was steadily rising. The E3 2003 "Hallucination" trailer's dark, fear-inducing setting and detailed, eerie 3D visuals had been well received, with the game in some ways benefiting from being a highly anticipated GameCube exclusive. Nothing more had been shown since E3 2003 six months earlier, although Capcom continuously reassured fans of its continued development.[10] Even financial investment firms took notice of the game's potential, with Japanese company UFJ Tsubasa Securities expecting *Resident Evil 4* to sell 1.8 million copies, based on what they had seen so far.[11]

But all of those expectations were suddenly upended on January 28, 2004, when Capcom held its Gamers' Day event in Las Vegas to show off its upcoming game line-up, including an update on *Resident Evil 4*. Here, Capcom unveiled a brand-new trailer and playable demo, but what attendees saw was nothing at all like the November 2002 and E3 2003 "Hallucination" trailers. In fact, this new trailer looked nothing like any prior *Resident Evil*. What Capcom unveiled shocked gamers and would permanently redefine what *Resident Evil* was, both as a video game and as a franchise. *Game Informer* magazine, which broke the story first, described the new *Resident Evil 4* as "The Shocking New Face of Survival Horror."[12]

In this latest incarnation, *Resident Evil 4* had taken on a completely new form distinct from its predecessors and previous builds. Gone were the hallucinations, puzzles, zombies, viruses, haunted mansions and neon lighting. In their stead was a new game taking place in a bright, outdoor environment resembling a rural European village. There was no Hook Man or any flesh-eating zombies. These were now replaced by dozens of humanoid villagers, all of whom could speak an audible form of basic Mexican Spanish. The perspective was like none of the previous *Resident Evil* games, either: while the game was still in third-person, the camera was locked to a fixed position behind the protagonist, giving players a clear view of the action in front of him, all in a mandatory widescreen-aspect ratio that was still uncommon in games. Aiming the weapon would bring the camera forward, just behind the protagonist's shoulder, somewhat resembling the two viewpoints employed in *Resident Evil: Dead Aim*. Health and ammunition counts were now displayed on a HUD in the bottom right corner of the screen.

Of all the elements shown in previous builds, the protagonist was the only one that survived the transition: Leon S. Kennedy, still sporting his brown leather jacket. The story was set in 2004, canonically several years after the previous games, and Leon was now a secret agent for the American government embarking on a mission to rescue the president's daughter, who had been kidnapped by cultists. According to the story, the Umbrella Corporation was no more, the epic showdown hinted at in the ending of *Resident Evil CODE: Veronica* apparently having occurred off-screen or not at all. While *Resident Evil* traditionally gave players control of combat-restricted characters who could do relatively little, Leon was now empowered by the new aiming mechanic and plentiful ammunition to take down as many enemies as his heart desired.

Gamers, journalists and other observers alike were shocked at what *Resident Evil 4* had become. It looked nothing like a *Resident Evil* game, seemingly having nothing in common except the name. Some fans were skeptical of this new direction, while some were curious. Others were excited at the new gameplay, especially those who disliked the traditional *Resident Evil* style. *Game Informer* was positive about the new direction, stating that "the controls are intuitive, the combat intense, and even with the loss of the exaggerated camera angles for dramatic effect, we still felt a blood-curdling sense of fear the entire time we played. It's a very claustrophobic experience. The enemies are always around you. And if they get close, they grab hold and leave you bashing buttons to get free." *Game Informer* reassured fans that *Resident Evil 4* was looking promising, even if the traditional horror elements that Shinji Mikami previously promised were gone: "Any concerns we had that the series would lose its hallmark horror with this new perspective were quickly thrown out the window after playing it."[13]

Capcom also now publicly revealed that Mikami was the director of this new vision for *Resident Evil 4*. They justified the change in direction as something he felt was necessary to do to retain the series' signature horror and shock value. "Mikami simply had become tired of spending too much time managing and not enough time being creative with his team," *Game Informer* explained, and later quoted Mikami as saying "I remember playing

[Resident Evil] Zero and saying to myself that this is just more of the same ... This is why I wanted to change the system. With the new system I once again feel nervous and scared when I play it."

By this point, *Resident Evil 4* had experienced life in four different phases, if one counts the concept that eventually became *Devil May Cry*. The project had been in development for nearly five years, having begun way back in 1998 after *Resident Evil 2* was released, so, for Mikami, *Resident Evil 4* was in many ways simply way overdue. The "Hallucination" concept had proven to be unfeasible on GameCube hardware, which made Mikami aware of the perils of basing a game's concept around a single story point. He therefore decided to write the new story himself, intentionally separating it from the rest of the series, while ensuring that it would have no direct bearing on how the gameplay was designed or how the game's engine was implemented. "I realized that in order for the project to succeed, the reboot would have to focus less on story and more on gameplay. Therefore, I wanted to take control of the new game's story," Mikami explains.

Capcom spent almost all of 2004 exhibiting *Resident Evil 4* at major game events. The playable demos shown at E3 and Tokyo Game Show 2004 revealed information about the supporting cast, including the president's kidnapped daughter Ashley Graham, as well as Luis Sera, a Spanish local with inside knowledge about the village. Impressions from major gaming media outlets were very positive; they praised the new gameplay and graphics, with IGN calling the graphics "unequaled" in one preview.[14] At the end of the year, Capcom unveiled that Ada Wong would be reprising her role as a spy with mysterious intentions, showing that the game had more ties with past games than it initially let on.

In August 2004, Capcom announced that *Resident Evil 4* would be released in North America on January 11, 2005, later that month in Japan and in March everywhere else. In one sense, the 2005 release date was a delay, given that, internally, Capcom had aimed for a 2004 launch; the official Japanese *Resident Evil 4* website had even included an Easter egg indicating a 2004 release, although this was never officially publicized. Capcom would ultimately end up with just under one year to sell Mikami's new vision for *Resident Evil* to its audiences. Media interviews looked promising, but Capcom and Mikami would not know for sure if they had made the right decision until after the game was released.

"POSSIBLY THE BEST VIDEO GAME EVER MADE"

January 2005: After nearly five years of development, *Resident Evil 4* was finally released for GameCube. Always intended to be somewhat different from its predecessors, *Resident Evil 4* had gone through several revisions under three directors before Shinji Mikami stepped in and took it in an entirely new direction altogether. With nearly nothing else out there that resembled what Capcom was aiming for with *Resident Evil 4*, it remained to be seen how audiences would react.

It turns out gamers were in for a treat. As they bought their copies and began diving into the world of *Resident Evil 4*, it became increasingly clear that the world of *Resident Evil* had changed for the better. Throughout the game – which could take anything from ten to over twenty-five hours to complete on the first try – players discovered there was more to the village than just a group of farmers. Leon explores a variety of environments, from the farm village to an ancient castle and an industrial mining island. While *Resident Evil 4* turned out to be considerably longer than any of its predecessors, Mikami managed to craft a carefully paced experience from beginning to end. No particular section of the game feels too long or too short, there is only minimal backtracking in any given area, and many of the set gameplay pieces are clever, well designed and effectively implemented.

One example of *Resident Evil 4*'s compelling design is in the initial encounter with Dr Salvador, the chainsaw-wielding *ganado* whose face is wrapped in a rucksack. Dr Salvador appears early on in the village scene, his chainsaw obviously capable of decapitating Leon. The standard handgun is barely effective against the enemy, but a cleverly placed shotgun and the presence of an explosive grenade gives players a fighting chance, while teaching them how to effectively maneuver through environments and utilize items to dispatch multiple enemies at once. Beyond its well-designed gameplay utility, such set pieces are memorable and enjoyable to play. Mikami's design also offers an additional layer of depth: some players might be too intimidated to fight Dr Salvador, even when armed with stronger weapons, so *Resident Evil 4* allows those players to simply avoid the battle until the internally timed set piece is over. No previous *Resident Evil* title offered anywhere near the level of depth that *Resident Evil 4* brings to the table in its first twenty minutes.

Fans have praised the game's groundbreaking attention to detail for the time. The non-Japanese versions are filled with numerous different kinds of violent and gruesome death sequences, such as decapitations, brutal stabbings, falls into chasms, suffocation in acid baths, being crushed by boulders, and more. In fact, there are so many ways to die in the game that fans have recorded twenty-minute YouTube videos depicting nothing but the game's death scenes.

Drawing inspiration from Western-developed third-person shooters, the game's weapons and item management system is more hands-on than in previous games. Players can obtain a larger array of firearms, with varying reload speeds, aiming accuracy, recoil and firepower, all of which can be individually upgraded in exchange for Pesetas, the game's currency, which players can obtain by killing enemies or selling jewels and other treasures Leon picks up throughout the world. Players can choose how and when to upgrade their weapons to suit their play-styles, and these weapons and supplies can be purchased or upgraded by visiting the enigmatic Merchant, a masked, seemingly human figure wearing a hooded trench coat who speaks with an exaggerated pseudo-Australian accent. The Merchant's humorous portrayal has made him a minor gaming-culture icon, and in 2005 the American comedian group Mega64 filmed a short video of one of their members dressing up as the Merchant, visiting a mall and saying the same lines, in the same manner, to ordinary people, eliciting both confused and amused reactions.[15]

Lastly, beating *Resident Evil 4* unlocks a few extra modes, such as "Assignment Ada," a short scenario featuring Ada as she retrieves a set of bioweapon samples for her employer, who turns out to be Albert Wesker. More substantial is "The Mercenaries," which borrows its name from the unlockable mini-game in *Resident Evil 3: Nemesis*, but takes the concept further. Players control either Leon, Ada, Krauser, HUNK or Wesker as they try to defeat as many enemies as possible within the time limit. Players can extend the time limit by breaking timer vases located throughout the stages, which are taken from the main game. Many players found The Mercenaries to be very replayable, and often felt encouraged to get high scores – a testament to the strong design elements of *Resident Evil 4*'s gameplay.

Once launched, *Resident Evil 4* became a critical and commercial success well beyond the expectations of the gaming community. Reviews poured in from all major North American media outlets, offering virtually unanimous praise for the game's quality and innovation. IGN's Matt Casamassina declared *Resident Evil 4* "the best survival horror game ever made."[16] Greg Kasavin called the game "an amazing achievement" when reviewing for GameSpot.[17] *Nintendo Power* believed it to be "possibly the best console video game ever made, and definitely the standard that horror titles will be measured by for years to come."[18] European game media were equally enamored. *Edge Magazine*, with its reputation for high standards, said the game was "filled with sights, sounds and thrills that will linger in the memory long after the content of more sophisticated titles has been forgotten."[19] In Japan, *Weekly Famitsu* awarded the game 38 out of 40 stars, its reviewers singing much the same praises as their Western counterparts. The game did receive some complaints, most notably about the long segments in which players must escort a vulnerable Ashley from one room to the next; others criticized the story for its lack of connection to previous *Resident Evil* titles. Still, the praise far outweighed the criticism.

Unlike the *Resident Evil* remake and *Resident Evil Zero*, which did not enjoy particularly high sales, *Resident Evil 4* became a commercial hit on GameCube, despite the system's long association with younger demographics. Notwithstanding certain developments that had worked against its commercial potential (a PlayStation 2 port was announced a few months earlier), *Resident Evil 4* on GameCube managed to be the top-selling game on any platform in North America throughout January 2005.[20] The game performed less impressively in Japan due to the aforementioned PlayStation 2 port, but global sales of *Resident Evil 4* on GameCube eventually reached 1.6 million units, an improvement on the other two GameCube games and on *Resident Evil Outbreak*, *Onimusha 3: Demon Siege* and even the initial release of *Devil May Cry 3: Dante's Awakening*. *Resident Evil 4*'s appeal and impact were so wide-reaching that it overcame the GameCube's stigma as a child-focused system for which only Nintendo games sold well, at the same time outselling all the other games Capcom released around the same time. Had there not been a PlayStation 2 announcement before its release, *Resident Evil 4* might have sold even more units on Nintendo's console.

Back in 2000, Mikami vowed that *Resident Evil 4* would be a "full model change," and thanks to the game's rare combination of innovation, creativity, quality and critical acclaim, he had succeeded by any standard. But he confesses that when he made his remarks, years before, he actually had no idea what they were supposed to mean, or what form they would eventually take. "I always intended for the phrase 'full model change' to be vague. It was always meant to be a simple concept, not a specific direction that limited me to one particular thing." By keeping all options open and being willing to course-correct when the "Hallucination" demo was imperiled, Mikami was able to pull a rabbit out of a hat. *Resident Evil 4* was always meant to be an important step in the franchise – more so than *Resident Evil Zero* or *Resident Evil CODE: Veronica* – but its impact went beyond the franchise, beyond Capcom, and permeated through the entire industry for years to come. No other *Resident Evil* game, except perhaps the 1996 original, could lay claim to such a presence.

Reflecting on the critical success of the game, Mikami feels proud to have created a game with as much influence as *Resident Evil 4*, although he concedes that it might not be the best game out there, even among Capcom's contemporary titles. "You know, I think *Okami* is better than *Resident Evil 4*," Mikami says without a tinge of sarcasm, referring to Hideki Kamiya's April 2006 PlayStation 2 title. For its part, *Okami*, which draws some inspiration from *The Legend of Zelda* series, has also been praised as one of Kamiya's best games. Sensing that his view may be hard to believe, Mikami adds: "I'm honored to have made *Resident Evil 4*."

MIKAMI'S HEAD: *RESIDENT EVIL 4* COMES TO PLAYSTATION 2

On November 1, 2004, Capcom Japan posted a press release on its website that shocked the video game community: *Resident Evil 4* was coming to PlayStation 2 and was no longer exclusive to GameCube. This decision came three years and two months after the Biohazard Strategy Presentation, where Shinji Mikami publicly pledged to develop mainline *Resident Evil* games only for GameCube. Technically speaking, this was a re-announcement of the game for PlayStation 2, given that *Resident Evil 4* had been planned for Sony's platform before that initial build became *Devil May Cry*.

The press release had a different tone from usual. Press releases usually talk about a game and its features, yet this seemed like a subtle attempt at damage control. Capcom cited "voices from loyal customers all over the world," followed with a seemingly unrelated blurb about the expansion of the video game industry through the upcoming Nintendo DS and Sony PSP next-generation handhelds. "Under these environments, we have come to this conclusion after deliberating over customers' needs, market environments, and various opinions from stakeholders such as shareholders or investors," Capcom explained. The implication was that Capcom's management had been pressured or influenced by shareholders to prematurely terminate *Resident Evil 4*'s GameCube exclusivity.

To those who had followed GameCube's dismal commercial performance since its launch, this change of policy should not have been terribly surprising. *Resident Evil* and *Resident Evil Zero* underperformed relative to Capcom's expectations, while other efforts, such as *PN03* and *Viewtiful Joe* failed to become breakout hits. GameCube sales were dismal for most of that console generation, and the system was gearing up to being Nintendo's worst-performing major product at that time. The *Resident Evil* series failed to generate any sustained popularity for GameCube among older audiences and, in turn, fans ignored the GameCube games in favor of other PlayStation 2 franchises or alternatives, such as *Resident Evil Outbreak*. By now, Capcom had already backtracked on its initial intention to keep some of the Capcom Five titles exclusive to GameCube: *PN03* stayed on the platform, but *Viewtiful Joe* was ported to PlayStation 2 in 2004, while *Killer7* was announced for PlayStation 2 before the GameCube version was even released, allowing the game to eventually be launched on both platforms simultaneously, in July 2005. That Capcom held out as long as it did before announcing *Resident Evil 4* for PlayStation 2 is remarkable.

One cannot imagine exactly how Mikami felt when the decision to put *Resident Evil 4* on PlayStation 2 was made by forces beyond his control. For nearly three years, he vowed that *Resident Evil 4* would never come to other platforms, with his most notorious assertion appearing in a summer 2002 interview with the Japanese magazine *Hyper Capcom Special*, where he was quoted as stating: "Make no mistake: *Resident Evil 4* is coming out for GameCube. It will not come out on other game platforms. If it does, I will commit ritual suicide."[21] Ritual suicide, in this case, refers to the Japanese terms "harakiri" or "seppuku", both of which are defined by *The Wisdom Japanese-English Dictionary* as "suicide by ritual disembowelment practiced by the Japanese samurai to avoid a disgraceful execution." (Mikami's statement was initially translated into English and disseminated throughout the internet as, "*Resident Evil 4* will definitely release only on GameCube, not on another console. If it happens, I will cut my head off." The word choice in the English translation certainly differs from the Japanese, yet the intent of the translation is ultimately the same.) Regardless of the method, Mikami was not being literal about ending his life over which platform *Resident Evil 4* would come out on; his comment was merely a figure of speech intended to reassure people that *Resident Evil 4* was a GameCube exclusive.

Following the PlayStation 2 announcement, Mikami maintained official silence on the matter, refraining from comment until an

April 2007 interview with *Famitsu*, where he took the opportunity to apologize to people who had bought a GameCube based on his promise that *Resident Evil 4* would stay exclusive to that system.[22] The apology was sincere and diplomatic, if belated. Behind the scenes, however, one former Capcom employee remembers Mikami feeling "humiliated, livid and betrayed." Another former employee, who worked with Mikami, mentioned that he had come very close to resigning from Capcom, a decision that was averted only due to other developments inside the company that were satisfying enough for Mikami to persuade him to stay.

The PlayStation 2 port of *Resident Evil 4* was scheduled for release at the end of 2005, allowing it to remain exclusive to GameCube for most of that year. With Mikami no longer involved with the franchise at this point, Capcom assigned a new producer to helm the project: Masachika Kawata. Having joined Capcom in 1995, Kawata had worked with the *Resident Evil* team since *Resident Evil 3: Nemesis*, when he was a background designer; he later worked on the *Resident Evil* remake as a lead designer for the game's CG-rendered visuals. Given GameCube's stronger horsepower over PlayStation 2, as well as the two systems' different architectures, a considerable effort would be needed for the port. What's more, *Resident Evil 4* was one of the most technologically optimized GameCube games ever released and a visual showcase for the system, especially among third-party games. A former Capcom employee recalls: "When we heard the game would come to PlayStation 2, most of us weren't sure whether it was even possible for the PlayStation 2 to run the game without severe compromises."

Unsurprisingly, the port suffered from a number of noticeable downgrades. The same former Capcom employee recalls that sound was the first element affected, the team being compelled to do this in order to preserve most of the game's look. By reducing the amount of hardware memory occupied by audio-related processes, the development team would have more resources to maintain stronger fidelity to visuals and gameplay. This explains why, despite the PlayStation 2's DVD having more capacity than the GameCube mini-DVD, the PlayStation 2 port's audio sounds muffled and compressed compared with the GameCube original.

Even with sound quality reduced, the team was still forced to make several visual compromises, including substantially lowering the game's polygon count, toning down the lighting effects and decreasing textural detail. Another downgrade was in the game's cut-scenes. On GameCube, nearly all of them were rendered in real-time, but the amount of system resources required to do the same on PlayStation 2 led the team to instead opt to replace the real-time scenes with compressed pre-rendered video recorded directly from the GameCube version. Not only did these recorded scenes look worse than the real-time versions, they transitioned in and out of gameplay less smoothly. Pre-rendered videos also led to cut-scenes always displaying Leon, Ashley and Ada's standard costumes, even if players had selected alternative attire. Initially, the development team tried to avoid making this compromise by using multiple DVDs. "There was brief talk about putting the PlayStation 2 version on two DVDs specifically to preserve the alternative costumes in the game," the former employee recalls. "We toyed with the idea of recording all the costume variants and shipping on two DVDs so it had all the videos. But in the end, we didn't think it would be worth it to double manufacturing costs just to appease the small number of players who select alternative costumes."

To offset the later release and technical downgrades, Kawata's team set to work adding new content exclusive to the PlayStation 2 version. The most notable addition is a scenario titled "Separate Ways" (known in Japan by the odd name "The Another Order"). This exclusive five-part scenario, directed by Kuniomi Matsushita, features Ada Wong as she experiences the events of the main adventure, similar to the Zapping System used in *Resident Evil 2*. As well as providing more insight into Ada's involvement in the story, "Separate Ways" repeatedly features Albert Wesker, who had previously been mentioned only in Leon's scenario, giving players a glimpse of to the exact nature of Wesker's motives. Other minor additions with the port include a new weapon and extra costumes, including a steel knight costume for Ashley that made her impervious to any sort of damage, alleviating one of the few complaints people had about the GameCube version – that too much time was dedicated to escorting Ashley throughout the game because that she was so vulnerable to enemies. There were also tweaks to the game in terms of enemy placement, weapon efficacy and item locations.

Despite the number of additions and modifications required, Capcom was able to release *Resident Evil 4* for PlayStation 2 in October 2005. The game had made it over in a recognizable and respectable form, trading downgraded visuals in exchange for extra content and a mostly identical gameplay experience. Reviews were largely just as positive as those for the GameCube release.

Commercially, the port saw very impressive sales in all regions. In Japan, it debuted with sales of nearly 243,000 in its first week, putting it instantly above the GameCube version, which had sold only 220,000 copies after eleven months on the market.[23] As of

2020, the PlayStation 2 port of *Resident Evil 4* has sold 2.3 million copies globally, compared to 1.6 million on GameCube, making it Capcom's best-selling game both for the PlayStation 2 and that entire console generation, even putting it beyond Capcom's *Onimusha* and *Devil May Cry* titles, which had been released years earlier. Capcom had clearly made the correct decision to reverse its GameCube exclusivity policy in favor of a PlayStation 2 port. After years of relatively underwhelming sales, *Resident Evil* had returned to the top spot among Capcom's franchises.

The success of the PlayStation 2 port would also benefit Kawata's career. Mikami had already distanced himself from the *Resident Evil* franchise following the release of *Resident Evil 4* on GameCube, which he had vowed would be his last-ever *Resident Evil* game. This allowed Kawata to become a vital figure in the series' development and a sort of successor to Mikami. Kawata was promoted to the role of producer and would have a hand in most *Resident Evil* games from 2007 onward.

CHAPTER 11: SOWING THE SEEDS OF A NEW ERA

DEADLY SILENCE: THE *RESIDENT EVIL* TENTH ANNIVERSARY

Between March 22, 1996, when *Resident Evil* was released for the original PlayStation, and January 11, 2005, when *Resident Evil 4* launched on GameCube, there were some six mainline titles, three first-person shooter spin-offs, two online-compatible offshoots, two handheld renditions, one remake, two cancelled prototypes and a number of derivative titles for mobile phones. The series had its origins on Sony's PlayStation, although Sega and Nintendo consoles received their own entries, some in more dramatic fashion than others. The industry never stood still, and technological improvements, coupled with advancements in game design and evolving consumer preferences, saw *Resident Evil* transform itself from a slow and methodical action-exploration hybrid to an action-packed shooter. Meanwhile, after a decade of involvement, Shinji Mikami, the father of the *Resident Evil* series, decided to leave it behind and move on to other games. A lot happened during those nine years, and while things were not always that rosy, Capcom ultimately came out as a stronger video-game company. Perhaps it is somewhat poetic that it is none other than the original game that serves as the bookend to the first decade of *Resident Evil*.

The original pops up at various points in the franchise's first ten years. It was ported to Saturn and re-released as a *Director's Cut* expansion in 1997, and it received another re-release, with an unfortunate new soundtrack, in 1998. Capcom also attempted to release a Game Boy Color version in 2000 before it was abandoned, and then there was the 2002 remake on GameCube. In August 2005, *Resident Evil: Director's Cut* even came out on an obscure Korean Samsung mobile phone. And in January 2006, just two months before the franchise's tenth anniversary, the original *Resident Evil* would receive yet another re-release, this time on a Nintendo handheld.

In late 2004, Nintendo released its first truly 3D portable console, Nintendo DS, which stood for "Nintendo Dual Screen." As the name suggests, the system has two screens stacked vertically on top of each other in a clamshell format; the lower one is a responsive touchscreen enabling new gameplay features and ideas. A few weeks later, Sony released PlayStation Portable (PSP), a more traditional, and more technologically capable, handheld. Nintendo's and Sony's competition now extended beyond the living room and into the realm of portable gaming.

As 3D-capable handhelds, both Nintendo DS and PSP presented Capcom with the first mainstream platforms that could handle *Resident Evil* games without large redesigns or compromises. It was a far cry from the days when the original *Resident Evil* had to be shoehorned into the 8-bit Game Boy Color or the offshoot *Resident Evil: Gaiden* was developed, which hardly resembled the series. Capcom wasted little time getting the ball rolling. In August 2005, the company announced that it was developing a port of the original *Resident Evil* for Nintendo DS under the title *Resident Evil: Deadly Silence* (also referred to as *Resident Evil* "DS": the initialism was often used in game titles for the handheld). The re-release, intended to commemorate the series' tenth anniversary, was launched on January 19, 2006.

2006 was an interesting year for the franchise. On one hand, having the entire original *Resident Evil* while out and about, in a car or onboard an airplane, was a novelty at the time. I happened to receive my own copy of *Resident Evil: Deadly Silence* a day before a family trip to Las Vegas in January 2006, and it felt very special to play through the original game on an airplane. At GameSpot, Greg Kasavin reported that the game was "surprisingly successful at translating the scary bits of the original to a much smaller format … It's pretty wild that now you can play a game like this on the go."[1]

On the other hand, despite the novelty of the handheld version, the original *Resident Evil* had long been superseded by the 2002 GameCube remake, while *Resident Evil 4* brought a paradigm shift to the series' gameplay style. Barely a year old, the latter was still fresh in people's minds and a major presence in gaming discourse of the time. There appeared to be little appetite for a return to the traditional *Resident Evil* style last seen in *Resident Evil Zero*. In reviewing *Deadly Silence*, Jon Wahlgren of Nintendo Life explained that while the game was "ground-breaking when it first hit the PlayStation in 1996, many of the game's mechanics are downright antiquated by now and can be off-putting to gamers who missed out on the series until Leon Kennedy shot up half the population in an unnamed European village. As a new game, *Resident Evil: Deadly Silence* isn't that great, but as an adaptation it works out very well."[2]

The most obvious improvements over previous renditions on PlayStation, Saturn and PC could be observed in the graphics. The character models showed more detail, while taking some cues from the designs in the GameCube remake. The pre-rendered backgrounds suffered from visual artifacts due to the compression required to fit the game onto a Nintendo DS game card, but the smaller screen masked the compression well. Elsewhere, Capcom implemented quality of life improvements that were not featured in past ports (or in future games, for that matter). Interestingly, these improvements turned the original *Resident Evil* into a game that was, in some respects, mechanically more advanced than both its sequels and its very own remake. The iconic door-opening loading sequences between rooms could now be skipped with the press of a button, which dramatically shortened gameplay time. Players could reload on the fly, a feature pulled directly from *Resident Evil 4*. The auto-turn introduced in *Resident Evil 3: Nemesis* was added into the DS port, and players could brandish the Combat Knife at any time, thus saving an item slot.

Capcom also introduced a "Rebirth Mode", which modifies the game scenario by rearranging item locations and adding first-person knife-action sequences, new cut-scenes and simple treasure-chest puzzles using the DS's lower touchscreen. Capcom even added a multiplayer mini-game in which players team up to kill zombies by wirelessly linking their DS systems. The port contains all the voice-acting and full-motion video cut-scenes of the original game, although for some reason every version – including the Japanese one – features the censored introduction video. Luckily, advancements in solid-state storage and compression techniques meant Capcom did not encounter any issues putting all of the original content onto a Nintendo DS card, unlike the months-long process needed to bring *Resident Evil 2* to Nintendo 64 seven years prior.

Resident Evil: Deadly Silence is, perhaps unintentionally, a symbolic manifestation of the creative and technical struggles found throughout the early history of *Resident Evil*. With it, Capcom finally succeeded in bringing the series to a handheld in its intended form; many of the improvements that came with the sequels eventually found their way back to the original; a non-disc storage format was no longer a liability. The only element that seemed to be missing was the original horror and shock value, which had dissipated long ago. Still, for dedicated fans, it was a blast from the past.

Resident Evil: Deadly Silence did not sell particularly well, which was unsurprising considering the differences between consoles and handhelds. The former have always been more conducive to cinematic experiences like *Resident Evil*, while the latter have succeeded with less cinematic and more socially driven experiences, such as *Tetris* and *Pokémon*.

Sony's PSP, the other major handheld of the era, was not left out of the running. In Japan, *Resident Evil: Director's Cut* was released digitally for PSP (and PlayStation 3) via the PlayStation Store, which offers emulated PlayStation games for download. North America and Europe received *Resident Evil: Director's Cut DualShock* instead, complete with its terrible soundtrack. *Resident Evil 2* and *Resident Evil 3: Nemesis* were released for the PlayStation Store in 2007 and 2008, making the PlayStation *Resident Evil* trilogy fully handheld.

SHINJI MIKAMI AFTER *RESIDENT EVIL*

The success of the first *Resident Evil* saw Shinji Mikami grow from a simple game creator and director to Capcom's first officer, producing and acting as an advisor for popular games ranging from *Resident Evil 2* all the way to *Dino Crisis, Onimusha: Warlords, Devil May Cry* and even *Phoenix Wright: Ace Attorney*, Capcom's attorney simulation title released for Game Boy Advance in October 2001. When Yoshiki Okamoto and Noritaka Funamizu, the old guard from the mid-1980s, departed Capcom in late 2003, it was Mikami and Keiji Inafune who succeeded them. But Mikami had never planned on becoming the figurehead of a blockbuster video-game franchise. While Inafune would continue to work his way up the company as a producer for the *Mega Man* and *Onimusha* franchises, Mikami had other intentions. He was not interested in remaining as a producer or businessman. His number-one goal was, and has only ever been, to make new and interesting games.

In an interview with *Weekly Famitsu*, Mikami revealed his feelings of alienation after becoming a producer. "There was a time when I wanted to leave Capcom because of that," he explained, before elaborating further. "I joined Capcom in order to create things, and I thought that going away from that would be counterproductive. It was hard, not being directly involved with the development process."[3] When Mikami brought the *Resident Evil* series exclusively to GameCube, he did so purely for creative reasons. It made little business sense to take the series away from the PlayStation 2, but Mikami didn't prioritize business. He felt a connection with Nintendo's approach to creativity, while disagreeing with Sony's and Microsoft's. He put his money where his mouth was and spearheaded the GameCube Capcom Five announcement in November 2002, which coincided with him directing *PN03*, which was released in March 2003. The obscure shooter saw virtually no success, though it brought Mikami perhaps more satisfaction that he had enjoyed in years. He was directing a game, and it was neither *Resident Evil* nor any other survival horror (as *Dino Crisis* also was). However, due to his failure to achieve popular hit titles in the years immediately after, Mikami decided to step down as the manager of Production Studio 4. He then thrust himself into the director's seat of *Resident Evil 4* to save the project from disaster.

In late 2004, when *Resident Evil 4* was announced for PlayStation 2, Mikami nearly quit Capcom in protest. He found the situation deeply embarrassing after years of promising that the game would be a GameCube exclusive. The PlayStation 2 port demonstrates that Capcom, like all other game companies, is in business to make money, regardless of how an individual creator might feel (even if it was Mikami's *Resident Evil* that had saved Capcom from bankruptcy eight years earlier). In spite of these setbacks, Mikami remained loyal to Capcom and hoped to find a means by which he could stay at the company while working on new content. He negotiated with the company's upper management, promising to finish development of *Resident Evil 4* in exchange for being allowed to move on to making entirely original games afterwards. Mikami was no longer interested in having a substantial influence in Capcom's business decisions and felt that there were other people talented enough to take the helm for the *Resident Evil* series after *Resident Evil 4*.

Mikami had one task left for the franchise, then: selecting a successor to carry the creative torch. "My last official decision involving *Resident Evil* was choosing the director of *Resident Evil 5*," Mikami recalls; the new game would be announced in July 2005, for the PlayStation 3 and Xbox 360 consoles. "The final version of *Resident Evil 5* was directed by Yasuhiro Anpo, but I actually had chosen a different person to be the director. It turns out that the person I chose was not the best fit for the job, which led to Anpo taking over."

Resident Evil 4 was finally released in January 2005, thus concluding Mikami's involvement in the franchise (he was not involved with *Deadly Silence*). It had been a little over ten years since his original boss, Tokuro Fujiwara, called Mikami into a meeting room to discuss the creation of a new horror game that could be the successor to *Sweet Home*. There were ups and downs during Mikami's tenure, but it was a job well done. No matter what challenges now awaited him, his legacy as the creator of *Resident Evil* was set in stone.

THE BEGINNING AND THE END OF CLOVER STUDIO

On July 1, 2004, Capcom announced the establishment of a new development subsidiary under the name "Clover Studio". The press release described Clover as "an independent studio funded by Capcom Japan," with producer Atsushi Inaba named as its president and CEO. Among the notable members joining the new studio were Hideki Kamiya and Shinji Mikami, who would transition from his position at Production Studio 4 to Clover following completion of *Resident Evil 4*. Other notable members included Hiroki Kato and Masaaki Yamada. Capcom's primary objective for Clover was to create new and original properties, as opposed to internal Capcom studios that focused on existing franchises such as *Resident Evil* and *Street Fighter*.

Clover's first project was a port of Kamiya's *Viewtiful Joe* for PlayStation 2, with extra features. The GameCube release the year before saw minor sales, but very positive feedback. Clover was also developing a sequel, *Viewtiful Joe 2*, for both GameCube and PlayStation 2. Afterwards, the studio began work on *Viewtiful Joe: Red Hot Rumble* for GameCube and PSP, as well as *Viewtiful Joe: Double Trouble!* for Nintendo DS. Aside from the *Viewtiful Joe* games, Clover began developing two other original titles: *Okami* and *God Hand*, which was directed by Mikami.

While *God Hand* and the *Viewtiful Joe* games were relatively small-budget projects with low expectations, *Okami* was given much more prominence from a production standpoint. Directed by Kamiya, *Okami* is an action-adventure title for PlayStation 2 overlaid with cultural motifs from Japanese history and featuring colorful cel-shaded graphics; gamers have observed similarities between *Okami* and Nintendo's *The Legend of Zelda* series. Eager to create an epic artistic hit, Kamiya poured a large amount of Clover's time and resources into *Okami*, and by the time the game was released, in April 2006, it had become Capcom's most expensive game to develop, going far beyond anything else the company had made up to that point. The game itself is long and expansive, requiring tens of hours to complete on the first try.

Reviews of *Okami* were very positive, reinforcing Kamiya's reputation as a creator of quality games. Unfortunately, *Okami* did not sell anywhere near enough copies to recoup Capcom's investment, with sales so underwhelming that one former Capcom employee in 2006 described *Okami* as having lost "a shit ton" of money. Kamiya had experienced setbacks before, particularly with *Resident Evil 1.5*, but the commercial bombing of *Okami* was an entirely different beast. Capcom's management was alarmed by its underperformance. Clover had been founded as a quasi-external studio in order for Capcom to retain its best talent without forcing them onto existing IP, but management now had serious questions about the viability of its investment.

Clover had one more game in the pipeline after *Okami*: Mikami's *God Hand*, a beat-'em-up action game for PlayStation 2. *God Hand* was essentially another *PN03*, being an action-focused game with little story, modest graphics and a high focus on gameplay. Released in September 2006, it had not been expensive to develop, but it saw low sales and divisive reviews.

After *God Hand*, Capcom had finally had enough. Seeing very little return on its investment in unique or original properties, the publisher decided to pull the plug on Clover Studio and close it down. Publicly, Capcom said the reason for the closure was for the company "to improve its overall development structure," implying that it had more to gain from integrating Clover back into Capcom proper rather than operating it as a separate entity. This was in fact true, to a certain extent; Capcom's management hoped that Clover's talent would to come back to the company's internal studios to work on existing IPs. However, for Mikami, this was the path he most desperately wanted to avoid; he saw no future for himself in working on more *Resident Evil* games. The others, including Kamiya, felt the same way. Their desire to pursue original content proved too great to give up, and thus Mikami, Kamiya, Inaba, Kato and a slew of others tendered their resignations, leaving Capcom behind. The legal process of shutting down Clover Studio was officially completed in March 2007, putting an end to a three-year venture that saw an exodus of talent from Capcom's orbit.

POST-CAPCOM: PLATINUMGAMES AND TANGO GAMEWORKS

With Clover Studio unceremoniously dissolved and its former talent resigned from Capcom and off on new ventures within the video game industry, Shinji Mikami, Atsushi Inaba and Hideki Kamiya formed a new company, Seeds Inc.. Meanwhile, Tatsuya Minami, the former producer at Production Studio 3, had left Capcom to found his own company, Odd Inc.. Additionally, Mikami had also created a company called Straight Story in order to allow himself to work independently as a game consultant.

Then, in 2007, Mikami, Kamiya, Inaba and Minami decided to merge Seeds and Odd to form Osaka-based PlatinumGames Inc., which would operate as an independent work-for-hire game developer focused on creating original, high-quality games on the level of the hits the founders had become known for. Minami would serve as the president of the company, with Kamiya as a game director and Inaba as a producer. Mikami opted to remain "special corporate officer," preferring to preserve his independence.

PlatinumGames would work with any publisher who could provide funding for new projects. The first major partnership was formed with Sega, with whom PlatinumGames would go on to develop a number of hit titles, including 2009's *Bayonetta*, a Kamiya-directed *Devil May Cry*-inspired hack-and-slash game. Mikami, although not an official PlatinumGames employee, would go on to direct *Vanquish*, a third-person shooter released in 2010. As of 2020, PlatinumGames continues to develop games for several publishers, including Nintendo and Square Enix.

Following the release of *Vanquish*, Mikami moved from Osaka to Tokyo, where he founded a new independent development studio, Tango K. K., along with twelve others who joined him. Mikami hoped that his new company would allow him to continue making innovative and original games, as well as raise an upcoming generation of young game creators. In most start-ups, the initial success and momentum of the company depends on its ability to secure funding. PlatinumGames had struck a deal early on with Sega, but Mikami faced more difficulty in getting Tango off the ground. Speaking to Polygon in 2014, Mikami conceded that Tango had experienced financial hardship not long after its founding. Fortunately for him, ZeniMax Media Inc., the parent company of prominent US game developer Bethesda Softworks, agreed to purchase Tango. "We were in trouble financially until Bethesda came along," Mikami told Polygon.[4] Tango K. K. was renamed Tango Gameworks, and thus became a subsidiary of ZeniMax. In a somewhat ironic twist, Mikami would go on to direct *The Evil Within* (*Psycho Break* in Japan), an original survival horror game reminiscent of *Resident Evil 4* and released in late 2014. Tango followed up with a sequel, *The Evil Within 2*, produced by Mikami and directed by American game designer John Johanas, another young creator whom Mikami sought to empower, just as he had done with Kamiya nearly two decades earlier. As of 2020, Mikami remains at Tango Gameworks, working on projects such as the action game *GhostWire: Tokyo*.

THE NEXT ERA
OF *RESIDENT EVIL*

The first twelve years of *Resident Evil*'s history, from 1994 to 2006, were a roller coaster ride for everyone involved. It all began when Tokuro Fujiwara refused to give up on his dream of bringing back *Sweet Home* and transforming horror games into their own genre. Capcom, which experienced financial turmoil in the mid-1990s, was on the brink of bankruptcy when *Resident Evil* launched on March 22, 1996, to strong reviews and higher-than-expected sales. The original game's success was made possible thanks to the efforts of its staff, including Fujiwara, Yoshiki Okamoto, Shinji Mikami, Hideki Kamiya, Hiroki Kato and Kazuhiro Aoyama. Each of these creators have since moved on to different opportunities for individual reasons, but their legacies are not forgotten, both in and outside of Capcom.

And this is where I would like to bring *Itchy, Tasty* to a close. The departure of the series' early creators, beginning in 2006, paved the way for the very different journey that *Resident Evil* would take over the next fourteen years. Capcom began this second period by riding the momentum it built with *Resident Evil 4*, releasing several successors on nearly every major console, to varying levels of critical and commercial success. New and familiar faces guided the franchise along as it encountered new challenges in a constantly evolving video-game market. And nearly a quarter of a century after the original *Resident Evil*, the series continues to shock and amuse gamers around the world.

The most satisfying feeling in carefully chronicling the first decade of *Resident Evil*'s history has come from all my interactions with the original developers. They were no longer just names in the game's ending credits or people who were interviewed on video game websites; they became *people* who meant something to me personally, even though we are not family or even friends. It has been a privilege to relive the experiences of the *Resident Evil* team, to hear how their passion (or indifference) has evolved over time. I want to thank them all for sharing their memories with me and with the rest of the *Resident Evil* community.

CATALOG OF GAMES

Original releases:

Resident Evil
Biohazard
Original release year: 1996
Platforms: PC, PlayStation, PlayStation Portable, Saturn
Director: Shinji Mikami
Producers: Tokuro Fujiwara, Yoshiki Okamoto

Resident Evil 2
Biohazard 2
Original release year: 1998
Platforms: Dreamcast, GameCube, Nintendo 64, PC,
PlayStation, PlayStation Portable
Director: Hideki Kamiya
Producer: Shinji Mikami

Resident Evil 3: Nemesis
Biohazard 3: Last Escape
Original release year: 1999
Platforms: GameCube, Dreamcast, PC, PlayStation,
PlayStation Portable
Director: Kazuhiro Aoyama
Producer: Shinji Mikami

Resident Evil: Survivor
Biohazard: Gun Survivor
Original release year: 2000
Platforms: PC, PlayStation
Director: Hiroyuki Kai
Producer: Tatsuya Minami

Resident Evil CODE: Veronica
Biohazard CODE: Veronica
Original release year: 2000
Platform: Dreamcast
Director: Hiroki Kato
Producer: Shinji Mikami

Resident Evil: Survivor 2 – CODE: Veronica
Gun Survivor 2: Biohazard – CODE: Veronica
Original release year: 2001
Platforms: Arcade, PlayStation 2
Directors: Tomoshi Sadamoto, Yasuhiro Seto
Producer: Tatsuya Minami

Resident Evil Gaiden
Biohazard Gaiden
Original release year: 2001
Platform: Game Boy Color
Designer: Tim Hull

Resident Evil
Biohazard
Original release year: 2002
Platforms: GameCube, Nintendo Switch, PC, PlayStation 3,
PlayStation 4, Wii, Xbox 360, Xbox One
Director: Shinji Mikami
Producer: Hiroyuki Kobayashi

Resident Evil Zero
Biohazard Zero
Original release year: 2002
Platforms: GameCube, Nintendo Switch, PC, PlayStation 3,
PlayStation 4, Wii, Xbox 360, Xbox One
Director: Koji Oda
Producer: Tatsuya Minami

Resident Evil: Dead Aim
Gun Survivor 4: Biohazard: Heroes Never Die
Original release year: 2003
Platform: PlayStation 2
Directors: Eiro Shirahama, Takuya Iwasaki
Producer: Tatsuya Minami

Resident Evil: Outbreak
Biohazard: Outbreak
Original Release Year: 2003
Platform: PlayStation 2
Director: Eiichiro Sasaki
Producers: Yoshihiro Sudou, Tsuyoshi Tanaka

Resident Evil: Outbreak: File #2
Biohazard Outbreak: File 2
Original release year: 2004
Platform: PlayStation 2
Director: Eiichiro Sasaki
Producer: Tsuyoshi Tanaka

Resident Evil 4
Biohazard 4
Original release year: 2005
Platforms: GameCube, Nintendo Switch, PC, PlayStation 2,
PlayStation 3, PlayStation 4, Xbox 360, Xbox One, Wii, Wii U
Director: Shinji Mikami
Producer: Hiroyuki Kobayashi

Re-releases:

Resident Evil: Director's Cut
Biohazard: Director's Cut
Original release year: 1997
Platforms: PlayStation, PlayStation Portable (Japan only)
Producer: Hiroyuki Kobayashi

Resident Evil: Director's Cut Dual Shock Ver.
Biohazard: Director's Cut Dual Shock Ver.
Original release year: 1998
Platforms: PlayStation, PlayStation Portable
Director: Kazuhiro Aoyama
Producer: Hiroyuki Kobayashi

Resident Evil 2: Dual Shock Ver.
Biohazard 2: Dual Shock Ver.
Original release year: 1998
Platform: PlayStation
Director: Kazuhiro Aoyama
Producer: Shinji Mikami

Resident Evil 2
Original release year: 1998
Platform: Tiger Game.com

Resident Evil CODE: Veronica X
Biohazard CODE: Veronica Kanzenban (Complete Edition)
Original release year: 2001
Platforms: Dreamcast, GameCube, PlayStation 2, PlayStation 3,
PlayStation 4, Xbox 360, Xbox One
Director: Hiroki Kato
Producer: Shinji Mikami

Resident Evil: Deadly Silence
Biohazard: Deadly Silence
Original release year: 2006
Platform: Nintendo DS
Director: Minoru Nakai
Producer: Minoru Nakai, Keiji Inafune

NOTES

Chapter 1

1   Scott Butterworth, "Resident Evil Creator Shinji Mikami Reflects on the Series'
     Roots," *GameSpot*, March 22, 2016, at https://www.gamespot.com/articles/
     resident-evil-creator-shinji-mikami-reflects-on-th/1100-6435918.
2   "The Making Of Resident Evil," *NowGamer*, May 10, 2010, at http://web.archive.
     org/web/20130205033720/http://www.nowgamer.com/features/895087/the_
     making_of_resident_evil.html.
3   Ayumi Saito, *Research on Biohazard 2 Final Edition*, Micro Design Publishing,
     Tokyo, 1998, p.148.
4   Butterworth, "Resident Evil Creator".
5   "The Making of Resident Evil", *NowGamer*.

Chapter 2

1   Hideki Kamiya: "'You're the dark horse of the new recruits. You're either going to
     fail spectacularly, or you're going to be a huge success,'" *Twitter*, January 24, 2018,
     at https://twitter.com/PG_kamiya.
2   Saito, *Research on Biohazard 2*, p. 148.
3   Matt Leone, "Shinji Mikami and the Fountain of Youth," *Polygon*, February 20,
     2014, at https://www.polygon.com/features/2014/2/20/5425802/shinji-mikami-the-
     evil-within.
4   "Resident Evil 2," *Metacritic*, at https://www.metacritic.com/game/playstation/
     resident-evil-2.
5   Matt Leone, "The President and Future of Platinum Games," *Polygon*, April 16,
     2013, at https://www.polygon.com/features/2013/4/16/4214960/tatsuya-minami-
     platinum-games.

Chapter 3

1   Damien McFerran, "Yasuhisa Kawamura and the Resident Evil That Never Was," *Eurogamer*, January 18, 2015, at https://www.eurogamer.net/articles/2015-01-18-inside-the-resident-evil-4-that-never-was.

2   Paul Birch, "Yasuhisa Kawamura Interview," *Project Umbrella*, at https://www.projectumbrella.net/articles/Yasuhisa-Kawamura-Interview-Project-Umbrella.

3   Ibid.

4   "Platinum Titles," *Capcom IR*, at http://www.capcom.co.jp/ir/english/finance/million.html.

5   "Resident Evil 3: Nemesis," *GameRankings*, at https://www.gamerankings.com/ps/198459-resident-evil-3-nemesis/index.html (link deactivated).

6   "Resident Evil: Apocalypse," *Box Office Mojo*, at https://www.boxofficemojo.com/movies/?id=residentevilapocalypse.htm.

Chapter 4

1   J. J. McCullough, "Nintendo's Era of Censorship," *Tanooki Site*, at https://jjmccullough.com/Nintendo.htm.

2   Rob Crossley, "Mortal Kombat: Violent Game That Changed Video Games Industry', *BBC*, June 2, 2014, at https://www.bbc.com/news/technology-27620071.

3   Roland Kelts, "The Unmasking of 'Japan's Beethoven'," *New Yorker*, May 2, 2014, at https://www.newyorker.com/culture/culture-desk/the-unmasking-of-japans-beethoven.

4   "Ghost Composer Takashi Niigaki Claims 'Japan's Beethoven' Mamoru Samuragochi Not Even Deaf," *ABC News*, February 6, 2014, at http://www.abc.net.au/news/2014-02-06/japans-beethoven-not-even-deaf-ghost-composer/5244282.

5   "Sony Computer Entertainment America Expands Extensive 'Greatest Hits' Software Library by Adding Three New Titles," *PlayStation*, September 10, 2003, at https://web.archive.org/web/20071012203154/http://www.us.playstation.com/News/PressReleases/127.

6   Richard Eisenbeis, "Why You Can't Rent Games in Japan," *Kotaku*, June 1, 2012, at https://kotaku.com/5914749/why-you-cant-rent-games-in-japan.

7   "Chuuko Geemu Sofuto Saiban wa Sorekara Dou Natta no ka (Go-hen – Saikousaibanketsu to Sono Go)," *Timesteps*, November 1, 2016, at https://timesteps.net/archives/usedgame02.html.

Chapter 5

1   "1997 Top 100," *Game Data Library* at https://sites.google.com/site/gamedatalibrary/games-by-year/1997-top-100.

2   *Project Umbrella*: "Director's Hazard," *YouTube*, July 26, 2013, at https://www.youtube.com/watch?v=ID3tBEDfeeo.

3   Hideki Kamiya: "Yeah. Too many zombies. RT @theredlotus: Was the 3D object handling the reason why RE2 never made it to Sega Saturn? I heard other devs talking about how difficult it was to program for the console," *Twitter*, January 26, 2018, at https://twitter.com/PG_kamiya.

4   Stephanie Strom, "Sega Enterprises Pulls Its Saturn Video Console From the US Market," *New York Times*, March 14, 1998, at https://www.nytimes.com/1998/03/14/business/international-business-sega-enterprises-pulls-its-saturn-video-console-us-market.html.

5   Dave Ragals, "Sega Unveils New Dreamcast Game Console," *CNN*, May 12, 1998, at https://edition.cnn.com/TECH/computing/9805/21/sega_dreamcast.

6   "Resident Evil Code: Veronica," *GameRankings*, at https://www.gamerankings.com/dreamcast/250618-resident-evil-code-veronica/index.html (link deactivated).

7   Leone, 'Shinji Mikami'.

Chapter 6

1   *IGN* Staff, "HotGen Tells Us It's Incredible!" *IGN*, January 6, 2000, at https://uk.ign.com/articles/2000/01/06/hotgen-tells-us-its-incredible.

2   *IGN* Staff, "Capcom's 2000 Releases," *IGN*, June 18, 2012, at https://uk.ign.com/articles/1999/12/15/capcoms-2000-releases.

3   *IGN* Staff, "Resident Evil Passes On," *IGN*, March 23, 2000, at https://www.ign.com/articles/2000/03/23/resident-evil-passes-on.

4   Matt Gander, "The Resident Evil That Never Was," *Games Asylum*, October 26, 2014, at https://www.gamesasylum.com/2014/10/26/the-resident-evil-that-never-was/.

5   "Retro: The Making of Resident Evil: Gaiden," *NowGamer*, June 27, 2011, at https://web.archive.org/web/20160306003515/http://www.nowgamer.com/retro-the-making-of-resident-evil-gaiden/.

Chapter 7

1   Matt Leone, "The Secret Developers of the Video Game Industry," *Polygon*, September 30, 2015, at https://www.polygon.com/2015/9/30/9394355/the-secret-developers-of-the-video-game-industry.

2   MrRetroGreg: "Japanese TV Commercials [1154] Biohazard Gun Survivor Baiohazzado Gan Sabaibaa," *YouTube*, October 15, 2016, at https://www.youtube.com/watch?v=cQFXRiYwhL4.

3   Jon Katz, "Voices from the Hellmouth," *Slashdot*, April 26, 1999, at https://news.slashdot.org/story/99/04/25/1438249/voices-from-the-hellmouth.

4   "2001 Weekly," *Game Data Library*, at https://sites.google.com/site/gamedatalibrary/games-by-year/2001-weekly.

5   Ryan Davis, "Resident Evil: Dead Aim Review," *GameSpot*, June 16, 2003, at https://www.gamespot.com/reviews/resident-evil-dead-aim-review/1900-6030112/s.

Chapter 8

1   "'Dengeki PS 20-shuunen' Sukuea ga 'FFVII' wo Hissagete PS ni Sannyuu Gyoukai ga Souzen to natte Ano Toki (1995/10-1996/3)," *Dengeki PlayStation*, June 18, 2014, at http://dengekionline.com/elem/000/000/862/862783.

2   "PlayStation," *Game Data Library*, at https://sites.google.com/site/gamedatalibrary/hardware-by-platform/playstation via Game Data Library.

3   IGN Staff, "Interview with Capcom Japan's Yoshiki Okamoto," *IGN*, May 29, 1997, at https://www.ign.com/articles/1997/05/29/interview-with-capcom-japans-yoshiki-okamoto.

4   *IGN* Staff, "N64 Enters the World of Survival Horror," *IGN*, January 8, 1999, at https://www.ign.com/articles/1999/01/08/n64-enters-the-world-of-survival-horror.

5   John Linneman, "DF Retro: Why Resident Evil 2 on N64 is One of the Most Ambitious Console Ports of All Time," *Eurogamer*, December 9, 2018, at https://www.eurogamer.net/articles/digitalfoundry-2018-retro-why-resident-evil-2-n64-is-one-of-the-most-ambitious-ports-of-all-time.

6   Todd Meynink, "Postmortem: Angel Studios' Resident Evil 2 (N64 Version)," *Gamasutra*, July 28, 2000, at https://www.gamasutra.com/view/feature/131556.

7   "Interview: Capcom chief lifts Resident Evil 0 lid," *CVG*, 30 August 2002, at https://www.webcitation.org/5ybfDs1rG.

8   Godzilla Ota, "'Baiohazaado o HD Rimasutaa' Intaabyuu Kanzenban 13-nenmae no Omoide ya, HD Rimasutaa-ban nara dewa no Omoide wo Kiku (1/2)," *Famitsu*, September 16, 2015, at https://www.famitsu.com/news/201509/16087589.html.

9   Capcom: "Resident Evil 0 – Developer Diary 2," *YouTube*, October 29, 2015, at https://www.youtube.com/watch?v=reRhy1WnUpQ.

10 *IGN* Staff, "N64 Enters the World of Survival Horror," *IGN*, June 22, 2012, at http://uk.ign.com/articles/1999/01/08/n64-enters-the-world-of-survival-horror.

11 "Baiohazaado Shiriizu ga Geemukyuubu dokusen kyoukyuu! Umi no oya de aru Kapukon – Mikami Shinji shi ga sono ito wo kataru!," *Dengeki Online*, September 2001, at https://dengekionline.com/soft/recommend/rec_mikami.html.

12 Wesley Yin-Poole, "Why Xbox Failed in Japan," *Eurogamer*, November 17, 2013, at https://www.eurogamer.net/articles/2012-12-13-why-xbox-failed-in-japan.

13 Ibid.

14 Ibid.

15 Hideaki Motozuka, "Meikingu," *Capcom Japan*, April 2002, at http://web.archive.org/web/20020611184435/http://www.capcom.co.jp/bio/making.

16 Matt Cassmassina, "Resident Evil (2002)," April 26, 2002, *IGN* at https://www.ign.com/articles/2002/04/26/resident-evil-3.

17 "Interview: Capcom Chief Lifts Resident Evil 0 lid," August 30, 2002, *CVG* at https://www.webcitation.org/5ybfDs1rG.

18 Matt Casamassina, "Resident Evil 0," November 11, 2002, *IGN* at https://www.ign.com/articles/2002/11/11/resident-evil-0.

Chapter 9

1   Tom Bramwell, "Resident Evil Outbreak Offline in Europe," March 29, 2004, *Eurogamer* at http://www.eurogamer.net/articles/news260304resieviloutbreak.

2   "2004 Top 500," *Game Data Library*, at https://sites.google.com/site/gamedatalibrary/games-by-year/2004-top500.

3   Ibid.

Chapter 10

1   Doug Perry, "Devil May Cry," *IGN*, October 16, 2001, at https://www.ign.com/articles/2001/10/16/devil-may-cry.

2   "10. Shinario no Hanashi," *Capcom Japan*, April 2002, at https://web.archive.org/web/20100306002121/http://www.capcom.co.jp/devil/column/vol010.html.

3   Ibid.

4   Doug Perry, "Resident Evil Series to Haunt PlayStation 2," *IGN*, December 4, 1999, at https://www.ign.com/articles/1999/12/04/resident-evil-series-to-haunt-playstation-2.

5   "Kapukon GC Shinsaku Happyoukai de, Kaku Taitoru no Direkutaa ga Sorezore Geemu Naiyou wo Shoukai," *Dengeki Online*, November 14, 2002, at https://dengekionline.com/data/news/2002/11/14/25bd4cb3a478b74c6badb3eb9356f952.html.

6   "Kapukon no Mikami Shinji-shi ga Jishinsaku wo Zokuzoku Happyou! (Kapukon Geemukyuubu Shinsaku Happyoukai Ripooto)," *Famitsu*, November 14, 2002, at https://www.famitsu.com/game/news/1137831_1124.html.

7   Birch, "Kawamura Interview".

8   Damien McFerran, "Yasuhisa Kawamura and the Resident Evil that never was," *Eurogamer*, January 18, 2015, at https://www.eurogamer.net/articles/2015-01-18-inside-the-resident-evil-4-that-never-was.

9   Birch, "Kawamura Interview".

10 *IGN* Staff, "The Most Anticipated Games of 2004," *IGN*, January 23, 2004, at https://www.ign.com/articles/2004/01/23/the-most-anticipated-games-of-2004.

11 *IGN* Staff, "Big Things for Resident Evil," *IGN*, January 20, 2004, at https://www.ign.com/articles/2004/01/20/big-things-for-resident-evil.

12 Andy McNamara, "And Then There Were Two…," *Game Informer*, March 2004.

13 Ibid.

14 *IGN* Staff, "E3 2004: Resident Evil 4," *IGN*, May 12, 2004, at https://www.ign.com/articles/2004/05/12/e3-2004-resident-evil-4.

15 Mega64, "Mega64: Resident Evil 4," *YouTube*, June 11, 2006, at https://www.youtube.com/watch?v=70Xx0qweowc.

16 Matt Casamassina, "Resident Evil 4," *IGN*, January 7, 2005, at https://www.ign.com/articles/2005/01/07/resident-evil-4-7.

17 Greg Kasavin, "Resident Evil 4 Review," *GameSpot*, January 10, 2005, at https://www.gamespot.com/reviews/resident-evil-4-review/1900-6115968/.

18 "Resident Evil 4," *Nintendo Power*, March 2005, retrieved from "Resident Evil 4," *Metacritic* at https://www.metacritic.com/game/gamecube/resident-evil-4/critic-reviews.

19 "Resident Evil 4," *Edge Magazine*, March 2005, retrieved from "Resident Evil 4," *Metacritic* at https://www.metacritic.com/publication/edge-magazine.

20 Tor Thorsen, "ChartSpot: February 2005," *GameSpot*, March 29, 2005, at https://www.gamespot.com/articles/chartspot-february-2005/1100-6120823/.

21 "Mikami Shinji x Minami Tatsuya," *Hyper Capcom Special 2002 Summer*, July 15, 2002.

22 Anoop Gantayat, "Mikami Alive and Well," *IGN*, April 5, 2017, at https://www.ign.com/articles/2007/04/05/mikami-alive-and-well.

23 "Top 10 Weekly Software Sales (November 28–December 4, 2005)," *Media Create*, at http://web.archive.org/web/20051212045944/http://m-create.com/eng/e_ranking.html.

Chapter 11

1 Greg Kasavin, "Resident Evil: Deadly Silence Review," *GameSpot*, June 25, 2007, at https://www.gamespot.com/reviews/resident-evil-deadly-silence-review/1900-6143721/.

2 Jon Wahlgren, "Resident Evil: Deadly Silence (DS)," *Nintendo Life*, March 10, 2010, at https://www.nintendolife.com/games/ds/resident_evil_deadly_silence.

3 J. C. Fletcher, "Shinji Mikami Talks About His Life Before Games and After Capcom," *Engadget*, November 11, 2010, at https://www.engadget.com/2010-11-11-shinji-mikami-talks-about-his-life-before-games-and-after-capcom.html.

4 Leone, 'Shinji Mikami'.

SOURCES

Anonymous, "10. Shinario no Hanashi," *Capcom Japan*, April 2002, at https://web.archive.org/web/20100306002121/http://www.capcom.co.jp/devil/column/vol010.html

Anonymous, "1997 Top 100," *Enterbrain* at https://sites.google.com/site/gamedatalibrary/games-by-year/1997-top-100 via Game Data Library.

Anonymous, "2001 Weekly," *Enterbrain* at https://sites.google.com/site/gamedatalibrary/games-by-year/2001-weekly via Game Data Library.

Anonymous, "2004 Top 500," *Enterbrain* at https://sites.google.com/site/gamedatalibrary/games-by-year/2004-top500 via Game Data Library.

Anonymous, "Baiohazaado Shiriizu ga Geemukyuubu dokusen kyoukyuu! Umi no oya de aru Kapukon – Mikami Shinji shi ga sono ito wo kataru!," *Dengeki Online*, September 2001, at https://dengekionline.com/soft/recommend/rec_mikami.html

Anonymous, "Chuuko Geemu Sofuto Saiban wa Sorekara Dou Natta no ka (Go-hen – Saikousaibanketsu to Sono Go)," *Timesteps*, November 1, 2006, at https://timesteps.net/archives/usedgame02.html

Anonymous, "'Dengeki PS 20-shuunen' Sukuea ga 'FFVII' wo Hissagete PS ni Sannyuu Gyoukai ga Souzen to natte Ano Toki (1995/10-1996/3)," *Dengeki PlayStation*, June 18, 2014, at http://dengekionline.com/elem/000/000/862/862783

Anonymous, "Kapukon GC Shinsaku Happyoukai de, Kaku Taitoru no Direkutaa ga Sorezore Geemu Naiyou wo Shoukai," *Dengeki Online*, November 14, 2002, at https://dengekionline.com/data/news/2002/11/14/25bd4cb3a478b74c6badb3eb9356f952.html

Anonymous, "Kapukon no Mikami Shinji-shi ga Jishinsaku wo Zokuzoku Happyou! (Kapukon Geemukyuubu Shinsaku Happyoukai Ripooto)," *Famitsu*, November 14, 2002, at https://www.famitsu.com/game/news/1137831_1124.html

Anonymous, "Interview: Capcom chief lifts Resident Evil 0 lid," *CVG* at https://www.webcitation.org/5ybfDs1rG

Anonymous, "Mikami Shinji x Minami Tatsuya," *Hyper Capcom Special 2002 Summer*, July 2002

Anonymous, "Platinum Titles," *Capcom IR* at https://www. capcom.co.jp/ir/english/finance/million.html

Anonymous, "PlayStation," *Enterbrain* at https://sites.google.com/ site/gamedatalibrary/hardware-by-platform/playstation via Game Data Library

Anonymous, "Resident Evil 2," *Metacritic* at https://www. metacritic.com/game/playstation/resident-evil-2

Anonymous, "Resident Evil 3: Nemesis," *GameRankings* at https:// www.gamerankings.com/ps/198459-resident-evil-3-nemesis/index. html (link deactivated)

Anonymous, "Resident Evil 4," *Edge Magazine*, March 2005, retrieved from "Resident Evil 4," *Metacritic* at https://www. metacritic.com/publication/edge-magazine

Anonymous, "Resident Evil 4," *Nintendo Power*, March 2005, retrieved from "Resident Evil 4," *Metacritic* at https://www. metacritic.com/game/gamecube/resident-evil-4/critic-reviews

Anonymous, "Resident Evil: Apocalypse," *Box Office Mojo* at https:// www.boxofficemojo.com/movies/?id=residentevilapocalypse.htm

Anonymous, "Resident Evil CODE: Veronica," *GameRankings* at https://www.gamerankings.com/dreamcast/250618-resident-evil-code-veronica/index.html (link deactivated)

Anonymous, "Retro: The Making of Resident Evil: Gaiden," *NowGamer*, June 27, 2011, at https://web.archive.org/web/20160306003515/http://www.nowgamer.com/retro-the-making-of-resident-evil-gaiden/

Anonymous, "Sony Computer Entertainment America Expands Extensive 'Greatest Hits' Software Library by Adding Three New Titles," *PlayStation*, September 10, 2003, at https://web.archive.org/web/20071012203154/http://www.us.playstation.com/News/PressReleases/127

Anonymous, "Takashi Niigaki Claims 'Japan's Beethoven' Mamoru Samuragochi Not Even Deaf," *ABC News*, February 6, 2014, at http://www.abc.net.au/news/2014-02-06/japans-beethovennot-even-deaf-ghost-composer/5244282

Anonymous, "The Making Of Resident Evil," *NowGamer*, May 10, 2010, at http://web.archive.org/web/20130205033720/http://www.nowgamer.com/features/895087/the_making_of_resident_evil.html

Anonymous, "Top 10 Weekly Software Sales (November 28–December 4, 2005)," *Media Create* at http://web.archive.org/web/20051212045944/http://m-create.com/eng/e_ranking.html

Birch, Paul, "Yasuhisa Kawamura Interview (Project Umbrella)," *Project Umbrella* at https://www.projectumbrella.net/articles/Yasuhisa-Kawamura-Interview-Project-Umbrella

Bramwell, Tom, "Resident Evil Outbreak Offline in Europe," *Eurogamer*, March 29, 2004, at http://www.eurogamer.net/articles/news260304resieviloutbreak

Butterworth, Scott, "Resident Evil Creator Shinji Mikami Reflects on the Series' Roots," *GameSpot*, March 22, 2016, at https://www.gamespot.com/articles/resident-evil-creator-shinji-mikami-reflects-on-th/1100-6435918

Capcom: "Resident Evil 0 – Developer Diary 2," *YouTube*, October 29, 2015, at https://www.youtube.com/watch?v=reRhyIWnUpQ

Casamassina, Matt, "Resident Evil (2002)," *IGN*, April 26, 2002, at https://www.ign.com/articles/2002/04/26/resident-evil-3

— "Resident Evil 0," *IGN*, November 11, 2002, at https://www.ign.com/articles/2002/11/11/resident-evil-0

—, "Resident Evil 4," *IGN*, January 7, 2005, at https://www.ign.com/articles/2005/01/07/resident-evil-4-7

Crossley, Rob, "Mortal Kombat: Violent Game That Changed Video Games Industry,' *BBC*, June 2, 2014, at https://www.bbc.com/news/technology-27620071

Davis, Ryan, "Resident Evil: Dead Aim Review,' *GameSpot*, June 16, 2003, at https://www.gamespot.com/reviews/resident-evil-dead-aim-review/1900-6030112/s

Eisenbeis, Richard, "Why You Can't Rent Games in Japan," *Kotaku*, June 1, 2012, at https://kotaku.com/5914749/why-you-cant-rent-games-in-japan

Fletcher, J. C., "Shinji Mikami Talks About His Life Before Games and After Capcom," *Engadget*, November 11, 2010, at https://www.engadget.com/2010-11-11-shinji-mikami-talks-about-his-life-before-games-and-after-capcom.html

Gander, Matt, "The Resident Evil That Never Was," *Games Asylum*, October 26, 2014, at https://www.gamesasylum.com/2014/10/26/the-resident-evil-that-never-was/

Gantayat, Anoop, "Mikami Alive and Well," *IGN*, April 5, 2017, at https://www.ign.com/articles/2007/04/05/mikami-alive-and-well
IGN Staff, "Big Things for Resident Evil," *IGN*, January 20, 2004, at https://www.ign.com/articles/2004/01/20/big-things-for-resident-evil

—, "Capcom's 2000 Releases," *IGN*, June 18, 2012, at https://uk.ign.com/articles/1999/12/15/capcoms-2000-releases

—, "E3 2004: Resident Evil 4," *IGN*, May 12, 2004, at https://www.ign.com/articles/2004/05/12/e3-2004-resident-evil-4

—, "HotGen Tells Us It's Incredible!" *IGN*, January 6, 2000, at https://uk.ign.com/articles/2000/01/06/hotgen-tells-us-its-incredible

—, "N64 Enters the World of Survival Horror," *IGN*, January 8, 1999, at https://www.ign.com/articles/1999/01/08/n64-enters-the-world-of-survival-horror

—, "Resident Evil Passes On," *IGN*, March 23, 2000, https://www.ign.com/articles/2000/03/23/resident-evil-passes-on

—, "The Most Anticipated Games of 2004," *IGN*, January 23, 2004, at https://www.ign.com/articles/2004/01/23/the-most-anticipated-games-of-2004

IGN Staff, "Interview with Capcom Japan's Yoshiki Okamoto," *IGN*, May 29, 1997, at https://www.ign.com/articles/1997/05/29/interview-with-capcom-japans-yoshiki-okamoto

Kasavin, Greg, "Resident Evil 4 Review," *GameSpot*, January 10, 2005, at https://www.gamespot.com/reviews/resident-evil-4-review/1900-6115968/

—, "Resident Evil: Deadly Silence Review," *GameSpot*, June 25, 2007, at https://www.gamespot.com/reviews/resident-evil-deadly-silence-review/1900-6143721/

Katz, Jon, "Voice from the Hellmouth," at https://news.slashdot.org/story/99/04/25/1438249/voices-from-the-hellmouth

Kelts, Roland, "The Unmasking of 'Japan's Beethoven'," *New Yorker*, May 2, 2014, at https://www.newyorker.com/culture/culture-desk/the-unmasking-of-japans-beethoven

Leone, Matt, "Shinji Mikami and the Fountain of Youth," *Polygon*, February 20, 2014, at https://www.polygon.com/features/2014/2/20/5425802/shinji-mikami-the-evil-within

—, "The President and Future of Platinum Games," *Polygon*, April 16, 2016, at https://www.polygon.com/features/2013/4/16/4214960/tatsuya-minami-platinum-games

—, "The Secret Developers of the Game Industry," *Polygon*, September 30, 2015, at https://www.polygon.com/2015/9/30/9394355/the-secret-developers-of-the-video-game-industry

Linneman, John, "DF Retro: Why Resident Evil 2 on N64 is One of the Most Ambitious Console Ports of All Time," *Eurogamer*, December 9, 2018, at https://www.eurogamer.net/articles/digitalfoundry-2018-retro-why-resident-evil-2-n64-is-one-of-the-most-ambitious-ports-of-all-time

McCullough, J. J., "Nintendo's Era of Censorship," *Tanooki Site* at https://www.tanookisite.com/nintendo-censorship/

Mega64: "Mega64: Resident Evil 4," *YouTube*, June 11, 2006, at https://www.youtube.com/watch?v=70Xx0qwe0wc

Meynink, Todd, "Postmortem: Angel Studios' Resident Evil 2 (N64 Version)," *Gamasutra*, January 28, 2000, at https://www.gamasutra.com/view/feature/131556

McFerran, Damien, "Yasuhisa Kawamura and the Resident Evil that never was," *Eurogamer*, January 18, 2015, at https://www.eurogamer.net/articles/2015-01-18-inside-the-resident-evil-4-that-never-was

McNamara, Andy, "And Then There Were Two...," *Game Informer*, March 2004

Motozuka, Hideaki, "Meikingu," *Capcom Japan*, April 2002, at http://web.archive.org/web/20020611184435/http://www.capcom.co.jp/bio/making

MrRetroGreg: "Japanese TV Commercials [1154] Biohazard Gun Survivor Baiohazzado Gan Sabaibaa," *YouTube*, October 15, 2016, at https://www.youtube.com/watch?v=cQFXRiYwhL4

Ota, Godzilla, "'Baiohazaado o HD Rimasutaa' Intaabyuu Kanzenban 13-nenmae no Omoide ya, HD Rimasutaa-ban nara dewa no Omoide wo Kiku (1/2)," *Famitsu*, September 16, 2015, at https://www.famitsu.com/news/201509/16087589.html
Perry, Doug, "Devil May Cry," *IGN*, October 16, 2001, at https://www.ign.com/articles/2001/10/16/devil-may-cry

—, "Resident Evil Series to Haunt PlayStation 2," *IGN*, December 4, 1999, at https://www.ign.com/articles/1999/12/04/resident-evil-series-to-haunt-playstation-2

Project Umbrella: "Director's Hazard," *YouTube*, July 26, 2013, at https://www.youtube.com/watch?v=ID3tBEDfeeo

Ragals, Dave, 'Sega Unveils New Dreamcast Game Console," *CNN*, May 12, 1998, at https://edition.cnn.com/TECH/computing/9805/21/sega_dreamcast

Saito, Ayumi, *Research on Biohazard 2 Final Edition*, Micro Design Publishing, Tokyo, 1998

Strom, Stephanie, "Sega Enterprises Pulls Its Saturn Video Console From the US Market," *New York Times*, March 14, 1998, at https://www.nytimes.com/1998/03/14/business/international-business-sega-enterprises-pulls-its-saturn-video-console-us-market.html

Thorsen, Tor, "ChartSpot: February 2005," *GameSpot*, March 19, 2005, at https://www.gamespot.com/articles/chartspot-february-2005/1100-6120823/

Wahlgren, Jon, "Resident Evil: Deadly Silence (DS)," *Nintendo Life*, March 10, 2010, at https://www.nintendolife.com/games/ds/resident_evil_deadly_silence

Yin-Poole, Wesley, "Why Xbox Failed in Japan," *Eurogamer*, November 17, 2013, at https://www.eurogamer.net/articles/2012-12-13-why-xbox-failed-in-japan

ACKNOWLEDGMENTS

This book would never have been possible if it were not for dozens of people who were only too eager to help me make it a reality.

First off, I would like to thank all the past and present *Resident Evil* staff who spoke to me and helped me assemble the rich narratives that have never been told before. A big thank you to Tokuro Fujiwara (Whoopee Camp), Yoshiki Okamoto (Mixi), Noritaka Funamizu (Indigo Games), Shinji Mikami (ZeniMax Asia K. K.), Hideki Kamiya (PlatinumGames), Kazuhiro Aoyama, Hiroki Kato, and Kenichi Iwao for sharing their memories and opening up such personal experiences to me. I also want to extend my gratitude to other staff interviewed for this book, including Lynn Harris and Barry Gjerde.

A special shout-out goes to the people who helped me get in touch with the above game creators: Jean-Pierre Kellams, Manami Matsumae, Joel Welsh, Andrew Brasher, Akira Kusaka, Shinsaku Ohara (ZeniMax Asia K. K.), Heidi Kemps, Noritaka Funamizu, and all my friends at Capcom.

Special thanks to Steph Prader for encouraging me to make this project happen and for sending me the *Resident Evil*-themed notebook used to take memos during every interview, my business partner Mohammed Taher (Brave Wave Productions) for his never-ending support and amazing photo-editing skills, John Linneman (Digital Foundry) for his technical expertise and Jeremy Parish (Retronauts) for advice on how to write a book. An extra-special thanks goes to Matt Leone at Polygon for hosting an excerpt of this book online in January 2019, and for his invaluable editing advice. Christine Bagarino, Tariq Lacy and Sam Byford were also vital in providing advice, and their contributions have been invaluable.

I also extend my eternal gratitude to fellow *Resident Evil* fans. This book is for you, first and foremost. Thanks to George Melita, Rodrigo Navarrete Boettcher, Rob McGregor, Shahan Garabet, Anders Leirvik, CarcinogenSDA, The Sphere Hunter, Tomáš Gažar, Juan Flores, Gabriel Camara, Paul Birch, Paul Freshwater and Luiz Brehm for their valuable advice, support and information.

And then there are the wonderful, wonderful people at Unbound, the crowdfunding publisher of the English version of this book. Mathew Clayton was instrumental in getting the crowdfunding campaign off the ground, while Ilona Chavasse and Gregory Souza offered valuable support. I also offer tremendous thanks to Hayley Shepherd and Alex Newby for their editing and invaluable attention to detail, and to Alexander Eccles for his input on the final text.

For visuals, I want to extend my gratitude to Cory Schmitz for his cover design, created in cooperation with Unbound's art director Mark Ecob, using the zombie illustrated by the immensely talented

Manuel Perez. The chapter icons were created by Dan Clarke of Arkotype as a gift that I can never hope to repay.

Special thanks go to Angie Madonna David and all my colleagues at Limited Run Games.

I would like to send the greatest thanks to the 1,007 people who helped bring this book to life from October 2019 through October 2020 by becoming a supporter on the Unbound website. Without your contribution, this book could not have happened, and for that I am eternally grateful.

And the ultimate thanks go to everyone at Capcom, past and present, for creating the *Resident Evil* franchise that millions of gamers have loved for a quarter of a century.

INDEX

Unbound is the world's first crowdfunding publisher, established in 2011.

We believe that wonderful things can happen when you clear a path for people who share a passion. That's why we've built a platform that brings together readers and authors to crowdfund books they believe in – and give fresh ideas that don't fit the traditional mould the chance they deserve.

This book is in your hands because readers made it possible. Everyone who pledged their support is listed below. Join them by visiting unbound.com and supporting a book today.

Asroyiel
Nathan Atherton
Jonathan Attfield
Sarah Aubin
Andrew Averyt
Ntinos Avo
Andrew Axon
James B
Ron Babb
Charles Babcock
Eb Ball
Jason Ballinger
Richard Barchanowicz
Christian Bardenhagen
Mike Bareham
Andrew Barreiro
Chris Bass
Richard Batten
Sonny Bauer
Gregor Beck
Johnny Beck
Dan Beckett
Beefsound
Beggy BeggBegg
George Bell
Jared Bell
Francisco Beltran (RESH)
Keaton Benfield
Aaron Bennett
Laszlo Benyi
Peter Berkman
Cory Bevilacqua
Neville Bezzina
Kimberly Biedka
Edward Biglin IV
Bradley Biglin Jr
Paul Birch
Thomas Birchall
David A Birkhead
Nickolaus Black
Max Blair
Philipp Block

Jeremy Blum
Jake Blunt
Liam Bolton
Davie Bones
Gareth Bowen
Dr. Tim Bowes
David Boycott
Gervaise Branch-Allen
Andrew Brasher
Alex Breen
Luiz Brehm
Jake Brew
Hugh Briant
Samuel Briffaut
Mike Brignall
Adam Britt
Chris Brodeck
Brittney Brombacher
Blake Brown
Chris Brown
Ryan Brown
Matt Brumit
David Bryan
BSAArklay
Heath Bsharah
Craig Bucknall
Cason J. Budder
Boris Buegling
Christian Bugs
John Bull
April Bunnell
Luke Burden
Nabeel Hasan Burney
Chris Burns
John J Burns
Jordan Busch
David Butt
Sam Byford
Mauricio Calderón Arias
Pamela Calixto
Noah Callard
Whitney Callari

Gabriel Camara
Adam Cammack
Nicholas Camp
Mikala Carr
Thomas Carr
Sergio M. Carreto
Ade Carter
Carter
Garry Casey
Jose Casillas
Bob Cassella
Kiel Cassidy
Ronell Casteel
John Adam Caston
Edgar Castro
Darin Cavallero
Cass Cayton
Mert-Can Celik
Luke Cenkus
Christopher D. Ceron
Michael Andrew Chadwick
Noel Chamberlain
Matthew Chambers
Lik Chan
Lucas Cheuk Man Chan
Adam Chandler
ChaoticClaire
Whitney Chavis
Caibin Chen
Lester Chen
Justin Cheng
Charle Cherry
Nick Chester
David Cheung
Alexander James Chhaya
Colton Childers
Douglas Chin
Dorian Chou
Keegan Chua
Anthony Cicanese
Gino Cioffi
Tom Clancy
Brian Clark

Dan Clarke
Darren Clarke
Simon Clarke
Adam Clarkson
Arthur Clarkson
Jack Claxton
Joel Clements
Alex Cliff
Dio Cobian
Daniel Codd
Billy Coen
Sam Coleman
Simon Coleman
Jackie Angelina Conill
Kevin Connell
Drew Cook
Mathew Copeland
April Corbet
James Corker
Valerio Cosentino Trento
Louis Costanzo
Joseph Coughlan
Richard Court
Richard Cowan
Kevin Cristol
Dennis Cronan
Victor Cruz
Erick CT
James Curran
Christopher Curry
Dean Cuthbert
Lewis Czugalinski
Chris D
Peter Dafnous
Dia Darko
Julien Davau
Jon Davies
Robin Davies
Jeffrey Davis
Adam Dawson
Tanner James Day
Ruben De Jesus
Nicholas De Leon

Andrew DeCrescenzo
Felipe Demartini
Gurvir Singh Deol
Mats Deslongchamps
Tom Deterling
Mark Devaney & Lucy Holton
Tara Devlin
Daniel Devora
David Diaz
Ava Dickerson
Andrew J Dickinson
Doug Dickinson
Eric DiGiovanni
Bradley Dimmock
Patrick Dingle
Dino Crisis
Brent Disbrow
Niamh Dixon
Bimandra Djaafara
Matthew Dobrzynski
Zane Doherty
Ernest Doku
Jeremy Dove
Steven Dowdle
Jonathon Doyle
Sam Drew
Joe Drilling
Taylor Dull
Carl Dungca
Jasmine Edwards
John-Carlos Eire
Adam El Araby
Dalia El-azzeh
Jack Ellis
Scott Elrick
Elyani
Stephen Ennis
Ricky Enriquez
Dolgan Erendzhenov
Chris Erickson
James Ervin
Matthew Espejo
Adam Evanko

Jacob Evans
John Evans
Joshua Evans
Julian Evans
Ross Evans
Colin Evo
Andrew Fahmi
Lorenzo Fantoni
Kristin Farina
Andrew Farrar
Blair Farrell
Charles Faubert
Ed Fear
Alvaro Fernandez
Tristan D. Fernandez
André Ricardo N. Ferreira
Matt Ficeto
Antonio Fierro
Travis Fike
Quentin Fillou
Andre Finger
David Firth
Sean Fish
Andrew Fisher
Mark Flanagan
Bryan "Ambitious Dreg" Fletcher
Zachary Flurer
Matt Fowler
Rob Fox
Connor Francis
Matthew Francis
Kirsteen Fraser
Neill Freer
Stephen French
Dan Fretwell
Clayton Freund
Alexandra Fridmundardottir
Dennis Fuchs
Tokuro Fujiwara
Isamu Fukui
Noritaka Funamizu
Jamie Galea
Bob Galjaard

Shahan Garabet
Michael Gargano
Austin Blake Garner
Jonathon Garrard
Jim Garretson
Cal Garrioch
Miguel Garza
Caleb Gauss
Tomáš Gažar
James Geary
Johan Geerts
Gegz
Chris Geiles
Jason Gentekis
Oliver Gerlach
Robert Getz
Domenic Giandomenico III
Peter Gibson
TJ Gibson
Oren Giladi
Craig Gilmore
David Giza
Linnea Glas
David Goldsmith
Mark Gomez
Yannick Gomez
Eduardo Gonzalez Garcia
Russ & Mo Good
Craig Gordon
Adam Gorman
Keelan Grace
Gavin Graf
Raywat Grajangduang
Steinar Granmo
Pablo Grattoni
Gavin Greene
Nathan Greenwood
Stephen Greenwood
Jeremy Griffiths
Lloyd Griffiths
Kevin Groll
Stian Grønås
Ryan Grove

Christopher Grunert Pedersen
Dean Guadagno
Christopher Guen
Marc Guerra
James Gwinnell
Matthew Gyure
Riku Haapalainen
Emrah Hacikerimoglu
James Hadley
Norman Häfer
Jarlath Hagan
Sean '[STARS]TyranT' Hall
Justin Halloran
Jozef Hamilton
Emil Hammar
Derek Hammeke
Simon Hammonds
Graeme Hanks
Kaydie Hansen
Timo Harbart
Allison Harris
Jaime Harrison
Phil Harrison
Stefan Harrison
Tomi Hartikainen
Michael Hartnagel
Hayley Harwood
Nicholas Hash
Ali Hashemi
Miguel Hasson
Rissie Havrilla
Jennifer Hawkins
Matthew Haywood
Julian Hazeldine
Andrew Hazlegrove
Julien Hébert
Brittany Heidler
Maick Hendrick
Rito Hendrix
Seth Henriksen
Dana Henry
Joel Hernandez
John Hesington

Eric Hesla
Rianti Hidayat
Adam Hill
Jennifer Hill
James Hine
Jacky Ho
Tan Hoang
Lucien Hoare
Natalie Hobson
Paul Hodgeson
Gregory Hogan
Scott Holcomb
William Holden
Spencer Holmes
Jonathan Holt
Steven Hopper
Zane Householder
Allister Howe
Frank Howley
HowTinDog
Tim Huang
Robert Hudok III
Adam Humphreys
Jonathan Hunsley
Nathaniel James Huston
Nathan Hymas
Henrik Hynninen
i'm man
Stefan Ignacio
Ik
Donald Illoh
Neil Irvine
Isis
Robert Iwataki
Scott Izynski
James Jackson
Alexander James
Koos "Koosjuh" Janse
Aaron Jarvis
David Jarvis
Miguel Jauregui
Mikey Jay
Andrew Jeffrey

Jim
Luis Jimenez
Adrián Jiménez Galán
Alberto JM
Peter Johansson
Stephen Johns
Cody Johnson
Daniel Johnson
Gregg Johnson
Oliver Jolley
Cody Jones
Emrys Jones
Greg Jones
Nicholas Jones
Fraser Jordan
Christopher Jungo
David Jupp
James Jursudakul
Leo K [Rogue]
Scott Kahlert
Hideki Kamiya
Jose Karica
David Katz
Aaron Kavanagh
Corey Kazaks
Sean Keane
Chris Keates
Shaun Keating
Brendan Kellegher
Remington Keller
Thomas-James Kelly
Wesley Kempton
Michael Kenny
Tamerlan Khadzhiev
Khizran Khalid
Armand Kiauleikis
Dan Kieran
Michael Kierstead
Melissa Kight
Michael Kilpatrick
Francis Kim
James Kim
Melanie Kimble

Dean Kimmins
Anthony King
Brett King
Elliott "Kip" Kipper
KittyRawr (Lilly)
Déarbhla Klue
Kris Knigge
Knight of Words
Antonia Knoblich-Hirst
Jordan Koeppl
Paweł Kozikowski
Ryan Kozimor
John Kozlowski
Kevin Kramer
Scott Krefetz
Patrick Kulikowski
Kiba Kurosaki
Henri Lähteenkorva
Ben Lancaster
Joey "3RDplayer" Lansing
Jeff Largent
Jake LaStella
Lucas Laujedo Garcia
Jordan Launstein
Andrew Lavigne
Brian Lavin
David Lawrence
Joshua Lawrie
Jérémie Le Goff
Charles Lee
Chun-hui Lee
Edward Lee
Josh Lee
Michael Lee
Ville-Veikko Lehtimaa
Brian Lelas
Rick Lemon
Casey Lent
Matthew Lenton
Matt Leone
Stephen LeTrent
Ryan H Lewis
Terry Lewis

Harold Li
Lady Lilith, Daughter of Hatred
Lawrence Lin
Andrew Lindsay
Charley Link
Shane Link
John Linneman
Ian Lipthorpe
Edward Lira
Michael Little
LoganLives
Nicholas Lohr
Corey Losey
Samy Lourdani
Michael Low
Ciaran Lowe
Matthew Loxley
Zach Lubag
Jose Miguel Vicente Luna
Matt Lyboult
Thomas Lynch
Alastair Macgregor
Joe Macgregor
Mario Maciel
Jem Mackay
Andy Maclean
John Madden
Jason Maddison
Andrea Maderna
Mark Magro
Dave Mahen
Vincent Maher
Ramtin Mahinpourian
Romain Mahut
Devon Maisonave
Rick Mallen
Luke R. Maloney
Anna Maness
Andrew Mann
James Mann
Samuel Manojlovic
Meylani "Spooky" Manzano
Scott Markle

Andrew Marmo
Ben Marrow
Sebastian Marsh
Jerrod Marshall
Andrew Martin
Ian Martin
Josh Martinez
Alex Massie
Mattafex
Tony Matthews
Daniel Maupin
Christian Mayer
Brian Mazeski
mb
John McArdle
Derek McCauley
Ron McCullough
Kevin McCusker
David McCutcheon
Jake McDaniel721@gmail.com
Jon McElroy
Rory McGill
Thomas "chaoslongshot" McGrady
David McGreavy
Ross McIntosh
Ben McIntyre
Zak McIver
Jason McKeon
Gillian Mclean
Martin McLean
Melody McMichael
Aaron McMullan
Darren McNally
Kris McQuage-Loukas
Kaitlyn Meehan
Ada Mejia
CJ Melendez
Siobhan Merrigan
Raja Miah
Adrian Michel
Shinji Mikami
Jason Miles
Torin Miller

William Miller
Cody Mills
Marcel Mink
Diego Miranda
Brandon Mitchell
John Mitchinson
Tyler Moccia
Eslam Mohammed
Anna Molinari
Lexi Momo
Louis Montambeault
Andrew Montemayor
Brooke Montroy-Malone
Paul Moody
Cruz Moore
Jeron Moore
Luke Moore
Tim Moore
James Moran
Scott Morrison
L.G. Moura
Kristian Mroczko
Mrsalbertwesker (Jackie Scott)
MrTrent from www.residentevilfr.com
Joseph Murphy
Jean-François Murray
Faisal Mustafa
Logan Myers
Kenneth Nabours III
Jacob Nachman
Nanovixen
François Natali
Marky Nations II
Rodrigo Navarrete
Carlo Navato
Alex Neale
Steven Neale
Nick Nelson
Neptune (Resident Evil Podcast)
Paolo Neri
Dominique Neuen
Mark Neugodov
John Nicholson

Ryan Nicholson
Ryan Nielson
Laura Nixon
Tim Nolde
Alexander Norris
Noscere
Brandon Numrich
Craig O Connor
Neville O'Connell
Erik Odeldahl
Jan Steffen Oeding
Tyler Ohlew
Brandon Olivarez
Cooper Opalinski
Efrem Orizzonte
Chris Orlando
Grayson Thomas Orr
Ronnie Othman
Henri Oung
Kyle Overby
Adam Overton
Jeremy P.
Jonathan Padilla
Anthony Padronaggio
Jacob Painter
Ashley Palacios
Jennifer Palmeri
Enrico Paolini
PapaDrewBear
Krzysztof Paplinski
Kia Pardo
Martin Paredes
Lauren Park
Miguel Parra
Niall 'Night_Hawk' Parsons
Graham Partridge
Matthew Patlan
Ian Patrick
Ryan Payton
Richard Pearce
Stepan Pech
Tim Pedersen
Fabrizio Pedrazzini

Charles Pellish
Seid Pepic
Justo Peral Garcia
Jose Perez
Manuel Perez
Michael Perez
Ana Pérez and Laura López
Carlos Pérez Olivares
Artyom Permyakov
Staffan Persson
Carl Petroff
Drew Pfefferle
Greg Philbrook
Shining Philistine
Brandon Phillips
Shawn Phillips
Gaetane Philoctete
Matthias Phung
Peter Pichler
Angelo "angecalo" Picone
Tanner Piecuch
Thomas Pierog
Baptiste Pierrel
Jon Place
David Plummer
Paco Polit
Patrick Polk
Justin Pollard
Steven Pollard
Mark Polley
John Pope
Matt Popple
Jose Portela
Peter Post
D Potter
Lucy Potts
Philippe Poulin (MegaPhilX)
Darren Power
Steph Prader
Jacob Probst
Brian Prouton
Nicholas Provan
Chris Pruett

Nicholas Ptacek
Simon Pulman
Don Purnell
Adrian Purser
Kimberley Purvin
Chevy Putman
Andres Quesada
Stephen Quinlan
Mick R.
Alex R.I
David Ramirez
Emiliano Ranzani
Tyler Rash
Jonathan Rauscher
Tom Redfield
Arron Reed
Jordan Rees
Nelson Regalado
Denis Reimer
Samuel Reinders
Remitonton Reminantoka
Weskers Report
Resident Evil Collection FR
McDougall's Revenge
Matthew Reynolds
Francois Ricchetti
Mark "Yoke" Rice
Ste Richards
Kristina Richartz
Juliana Rickle
Andrea Rigamonti
Graeme Ringland
Kenneth Ringwald
Matthew Rios
Patrik Riström
Christopher Rivera
George Rivera
Ewen Roberts
Maria Roberts
Dean Robertson
Jeff Robertson
Fred "GH101" Rojas
Victor Romero

Tyler Romo
Roofress
Juan Rosa
Joel Rose
Tabby Rose
Matt Rossall
Matthew Rudkin
Kristine Rudling
Victor Manuel Ruiz Cota
Luca Rungi
Matthew Russo
Mark Lester Ryan
Zane Sade
Danar Sadewo @wildestcatever
Esteban Salazar
Robert Preston Hayden Salazar
Alyssa Salcedo
Esteban Sanchez
Julian Sapien
David Sarnoski
Bogdan Saushkin
Loucas Savvides
Andrew Schiffel
Stacey Schlanger
Adrian Schmettau
JR Schmitt
Joshua Schrier
Keldon Schroen
Charles Schwilling
Thor Segui
Kayla Severson
Tyler Shank
Matthew Shaver
Stephen Shelburne
Ben Shelley
Ryan Shepherd
David Sheppard
David Shevlin
Kazuhiro Shirakawa
Kirby Shrable
Kevin Shropshire
Sean Sicher
Kathryn Sidwell

Leonardo Silva
Rob Silvestris
Andrew Simmons
Matthew Sinclair-Thomson
Hardeep Singh
Chris Sirmans
Brian Skahan
Skayra
Erin Skoog
Jeremy Sliwerski
Jordan Darrell Slone
Quinton Smalley
Aaryn Smith
Cory Smith
Gary Smith
Heather Smith
Kara Smith
Lindsey Smith
Michael Smith
Nathaniel Smith
Syd Smith
Michael Smoley
Ruth Snape
Lorelai Snark
Dan Sneddon
Audi Sorlie
Christopher Sousa
Achille Spampinato
Reverend Speed
Andy Spence
Joey Spencer
Stephanie Spencer
Michael Stadler
Luke Steele
René Steffek
Don Steiner
Robert Steinman
Konstantin Steshenko
Ash Stansby Stewart
Cody Stokes
Lucas Stonehouse
Jochen Storr
Samantha Stroud

Elaine Stryker
Stephen Sturges
Brian Sullivan
Mark D. Sullivan
Mingjen Sung
Eugenia Suo
Max Sutcliffe
Tim Suter
Christopher Suursoo
Tim Swanson
Paul Swiers
James Sykes
Mark Syvuk
Jamie Szabó
Michael Szalkiewicz
Joseph Tartaro
Don Taylor
Peter Taylor
TheLevelBest
Brody Thomas
Cibu Thomas
John Thomas
Kennedy Thomas
Trevor Thomas
Thomas
Andrew Thompson
Charles Thompson
Jan-Niklas Tielke
Darrick Tigner
Raymond Tobias
Alexei Toma
Johan Toresson
Shyann Trantham
Thomas Tranum
Ricardo Trujillo
Evan Turner
TxK_Keys
Unfamiliar Cornball
Richard Upchurch
Joe Upham
Brian Valdillez
Ferdinand van den Haak
Coen van der Heijden

Simon van der Liek
Davy Van Obbergen
Heather Vandagriff
Zoltán "Teflon" Várhelyi
Ray Vasquez
Timothy Veilleux
Saulius Vekteris
Sean Velasco
Gene Venables
Nicholas Venice
Yordi Verhoene
Hailey Vert
Nikita Vinokurov
Kyler Vo
Dave Voyles
Daniel Vuckovic
Anna Vuong
William Wade
The Waffling Taylors
Matt Walker
Daniel Wallace
Trevor Wang
John Ward
Wario64
Walker Warren
Andrew Warwick
Aydan Watkins
Rob Watkins
Grant Watson
Stuart Watt
Gustav "Le Bagronk" Wedholm
Alexander Weick
Bernard Welsh
Kurt Wentzel
Nathan Werfalli
Teajay Werle

Matthew Werner
Josh Wetuski
Daniel Wheeler
Houston Wheeler
Where's Barry
Adam White
Dylan White
James White
Jonathan Whitt
Jamie Whitworth
Jeff Wiggins
Tony Wilczynski
Ben Williams
David A Williams
Ian Williams
Thom Willis
Carl Wilson
Danny Aaron Wilson
Chris Winnington
Vivian Wolf
Sebastian Wolff
Martin Wong
Nigel Woodall
Ross Woodruff
Derek Woods
Landon Wright
MegaMichi Wunderle
Jarin C. Yarbrough
Charles Younts III
Rex Yuan
Joyce Yuen
Angelo Paul Zampogna
Timo Zander
Justin Zebrak
Γρηγόριος Κάρτσιος